THE THREE KINGS

BUSBY   SHANKLY   STEIN
THE MAKERS OF MODERN FOOTBALL

THE THREE KINGS
LEO MOYNIHAN

Quercus

First published in Great Britain in 2019 by Quercus.

Quercus Editions Ltd
Carmelite House
50 Victoria Embankment
London EC4Y 0DZ

An Hachette UK company

A CIP catalogue record for this book is available
from the British Library.

HB ISBN 978 1 78747 565 6
TPB ISBN 978 1 78747 566 3
Ebook ISBN 978 1 78747 567 0

10 9 8 7 6 5 4 3 2 1

Pictures are © and courtesy of, in order of appearance –

1 – Jimmy Taylor: 2 – Daily Mail/Shutterstock: 3 – The Celtic Wiki:4 – Shankly.com:
5, 6 – Colorsport/Shutterstock: 7 – PA Images: 8 – Robin Marwick Collection, North Lanarkshire Archives:
9 – Liverpool Echo: 10 – The Celtic Wiki: 11 – Mirrorpix: 12 – Celtic Quick News:
13, 14 – Getty Images: 15 – Rexscanpix/Shutterstock: 16 – Examinerlive.co.uk:
17 – PA Images: 18 – Liverpool Echo: 19 – Getty Images: 20 – Paul Lewis/Shutterstock:
21 - Barry Greenwood/Associated Newspapers/Shutterstock:
22 – Colorsport/Shutterstock: 22 – Daily Record

Typeset by CC Book Production

Printed and bound in Great Britain by Clays Ltd, Elcograf S.p.A.

'Give me the man as a friend and a neighbour
Who toils at the loom – with the spade – or the plough;
Who wins his diploma of manhood by labour,
And purchases wealth by the sweat of his brow.'

'Judge Not a Man', John Bedford Leno, 1857

Contents

Prologue: Three Games in May   1

Chapter 1: Kings of the Underworld   12
Chapter 2: Their Brains Are Closer to the Ball   29
Chapter 3: Sacrifice   46
Chapter 4: Jock's on the Road   63
Chapter 5: Round the Back   74
Chapter 6: Natural Enthusiasm   90
Chapter 7: Making it in Paradise   105
Chapter 8: His Babes   118
Chapter 9: Cleaning the Toilet   136
Chapter 10: Playing Cowboys with John Wayne   151
Chapter 11: The Swinging Sixties   164
Chapter 12: Immortality   180
Chapter 13: Odyssey   194
Chapter 14: Letting Go   209
Chapter 15: The Kings Are Dead   227

Epilogue: Long Live the Kings   244

Acknowledgements   251
Bibliography   253
Index   255

Prologue:

Three Games in May

Three men stand in the dark but they are not afraid, for these men know real darkness.

They have stood below ground, they know what it is to taste dust, to breathe dirt. They have known others who went to work in that darkness but whose lifeless bodies were carried to the surface.

They know that even in darkness there is light. Down in the pits and at the coalfaces of Scotland's Central Lowlands they have seen the best of men. Felt the heat. Wished away the fatigue. They have seen camaraderie, life-affirming friendships, organization, laughter and the sort of hard work that few could comprehend.

Three men have their football teams with them – men from differing backgrounds but made of similar stuff. The sport that always offered them a way into the light now offers them even more. Glory awaits. It is time to go to work.

Estádio Nacional, Lisbon
5.21 p.m., 25 May 1967
Celtic vs Internazionale

A gust of warm Iberian air flows through the tunnel as if to usher in the enormity of what is about to begin. Jock Stein looks at his team lined up ahead of him in single file. They bounce up on their toes; their studs hit the concrete floor, sounding like large Scottish drops of rain on an outhouse tin roof.

Would it be better if it was raining? Would it be better if they were back in Scotland? Is this occasion asking too much of them? He turns to his right and sees the opposition. Internazionale of Milan. European champions in 1964. European champions in 1965. World champions in 1964. World champions in 1965. Another gust of warm Lisbon air fills the tunnel. The Italians stand motionless. They won't have noticed it. To them this is the norm.

Stein, always the keenest of footballing students, knows his opponents. There they stand with names like Italian sports cars. Facchetti, Domenghini, Biccili. Dark wavy hair, focused eyes, chiselled jaws, tanned, oiled legs. Their blue and black striped jerseys hang on their muscular torsos like designer clothes on catwalk models. There they stand.

Sandro Mazzola. Inter's number 8. The great Italian inside forward. All bustle and goals. He is still, focused, relaxed. The iconic colours he wears are bright, but with that pencil moustache he looks more like a black-and-white film matinee idol waiting for Sophia Loren outside a Milanese boutique before an evening of saffron-infused risotto.

Stein turns back to his team. Names like Auld, Clark and Chalmers. More a firm of solicitors in Motherwell than Italian motor moguls. They bounce on their toes, moving faster now, their pale legs in total contrast to the sun-kissed limbs of their opponents. They look at each other and offer gummy smiles. Their front teeth sit safely elsewhere for the next two hours. He looks at them. His shoulders swell. Right now he wouldn't swap a single one.

He thinks of the people watching back home in Glasgow, in Scotland, in England, around Europe. Words like *underdogs* are used about his team. He gets that. He has no time for the adjective himself but knows people use it to describe the men he is about to send out into this Lisbon evening. It's rare for such terms to be tagged to his Celtic side. This season alone they have won three trophies. Four if you count the Glasgow Cup, which he does. But this is different. This is Internazionale, and so the word hangs there above him in the warm evening air. *Underdogs.* He hates it.

Perhaps he learned to hate it as a younger man working at a North Lanarkshire coalface. Men who strove, grafted, toiled and pushed themselves underground may have been seen as underdogs too. Pitied even. As if they had drawn life's shortest straw. Perhaps they had, but the men he knew from his days underground were anything but underdogs. Not a chance.

Stein looks to his right. There's Inter's coach, Helenio Herrera. Smartly dressed. Cool. Calculated. A bit arrogant, but that's all right. He's a two-time European Cup winner. He's earned Stein's respect, of course he has, but Stein feels a tension, as if that respect isn't reciprocated. He'd promised Stein a trip to Milan to watch his side play but that never materialized. He's told people his side has the lucky dressing room. Lucky? Stein grins at the absurdity of that. He doesn't care for all that pre-match silliness but there is something about Herrera that grates. What is it?

Maybe it's his style of play. After all, it's what happens on that pitch that matters tonight. Inter's coach, born in Argentina to Spanish parents but a keen advocate of Italian *catenaccio.* The clothes and the past medals and the lucky dressing rooms don't matter. He's defensive and Stein's team know only how to attack. As one. Perpetual movement from front to back. Stein looks at his players and a wave of confident defiance blows back the warm air from whence it came.

Publicly, Stein has said he wanted to play Inter. Play the best. He knows his team, knows the energy they have. Yes, he wanted to play the Italian champions because he is a football man, and he is fascinated to see how these god-like men from Milan will cope with a team whose energy they will never have encountered before.

What are his team thinking? He wonders how each one feels. Jimmy Johnstone, his mercurial little winger, the epitome of Scottish trickery. Tommy Gemmell, his long-legged fullback, the most jovial man in Glasgow unless you're a poor winger trying to get the better of him on a Saturday afternoon. Stevie Chalmers, his centre-forward, perhaps only playing due to an injury to Joe McBride but now charged with pulling bricks from Milanese walls. And his captain, Billy McNeill, a player he had coached as a boy and now about to be the first man to lead out a British team for a European Cup final.

Stein checks his thoughts. Don't get carried away with senti-mentality. The whole week has been about normality. Keep the players focused on their own jobs, on what makes this team so good. Individual brilliance propped up by unerring togetherness. A work ethic and levels of fitness that might just suck the air from the tyres of a few Italian sports cars. 'Chase paper on a windy day,' he had heard one of his players say. He liked that. That will do him.

Preparation had gone well. The team were relaxed, undaunted by the occasion. Stein's old friend Matt Busby had once described a trip to Lisbon with his Manchester United team where he had let his players enjoy themselves at a swimming pool in the afternoon. They lost the game 5–0 and Matt laid the blame on the sun's sapping rays. Stein's players would stay in the shade until after 5 p.m.

Training had gone well. Inter's players had requested to watch one session and walked away not knowing whether to be pleased or concerned about just how relaxed their opponents had been. '*Festa!*' one Italian onlooker had said. *Party!* Stein was satisfied with that too.

He thinks of another word that he'd noticed tagged onto this travelling team. *Pioneers.* This club, his side, the first British club to make a European Cup final. Others had got close – great teams – but his was the first. The word made him think. He had worked in the pits until he was almost thirty. While others took their footballing ability to England he had stayed at home.

What if they won it? No, no predictions. That had been drummed into his team, and he wouldn't dare to dream.

He looks at his team again. All but one born within ten miles of Celtic Park. Bertie Auld, his dynamic midfielder starts to sing, 'Hail, hail . . .' The Celtic song. They all join in: 'Hail, hail, the Celts are here!' For the first time the Italians look unsure. For the first time the Italians look like they too are stepping into new territory.

His team. Eleven men in the green and white hoops of Celtic Football Club vying to be the best in Europe. A chink of light beckons them towards that dream. He wouldn't swap one of them. They are ready. On you go, boys. They walk towards the light.

Wembley Stadium, London
7.37 p.m., 29 May 1968
Manchester United vs Benfica

At last. At last his club have the chance. The roar of the crowd fills the tunnel. A quarter of a century earlier the roar of wartime bombing raids had devastated a football club, but here they are. The pinnacle is in sight.

From the day in 1945 that he had walked into Manchester United's life, Matt Busby had wanted them to be the best. He immediately saw past the rubble. Build it up. Make them great. The best around. First domestic greatness. FA Cup winners. League champions. That's fine, but soon his mind expanded. Europe. Be the best in Europe.

Busby stands in the darkness and looks ahead. He always has. How he had envied Hibernian FC of his native Scotland when they travelled to Germany for a first taste of the European Cup in 1955. How he had scoffed at the dull-minded souls at the Football League for denying English clubs the same opportunity.

Busby knows darkness. From the pits of Bellshill where he had grown up and reluctantly worked, to the days after Munich, the ultimate darkness when tragedy enveloped him and his people's lives. Darkness so black that he wondered whether he wanted to even be. But now, here in the bowels of Wembley Stadium, with his wonderful team ahead of him, this is right. Time to climb and stand proudly on top of the game.

The final. The word seems poignant. Is this the last great occasion of his career? Is this his last chance? It feels right. He's not overconfident, it just feels right. Real Madrid have been beaten. Real Madrid, the team, the institution that he had enviously watched win the first five European Cups, they have been beaten. Bill Foulkes – a survivor from the darkness of Munich – had scored in Spain's capital. This feels right. Bobby Charlton, that most buoyant of his Babes is now standing steadfast at the front of his team and ready to lead them out.

He hears the roar again. Over 90,000 people are out there and most are rooting for his team. Since they overcame Madrid he has been the country's focus. *Win this for Matt*. That won't do. Everything has always been about Manchester United, that is what this is about. The club he found floundering in the embers of war, that's what it has always been about. Making them the best around.

They must win. It won't be easy, but as he stands there in the darkness, the air of confidence that has filled his footballing lungs since defeating Madrid remains. He had been to see Benfica win their semi-final against Juventus. They are a great team, full of wonderful talent, but Busby left behind any feelings of inferiority a long time ago.

He knows they can win. Two years earlier they had overcome tonight's opponents in this same tournament. A fleeting thought crosses his mind as he recalls the previous summer when they lost to them in a friendly in Los Angeles. The thought is dispatched. A mere friendly; this is the final of the European Cup.

Busby's thoughts turn to preparation. It had been a tense day at their hotel in Berkshire. The usual afternoon nap had proved impossible, and his players had paced the grounds. That's OK. They're ready. They're eager.

His team talk had been concise. Nothing fancy. No need and certainly not his style. It's another game. He knows that's nonsense of course, but no occasion warrants hysterics. To win, to be the best, they must be themselves.

He thinks about where he is. Wembley. He loves Wembley. The grandeur, the size of the pitch that asks for so much more than mere ability. His players must use their minds. Concentrate. That's the message. Each pass must be measured. Find your teammate. Fail to do that and you'll run yourself into the ground. Lose concentration on this pitch and it becomes quicksand.

Work together, defend together and attack together. His mind flicks back to life in the Bellshill pits. That's the key. *Work together.* It's what they have always done and tonight will be no different. Nobby Stiles will look after Eusébio. He must. Bobby Charlton will lose the shackles he wore two years earlier for England in the World Cup final. There's no Denis Law, but Aston and Kidd will move and run and torment.

He realizes that his work – for now at least – is done. You prepare, you talk, you nurture, you hope. Now it's these men in front of him who have to play. Busby, once such a fine player himself, knows that, and the thought only fills him with further confidence.

No time for sentiment but one last reflection about the years gone by, about those not here tonight who would have been. Who should have been. They are never far from his mind, but this is all about now. The pinnacle is in sight. Out you go, lads.

His team walk towards the light.

Wembley Stadium, London
2.53 p.m., 4 May 1974
Liverpool vs Newcastle United

Ahead of him, at the end of the stadium tunnel, he sees a chink of green. The pitch. Behind him is a football team. Resplendent in red. He smiles. This is exactly how it was meant to be. Brought up in an Ayrshire village surrounded by green hills, the idea of standing and waiting to walk a team – the best team! – out at this old symbol of the British empire would have been bordering on insanity, but not for Bill Shankly. This is where he was always supposed to be. Some may call it destiny. Shankly scoffs at the word. To him this was down to sheer wonderful bloody hard work.

He straightens his tie. He looks back and waves to a few officials, shouts a hello to the referee. Yes, this is his place. Where he always knew he'd be. His team pick up on and feed off his confidence. In the dressing room just minutes before he had paced the floor, scowling at them, barked how good they were. How no one in the world could beat them. Now, standing behind him they look good. He knows they believe in him. Leeds might be league champions but this Liverpool team, well they are the best around.

He's been here before. The FA Cup win in 1965 was Liverpool's first, and he would never forget it, but this was something different. This was another team. Young, eager, brilliant. On the cusp of something even more special.

Not that it's been an easy year. The squad of players he is about to walk out onto the most famous turf in world football are winners, of that he is in no doubt, but there are egos – big personalities – and it has been his job this season to tame them. He has a boot room of course, a small band of brilliant men who can look after the football and tactics and idiosyncrasies of the game he has always loved, but as he waits to walk them out, it is the way he has manipulated and shaped those egos into a winning unit that fills him with pride.

Right behind him is Emlyn Hughes. Enthusiastic, skilful, Shankly's image on the pitch. Further back, Tommy Smith – rock solid, proud, the man Hughes had replaced as skipper only months earlier. The dressing room after that announcement had been tense, volatile even, but Shankly had no time for petty disputes and brought his team into line through sheer weight of personality. He isn't interested in making friends; it's winning that interests him. And now they stand behind him awaiting glory. Yes, this is where Bill Shankly was destined to be.

If anything, he likes the needle that goes with the game. He isn't one to go after other managers or anything like that – he has nothing but admiration for anyone who works in football – but he encourages a level of competitiveness that sometimes spills over into trouble. Just days before, at Melwood, the Liverpool training ground, the team had played their usual five-a-sides and Shankly himself was rambunctious in a challenge on Kevin Keegan. His star man. Not some snotty-nosed youth-team player eager to please, but his team's poster boy. *Crack*. Shankly led with the knee, and Keegan was left feeling his back and wondering about his cup final chances.

Intense. That's how it should be. Be on it. Get at them. Move. Work. Support the man and the ball. The men behind him know exactly what is expected of them and he hopes the opposition – whatever front they put on for the cameras – knew what to expect from them too.

Ah yes, the cameras. Shankly has done a lot of talking to the cameras. He has praised his opponents' exciting young players, complimented their style of play, the city of Newcastle itself, their fans. The night before though he had said on camera that he thought manager Joe Harvey looked nervous, and for a moment he had felt bad about that. But as he stands there, in the tunnel, Shankly knows that it's all part of the game, and like his days as a child when he stole turnips from the local farm in Glenbuck, he loves the mischievousness of it all.

After all, hadn't Newcastle players said in interviews that Tommy Smith was past it? And as for Malcolm Macdonald – or Supermac as he liked to be called – hadn't he told anyone who would listen that he would tear this Liverpool defence apart? Shankly stands in that tunnel and smiles. Yes, he loves the needle. He uses it.

Shankly doesn't worry about how they'll play, this team of his. Perhaps even better than his first glorious 1960s incarnation. That's an argument for another day, but he knows this team will perform on this, the biggest stage of all. Months earlier they had run out onto Newcastle's big pitch and played their hosts off the park. On Wembley's massive pitch they will do the same. On that damp day in February they had drawn 0–0, but this time the goals will come. He knows it.

The fullbacks will bomb forward. The centre backs will marshal Newcastle's forwards while getting on the ball, wanting it, starting attacks as well as stopping them. The midfield three will move all day – probing, stopping, passing. The strikers will stretch, confuse and get at their opponents. 'Kevin, I want you to drop hand grenades all over their back line,' he'd said just minutes before. He knows Keegan's hand is on the pin ready to pull.

Shankly looks straight ahead. *There's that pitch.* Greener and lusher than the rolling hills of Glenbuck where he had grown up. Among those hills he had experienced hard work, he had experienced the merit – no, the fundamental importance of hard graft and togetherness. Those days and their people are everything to him but he knew he'd always end up here.

The referee gives him a nod. He walks his team towards the light.

Chapter 1:

Kings of the Underworld

U ttered by a doctor visiting a miner's cottage in the Lanarkshire village of Orbiston before the sun had introduced itself to a May morning in 1909, the words 'A footballer has come to this house today' were among the first heard by the newborn ears of a young baby who would soon be named Matthew Busby. Fifty-eight years later, dressed in white-tied regalia and accepting the freedom of Manchester, Busby stood and spoke of that moment and joked that the doctor had probably said those same words in every home in which he helped bring a new boy into the world.

We'll never know if in fact the astute medic saw something particular in Busby's newborn thighs that suggested he would go on to dominate the midfields of Manchester City, Liverpool and Scotland, or if indeed it was a line delivered to put a smile on the face of otherwise terrified new fathers, but if the former then the doctor's words were surely born from the experience of anyone who took an interest in football in this particular region of Britain. If Glasgow is rightly seen as one of British football's most productive engine rooms, then the Central Lowlands counties of Lanarkshire and Ayrshire have provided many of its vital components. Doctor or schoolchild knew that footballers came to many houses in this area south of Glasgow, and they always had.

Alex Brown and Alex Tait, both FA Cup winners with Tottenham in 1901; the brilliant pocket-sized Alex James of Arsenal and Hughie Gallacher of Newcastle and Chelsea; Billy McNeill, that most dominant of the Lisbon Lions; Davie Cooper, Rangers' and Scotland's irresistible winger in the 1980s – all can call Lanarkshire or Ayrshire their place of birth and upbringing, and all are part of a far longer list of players that includes three men who played the game at a fine level but whose footprints on the sport were firmly set as remarkable managers.

Matt Busby, Bill Shankly and Jock Stein. Gargantuan names. Gargantuan football men. Born and bred within forty miles of each other in a heavily industrialized part of Scotland that offered scant options for most school leavers. 'I was like everybody else from a mining family,' Stein would say. 'The next step when you left school was to go into pits. It was as simple and straightforward as that.' Mining for coal in the many pits that beckoned teenage boys was pretty much it unless you had a talent for the game of football, a sport ingrained in people's lives like black soot under the fingernails of colliers.

Long before young men daydreamed about wearing studded boots or occupying penalty boxes for fun, let alone being paid for the pleasure, mining in Scotland had been the driving force behind the country's industrialization. In the part of Lanarkshire where Matt Busby and Jock Stein were born, a life working in the darkness up to a thousand metres below ground was pretty much assured. These were the working conditions that all three men experienced, and their communities helped shape them as men, footballers and managers. Hard work, close-knit lives that depended on teamwork, the ability to face down those who sought to exploit you and your neighbour: all were part of a miner's and his family's everyday life, and these three men would take those experiences and lessons from the pits of Lanarkshire and Ayrshire to football pitches all over the world.

Mining in Scotland can be traced back to the twelfth century, when entrepreneurial monks utilized the shallow deposits and outcrops of minerals on their lands, cutting tunnels into hillsides and banks, before selling on the results. In the sixteenth century South Lanarkshire, with its abundance of lead, coal and even silver gained the nickname God's Treasure House in Scotland, but with such riches, the exploitation of serf labour followed.

As the industry grew, more and more colliers were sent to work in the darkness, dirt and danger of mines. In 1606, the year William Shakespeare penned *Macbeth*, a play that screamed of the consequences of greed and ambition, a Scottish law was passed decreeing, 'No person should fee, hire or conduce salters, colliers or coal bearers without a written authority from the master whom they had last served.' Basically, any worker choosing to abandon their employment without leave would be charged with a crime, deemed as stealing themself from their master. The same act also gave coal masters the power to apprehend 'Vagabonds and sturdy beggars' and put them to work in the mines that they owned. In 1641 the act was extended to stipulate a full six-day working week, with Sunday the only day off so as workers could attend church.

Resistance would come, though. The Duke of Hamilton's colliers in Lanarkshire were, as early as 1701, described as 'Something troublesome and mutinous . . . especially when ships was waiting upon the coales.' Even then, miners would try to be as trouble- some as possible to help reduce food costs and influence wage levels, something perhaps recalled by Jock Stein when he – a top football manager driving his Mercedes around the roads of Scotland and northern England during the miners' strike in the mid-1980s – showed his displeasure at strike-breaking lorry drivers taking coal through picket lines by dazzling them with the full beam of his headlights.

With the Industrial Revolution and the construction of the railways, the Central Lowlands became the hub of Scotland's heavy industry. Bountiful quantities of mineral wealth were discovered and exploited, the Scottish coalfields stretching from Ayr to Fife on the east coast, and it was in Lanarkshire that the most valuable of Scottish coal seams were found. Industry ruled, and Scotland's black country was its dark, beating heart. By 1879 in Lanarkshire alone there were 314 ironworks with 5,149 puddling furnaces and 846 rolling mills, and by 1881, 392 coal pits and 9 fire-clay pits. In 1910 there were 200 collieries in the county, producing more than half of all of Scotland's output.

Not only was output impressive, so was the coal itself. Lanarkshire coal was especially high in quality, coming from a field whose basin near Bellshill contained numerous thick and valuable seams. This was mining nirvana, and by the time the doctor was declaring that a footballer had come to the Busby household, a life working underground was seen as that child's most likely future.

The Industrial Revolution had driven the British empire forward and Scotland was very much cranking its pistons. In 1888 Glasgow welcomed Queen Victoria to formally open the City Chambers, all marble staircases and lavish decor. A huge crowd gathered to catch a glimpse of the monarch and marvel at the building's imposing facade. Thousands gasped at the opulence of building and regal visitor alike, while local dignitaries quickly and proudly labelled Glasgow the 'Second City of the Empire'.

*

Over forty years prior to Victoria's visit and amid far less grandeur George Busby had come to the city on the Clyde from across the Irish Sea, escaping the famine that had so decimated his country of birth. The Great Hunger was caused by a potato blight that affected much of Europe but whose impact was most keenly felt in Ireland, where the population fell by almost 25 per cent, while the British Whig government's neglectful (they called it laissez-faire) response only helped seal the fate of the million people who died. 'The judgement of god,' argued Charles Trevelyan, the colonial administrator charged with overseeing government relief, 'sent the calamity to teach the Irish a lesson.'

By the time George's great-grandson Alex Busby was born in 1889 the prejudices, assaults and harassments suffered by those early Irish immigrants had faded and communities formed. George's descendants had made the short journey south to Lanarkshire, and Alex came into a world somewhat easier than those who had left the land of his great-grandfather, just decades before. For years many Scots had shared the British government's view of the Irish. They were lazy, they were immoral, and they were too partial to drink. In Lanarkshire and Ayrshire among mining folk further reasons for distrust spilled over into issues of work. Hired by exploitative employers to break the unions in the early part of the nineteenth century, Irish workers in these communities were long labelled strike-breakers, adding fuel to the xenophobic bonfire. In 1835 one prominent Scottish judge was moved to write in his journal that the influx of Irish immigrants to his country had helped prove 'That a man might be a Catholic without having the passions or the visible horns of the devil', but no matter; it would take generations for ingrained mistrust to subside.

Alex grew up in Orbiston near Bellshill and began in the mine, digging alongside his neighbour Jimmy Greer. Also at the mine but working at the pithead was Jimmy's daughter Helen. Known by all as Nellie, she and Alex had caught each other's eyes to the extent that in the early days of 1909 – just five months prior to the birth of little Matthew Busby – they became man and wife at a simple service at nearby Mossend.

Life for the young family – Alex was twenty, Nellie seventeen – was lived in one of the many cottages built by the owners of the Orbiston and Hattonrigg mines. The Old Orbiston rows consisted of sixteen one-room and sixteen two-room houses. The Busbys had the luxury of two rooms and got on with their lives. Matt's gaining of three sisters in quick succession added to the overcrowding, but no matter, this was life and it was lived. A shared lavatory was at the end of each row of houses, and baths were taken in galvanized tin tubs, and of course there was plenty of coal with which to warm water for washing after long shifts underground.

Alex and Nellie worked hard at the pit and at home, and were able to move from the rows to nearby Crofthead Cottage. For Matt the toddler his little corner of the universe was a happy one.

On 2 September 1913 a locomotive travelling from Scotland to St Pancras in England's capital ploughed into a train at Ais Gill near Carlisle. Fourteen passengers were killed in a tragedy that went a long way to improve safety on British railway lines. Later that day, seventy miles north of the accident, Barbara Shankly, a kind woman who would under normal circumstances have felt deeply for those affected, was otherwise engaged giving birth to her ninth child, a boy she and her husband would name William. Bill, as he would be known, of course knew nothing of the crash, but by sheer force of personality and talent, he would go to have his own huge impact on Scotland, England and even – briefly – Carlisle.

For now though, life was the rural village of Glenbuck in Ayrshire, a mile from the Lanarkshire border. The road that linked the two counties was shingle, in Ayrshire white, in Lanarkshire red. The colours offered omens for young William's future, but as Barbara swaddled her new baby and let him sleep, Glenbuck, its population of 700 added to by one, got on with things as it always had, although the village had begun a decline that would eventually see it disappear altogether. Life was changing. The mines that had helped the place boom at the end of the nineteenth century were in decline and people were moving on.

As far back as 1650 there is recorded evidence of around forty stout Glenbuck dwellers making their living from surface mining and despite the harsh boggy surroundings, basic agriculture. Plentiful water though would attract the textile industry and help the development of a village toiling to make some sort of mark. Thanks to weaving, the bogs were drained and farmland increased, but it was the discovery of limestone, iron and of course coal that started to attract attention from afar. The population grew to 580 in the late eighteenth century and when an Englishman, John Rumney, from Workington (once again, given Shankly's eventual career path, a strange coincidence) founded the Glenbuck Iron Company, village life picked up considerably.

Pits were sunk, and a quarry established. Glenbuck Loch was created and cottages were built, but for those who called it home, life in the village rarely ran smoothly, and the iron enterprise got into trouble. In 1820 an observer wrote of Glenbuck that it stood 'In a wild and secluded situation between the mountains ... the iron works having been abandoned, the village has fallen into decay.' By then the population had dropped to less than 240.

Each of those steadfast souls had plenty of spirit, but what changed their lives, and the short history of the place in which they lived, was that they had coal beneath their feet. The coal plus a new railway line heading east to service the mines meant that the little village of Glenbuck could at last flourish. Mines were opened, more shafts sunk; a church was built, a public hall too. There was a bakery, a fish and chip shop, a greengrocer's, a sweet emporium and a butcher's. As the nineteenth century became the twentieth, you could say business and life in Glenbuck was booming. By 1900 the population was a lofty 1,700.

Once again, things would change. Years later, in his auto-biography Shankly explained his hometown's decline. 'People would move to other villages, four or five miles away, where the mines were possibly better.' But while plenty of men and their families moved away from Glenbuck to more prosperous parts of Ayrshire and Lanarkshire, Shankly's kin remained, happy to live out their lives amid its green hills and babbling streams. A major reason young Shankly continued to call Glenbuck home was that his father wasn't a miner. A one-time postman, John Shankly had drawn on the village's textile heritage and become a tailor. Shankly himself would grow up always looking immac-ulate, surely a nod to his father's skills.

John was a quiet man. To rile him one would have to talk ill of his family or his country, and in Glenbuck people rarely chose to do either. What they would do is come to him for alterations and new clothes. Take in a jacket, tailor a whole suit. Often he would accept less money than his craft deserved, but whatever he did make, it always went to the family. John didn't smoke and unlike many wouldn't take a drink. An eight-mile walk to the cinema was a relaxation for John and a love for the screen was a passion that Bill inherited.

Surprisingly, when you consider all five of his sons played the game professionally, John wasn't a football man. He played as a child and would watch it, but he was a keener runner, a quarter-miler and very fit even into old age. Bill took a lot from his father, but it was his mum, Barbara, who he later called his 'greatest inspiration', who did so much to shape him as a man and even manager. Loyal, calm under pressure, generous and with an incredible commitment to hard work, Barbara Shankly was like so many matriarchs in the area. She kept her family and her home happy and far more comfortable than circumstances should have allowed.

Up in Orbiston, Matt Busby's happy home life owed much to his own mother. Nellie's family had come from the Northern Ireland county of Antrim. They were Roman Catholics, and in the face of many of the prejudices that that background inspired, her father Jimmy had settled in Orbiston, where he and his family became members of a proud mining workforce and community. Nellie had given up her job at the pit to raise her family, and that home included her father, who in her mind too often lived up to Protestant stereotypes by frequenting one of the forty pubs in the Bellshill area.

Nellie loved her father and remained a fervent Catholic all her life, instilling that religion in Matt and her other children. She was eager to raise her family in the right way. A keen advocate of education, Nellie was – partly for tragic reasons – to be a guiding light for the boy she called Mattha, and like Barbara Shankly, she epitomized the many strong women who kept mining homes together. When in August 1914 Britain and Germany went to war, such was the importance of their work to the economy and the war effort that miners were at first dis-couraged from enlisting. Alex Busby though took the journey to nearby Uddingston to sign up for the Royal Irish Regiment and within a week was in County Tipperary for basic training, but would return home only two months later, deemed unfit for war service due to varicose veins.

Alex returned to the mine; Nellie worked at home; young Matt and his sisters lived their young lives, oblivious to the carnage happening on the fields of northern Europe. Aged just seven though, that carnage came very much into Busby's world when he and his sisters lost their uncle, Private Willie Greer in the early days of the Somme. And as the war dragged on and casualties mounted, his father would once again leave the village and this time head to battle. Alex Busby was killed in April 1917. Further tragedy befell Nellie just months later when she lost another brother, Thomas, also killed on the Western Front. 'First Uncle Willie, then my father, then Uncle Tommy,' said Matt Busby years later. 'Every man a miner, and they all left widows.'

For the widows the time to grieve was a luxury they could not afford. Nellie had received a government allowance while her husband was away, and now a widow-and-orphans pension was available, but it wasn't enough. It was time to go back into employment. To Matt, a small boy starting school, cloth-capped and short-trousered, the world must have seemed a cruel place. Life had been tough and taken a lot from him, but not for the last time in his life Matt Busby refused to buckle, and instead walked tall through adversity and tragedy. Nellie got on with bringing in what income she could while Busby himself did some caddying at the local golf club. She then remarried, her second husband Harry Mathie, a miner at the pit where she once again worked.

Busby's grandpa Jimmy Greer became an especially important male figure in his life, but Nellie's work at the pit was more than matched by her graft at home, and she maintained her children's pre-war way of life. As the oldest male child, Busby had to grow up quickly. Responsible, hard-working and a role model for children beyond even his family's four walls, his half-brother Jimmy Mathie particularly idolized him. Matt was a keen young footballer, quietly wise, with a tenderness of thought and action. He was also doing well academically and won a place at a good school in Motherwell. Every morning before seven Busby would leave the house to walk the three miles to his studies, and every afternoon for the last several hundred yards home he was accompanied by the adoring Jimmy. Busby had a way about him. Teachers even recommended he follow them into their profession.

If Busby's family experiences shaped him to become a wise leader of men, the same could be said of Shankly. Unlike his future friend, young Bill didn't need to grow up early, but as the penultimate child in a family of ten, sheer personality and an ability to be heard were vital if the young man was to get on. And Bill got on.

'If the whole world was like my family, there would be no trouble,' Shankly later stated. But that isn't to say from an early age he didn't understand that to succeed, rules were there to be manipulated, and that living off your wits could bring results. Working as a collective was what his football teams would always strive to do, a trait that he learned could bring success.

Winters could be especially hard in Glenbuck. Finding enough to eat was a genuine concern, and to the children the many farms and vegetable fields that surrounded the village must have glinted like jewellery to magpies when real hunger kicked in. The local constable had his work cut out. Working together, the youngsters would monitor the policeman's whereabouts and usually under the cover of night get away with many a potato or turnip. Visiting salesmen would also fall foul of young Shankly's Glenbuck crime spree. The wagon from nearby Strathaven would leave slightly lighter of scones, cakes and currant cakes. One day a huge bunch of bananas disappeared from a grocery wagon from Clydeside. 'It took four or five of us to carry it,' Shankly boasted in later years, 'and the bananas lasted for weeks.' From a young age Shankly was reaping the rewards that came from teamwork.

He knew right from wrong though. Misbehaviour at school would often result in the question, 'Do you want your punishment from me or your father?' The answer was always emphatically in favour of the teacher. Not that the leather strap used across the hands at school was a pleasant alternative, and should the misdemeanour be especially egregious, a visit to the headmaster, Mr Roger, all six foot of him with his terrifying catchphrase, 'Woe betide you,' was enough to ensure any transgression wasn't quickly repeated.

Shankly wasn't as able at school as Busby but he was a keen student with a great memory for facts, although 'If I did not consider it important, it went right out of my head.' Geography especially had his ears pricked. He loved to hear about England and Europe, but any wanderlust was for the future. To fourteen-year-old boys leaving school in places such as Glenbuck and Bellshill, the most likely journey was the walk from the school gate to the mine.

In the early October of 1922, when Shankly was just nine, it is safe to say that the young boy had no interest in baseball's World Series. The event that year across the Atlantic was the first to be broadcast on radio's still modish airwaves, but those early crackling sounds of an all-New-York affair as the Giants outmanoeuvred the Yankees and their feared outfielder Babe Ruth wouldn't have been heard across Scotland's Central Lowlands. The series was won 4–0 by the Giants, the only tied game coming on the afternoon and evening of 5 October at Upper Manhattan's Polo Grounds. A million miles away on the Glasgow Road in Burnbank, Lanarkshire, Jane Stein – like the Giants' pitchers – had a babe on her mind.

According to Lanarkshire lore, John Stein – named after his father and not called Jock for years to come – would be blessed with the sort of fortune that didn't require hard slog. A removable 'lucky cap' or extra flap of skin on the baby's head was and is said in these parts to be a sign of good luck. The midwife whose wrists were no doubt strained by handling a baby they would one day call 'the Big Man', noticed the flap and – like the doctor quick to pronounce Matt Busby a definite footballer – assured the new mother that the baby she now cradled in her arms had a one-way ticket to greatness.

'People in Lanarkshire knew that a lucky cap brought good luck, and at one time men going to sea used to try and get hold of one, as they believed that it would get them safely through any long voyages,' recalled Stein's sister Margaret McDade in Ken Gallacher's biography of her brother. 'Maybe it did, maybe it didn't – but it brought our John good luck in his life. He was very superstitious, you know, which may have come from that happening when he was born and my mother always going on about it.'

Good fortune, to outsiders at least, was not a feature of villages such as Burnbank. Four miles south of Orbiston and thirty miles north of Glenbuck, Burnbank was once a rural place with farms that served the local lace industry. It had been swallowed up by the industrial juggernaut that had left its mark over much of England, Wales and Scotland, and while Stein was born into a happy and loving home, the notion of a life blessed with luck could easily be discarded as superstitious claptrap.

Stein attended the local primary and moved on later to Greenfield School, an institution apparently for those less intellectually blessed. Not that Stein wasn't bright. Archie Macpherson, a friend and another of his biographers, wrote, 'Judging by the shrewdness, alacrity of mind in argument and the wide general knowledge he displayed at his managerial peak . . . it is tempting to reach the impression that sitting in the classroom of either of those schools was an intelligent child whose abilities might have taken him on an entirely different route, with the right prompting.'

Prompting. This was too often merely a stern shove to the nearest mine, and in 1927 Shankly went to work, following the same path as Busby had taken two years before. For parts of Britain life in the 1920s was befitting of Lloyd George's boast that it would become a 'land fit for heroes'. So-called bright young things were living life to the full, while the novels of P.G. Wodehouse and Nancy Mitford spoke raucously of a roaring decade where clubs were popping up across Soho in London allowing revellers to perform dances with names such as the Texas Tommy and the Black Bottom.

While the teenage Busby was working underground at his own black bottom, the frivolities of life in distant places such as Soho would have been mythical at best. By the middle of the 1920s, demand for coal had flattened. The Orbiston pit was closed. Nellie Busby sought work at the steelworks instead while her son moved to Parkhead, a nearby colliery. Busby never pretended to enjoy working underground. He never romanticized the toil he endured and witnessed, but he did have huge respect for it and for those who worked in the pits, and even as a teenager he would stand up for their rights.

In 1926 Chancellor of the Exchequer Winston Churchill reintroduced the gold standard, triggering off a chain of events that saw interest rates rise, the pound rise to levels which made British exports uncompetitive, and mine owners who demanded profits choosing to increase working hours while lowering wages. The miners and unions weren't going to take this lying down and in May that year, just weeks before Busby's seventeenth birthday, he joined the General Strike called by the Trades Union Congress. While the TUC strike would last only nine days, the miners were left to fight alone for months before hunger and hardship forced the men back to work. It was a defeat that galvanized the Labour movement and an experience that helped shape Busby's lifelong socialist views.

Stein and Shankly would share those politics, and the latter took to the mines with an enthusiasm he brought to most things in his life. Boys left the short shorts of their schools behind and donned longer versions, often fitted with extra patches on the knees for protection. Jackets belonging to their fathers were passed down, turned up at the wrists and given enlarged pockets to house a piece (lunch) box, and a flask for tea.

Frank Hillan, who in 1914 started work as a drawer in the Lanarkshire coalfield, driving a pony from the coalface to the 'main road', spoke of the ordeal undergone by so many children who faced what must have been a terrifying new reality. 'I'll never forget the first morning when I started at the pit in Coalburn,' he recalled. 'When I went down in the cage to take us underground, it dropped so fast that I thought everything had left me. I swore that if I ever got back up the pit, I would never go down again – but the next mornin' I had to. I remember how the boys startled at every noise. Even a drop o' water falling on a stone could be quite frightening.' Even Bill Shankly, a man not keen on admitting to fear, must have felt a tinge of trepidation when he entered the cage; his first six months working had been spent at the pit head emptying the trucks of coal. Soon like Busby, and later Stein, Shankly was underground.

One luxury came in the shape of electricity, a utility not affordable in most homes, but otherwise the work was far from light. Shankly would run full trucks of coal to the cages and then bring the empty trucks back. A normal working day might see him run twelve miles. Those footballers who later ran for miles on the pitch carrying out his instructions would vouch that such enthusiasm was deemed the norm on the field of play.

During the shifts, rats would play at their feet and compete for lunchtime scraps. 'You would be down there eight hours and you would have your grub to eat there and a tea can wrapped up in a big, thick newspaper to keep it warm for a couple of hours, perhaps even less,' Shankly later recalled. 'You had to drink your tea maybe an hour after you'd started, otherwise it would probably be cold. You had to eat where you were working and there was no place to wash your hands. It was really primitive. The longest break you would get for anything would be half an hour, but if a man was digging coal on piecework he could stop to eat any time. If there were six men doing a job, three could take a break while three worked.' Some of the rats would sit on the miners' laps to get a crumb from a sandwich.

The stench of fungus filled their nostrils, thick air blackened their lungs. The sound of booming gelignite pierced their ears. The men would return to the light or the darkness of late afternoon and scrub the day's work from their bodies, although being actually clean was a heady ambition.

Busby, Stein and Shankly all worked underground to bring money into the homes and families that had brought them up. There they witnessed a camaraderie they might not have seen elsewhere. They learned about teamwork, not your everyday office or even sporting variety, but teamwork that could and did save lives. Not one of them eulogized the life, but it was a time and an experience that shaped them.

In 1980 the Welsh actor Richard Burton, the son and brother of miners, guested on Dick Cavett's chat show in America. Talk was of course about his life on the stage and in the movies, but a sparkle similar to one of his wife's diamonds appeared in his eye as he began to talk of those who worked under the surface of South Wales. 'Miners believed themselves to be the aristocrats of the working class,' he said. 'They felt superior to all other kinds of manual labourers. They were skilled workers and that coalface was a magical creature.' Cavett then asked if Burton had feared following his family underground.

'No,' was the stern response. 'The opposite as a matter of fact. Every little boy's ambition in my valley was to become a miner. There was the arrogant strut of the lords of the coalface. They had these muscular buttocks and the bow legs and they walked with a kind of arrogance . . . They were the kings of the underworld.'

Below ground, in the darkness, the stench-filled air filling their organs and senses, Busby, Shankly and Stein saw first hand the pride with which work could be carried out. They saw these aristocrats and were proud to call them mates, but each had something else on his mind. An ambition to leave the rank dust behind. Football had been part of their lives since they were small boys and they were all under its spell. Now, as young men looking for a way out of a life otherwise pre-planned, football would be their shared salvation.

Chapter 2:

Their Brains Are Closer to the Ball

Matt Busby sits on a bed in Moss Side, Manchester. Melancholy fills the room. It is midnight but his bag is packed. He's already made his debut for Manchester City and on his way to succeeding in a career he'd always coveted, but this isn't how it was supposed to be. Christmas is coming and pneumonia has recently been his only yuletide gift. His spirits are low. He's written a letter to Jean, a girl he'd met whom now he misses as much as home, to say maybe professional football isn't for him. He wants to come back.

Phil McCloy walks into the room. McCloy is a teammate but perhaps more importantly he's from Uddingston in south Lanarkshire. It's getting late, but McCloy, thirteen years Busby's senior, is happy to talk. 'You can still make it,' he says. 'Give it a little longer. What have you got to go home to, Matt?' Busby thinks longingly of Jean.

Three years later Bill Shankly is playing cards, a game of brag. It's his first full weekend away from home. The card table is at Carlisle's Brunton Park stadium and his opponents are his new teammates in the professional game. He's losing. He has lost before, but this isn't home and he fears foul play. Wily old footballers rounding off their playing careers happy to clean out young bucks just making their way. And that's what they do.

This isn't easy. For now he's penniless, miles from home; the training kit is shoddy, the training not much better. Later, looking back on these early pigeon steps into professional football, he'll find a word that sums it up: 'Grim.'

Two men facing the reality of their dreams. For Bill Shankly, the unglamorous nature of his early foray into the game was merely a blip; the bigger picture hung gold framed in his mind's eye, and nothing was going to change that. 'It didn't deter me,' he later said of the early days at Carlisle. 'That was only a stepping stone.'

Busby's melancholy start to his professional football life, on the face of it perhaps spoke of a less certain individual. Yet this was a teenager who by joining Manchester City was not balanced on a stepping stone, but already at one of the country's major football clubs. City had won the Second Division in 1928, and so here he was, almost twenty, straight into the top flight. McCloy's words though that night would sink in. Busby would unpack his bags.

Both men left home, both men saw the stark reality of the life they had chosen but both men had something ingrained in them, something Jock Stein – at this point a schoolboy in Burnbank dreaming his own dreams of a similar chance in the game – also possessed. That something was a deep love of football. A love of playing it, discussing it, dismantling it and reassembling it. Like so many Scots, the game of football was for them a driving force. If those drawing up its early rules had worn the robes and mortar boards of England's lofty universities, then football's technical soul sported kilts and sporrans.

It had been a band of Scots gathered at Queen's Park in Glasgow in 1867 who made amendments that they felt would improve football's inchoate and somewhat barbaric rules. In doing so they sought a more deft approach, where the arts of passing and dribbling might be developed, and in time it was Scots travelling south to England and the fledgling Football League clubs who shaped the game, both by playing and managing. The Scottish novelist William McIlvanney, speaking on his brother Hugh's excellent documentary *The Football Men*, likened Scottish football folk to his country's engineers in as much as you could find them all over the world. 'They knew how things worked,' he said of Busby, Shankly and Stein. 'These men all had to very carefully work out the mechanics of what the game was.' There was a nimbleness to how Scots thought about the game. The passion for it burned bright, but the way the game was allowed to seep into the minds of those who let it and become part of their very way of thinking created more than mere footballers and managers. These were football doyens.

Like eighteenth-century Indians being handed a cricket bat, the Scots discovered a passion and created something better than what was already there. The football writer and Sir Matt Busby biographer Patrick Barclay, himself a keen Dundonian, is in no doubt of the country's role in football's development.

You have to bear in mind that Scotland was probably the capital of football. If there had been FIFA rankings, Scotland would have been at or near the top all the time. Football took off in Scotland like nowhere else. It is difficult to exaggerate how football's boom took off in Glasgow and its environment more than anywhere else in the world.

And so football was the entertainment to these

working-class people. Miners couldn't afford anything else anyway. Cinemas had started and could sometimes be visited but their only other form of entertainment was smoking. That was it.

But why did Scots become almost genetically obsessed? 'Maybe it is because we were smaller and our low centre of gravity meant our brains were closer to the ball.' Barclay laughs.

It was traditional though to have a very technical style of football. That originated in Scotland. It grew and grew. Matt [Busby] caught football from his environment. It was something that Scotland became good at and that fostered its popularity. World crowd records were always broken in Glasgow, year after year after year. It was probably the most phenomenal football boom in the history of the game.

Rugby in Wales is part of the fabric of society. In Scotland with football, it was the same. You can go back to the 1920s and 1930s and the coffee houses of Vienna being the intellectual cradle; OK, the coffee wouldn't have been as good in Scotland, but the talk was as enthusiastic and all enveloping as a part of society.

If football had become Scotland's intellectual property, Matt Busby's early discussions were with the very best of professors. Alex James of Mossend and Hughie Gallacher of Bellshill epitomized everything their country wanted from the game. Both diminutive and skilful (their brains very close to the ball), Busby grew up looking up to these older boys and taking in the things they were doing on their way to brilliant careers.

Alex James played for Orbiston Celtic, a local side who played their games on a Saturday alongside the village spoil tip. Matt was afforded the honour of laying out the kit for James and his teammates, and it was obvious from a young age that his affection for the game, his ability playing it and his empathy for those who did likewise might mean more to his future than merely finding a hobby. A combination of railway football specials and the newish Saturday half-holiday meant heavenly trips to Glasgow to watch Celtic, an obsession he had inherited from his father. Busby would watch his heroes in green and white hoops, and when he took on fellow local dreamers in games in which rules such as the number of participants and the length of the battle were never strictly observed, he'd fantasize about being one of them.

One day Alex James at Orbiston Celtic misplaced his boots, and young Busby sprang into action, running home and lending the future Arsenal star his pair. The whole town would hear of this act of generosity, perhaps offering local wags the prophetic line that the great Alex James was fit to lace young Matt Busby's boots.

Hughie Gallacher, who worked down the Hattonrigg pit from the age of fifteen, was the other starlet Busby watched regularly at close quarters. Soon the little striker would be heading to Newcastle and Chelsea and en route would win the Scottish Cup for Airdrie. These weren't just footballers affecting a young life; this was greatness inspiring greatness. 'My football thinking,' Busby said years later, 'has been influenced by close contact with great men from my boyhood.'

Busby had met Jean at the Bellshill miners' club, celebrating an under-18 Scottish Cup win by a team called Alpine Villa, the best youth team around and one that he and his best friend Frank Rodgers had been proud to join. Both were taking steps towards football as a career. Meanwhile Nellie Busby, at this stage not seeing football as anything but a passion, was planning to emigrate to America. She saw a future there for her family, a future that didn't involve mining. For Nellie, knowing how much his teachers thought of him, the idea of her grown-up son teaching in an American high school must have appealed.

The family were on a six-month waiting list for visas. Busby had left school and was working underground, but with the soot of the working day covering his body and clothes it was time for the young man to come clean. He told his mum of his sporting ambitions and with the support of Nellie and his family, it was agreed they would stay. Busby worked the week in the darkness but his weekends were given to the light of the game he adored. For Hughie Gallacher, for Busby, Shankly and Stein, for so many men who worked where dust and darkness owned their lungs and eyes, football was the oxygen tank and the light they could return to.

In 1929 D. H. Lawrence, the son of a Nottingham miner, wrote an essay called 'Nottingham and the Mining Countryside'. In it he bemoaned the effect that industrial mining had had on both the landscape and on the heart and souls of his father's generation: 'The great crime which the moneyed classes and pro-moters of industry committed in the palmy Victorian days was the condemning of the workers to ugliness, ugliness, ugliness: meanness and formless and ugly surroundings, ugly ideals, ugly religion, ugly hope, ugly love, ugly clothes, ugly furniture, ugly houses, ugly relationship between workers and employers. The human soul needs actual beauty even more than bread.' Lawrence thought miners actually placated that need underground. 'I know that the ordinary collier, when I was a boy, had a peculiar sense of beauty, coming from his intuitive and instinctive conscious-ness, which was awakened down pit.'

Richard Burton concurred with Lawrence in his appearance on the *Dick Cavett Show* in 1980, when he gushed about his father and the coal seam he used to work in South Wales. 'My father used to talk about it, as some men would talk about women. He'd talk about the beauty of this coalface.' Busby, Shankly and Stein, like Hughie Gallacher before them, understood that beauty, but while the miners that Lawrence observed came up from their cage to an ugly reality, these men had football, and football would feed their souls very nicely indeed.

From Alpine Villa, Busby took his passion to a top junior club, Denny Hibernian, but only for a handful of times as professional clubs were now very much taking a look. A dream move to Celtic wasn't possible simply because they found out he had trialled at Rangers, whose interest waned on finding out he was a Catholic. It would have to be south, and when Alex McNeill, the secretary at Denny Hibernian, got in touch with an old friend at Manchester City called Jimmy McMullan, a trial was arranged.

Busby travelled south to play a trial game at Burnley's Turf Moor, catching City's eye and warranting the offer of a move. Matt Busby, one-time possible school teacher and more recently probable miner was going instead to be a professional footballer. His mother was amused, while Jean must have wished Celtic would reconsider. There was talk that the Glaswegian giants were thinking again, but their change of heart was too late. Matt's half-brother would later say that he found Matt in tears on hearing that news, but his tears would have to dry, and dry quickly. A train was waiting to take him to a strange city in England's north-west.

Bill Shankly's passion for football and his sense of destiny were certainly fuelled by his family, but the geography (that subject that he'd especially enjoyed at school) he was born into had a huge say in the path he chose. There is no doubt that the mining towns and villages where these men grew up were the stick, and football the carrot hanging in front of them, but in Glenbuck the result was extraordinary. That this village in its short lifespan, its population never higher than 1,700, should produce fifty professional footballers suggests something remarkable about the place. It was said in Yorkshire that if you were after a fast bowler, you need only whistle down a mine. In Scotland if it was a footballer you were after, in Glenbuck you didn't need to whistle.

Amid its green hills and slag heaps, even the smallest patch of flat land in Glenbuck merited a game. Inter-pit matches were a combination of guile, grit and sheer bloody murder. Spireslack versus the Davy and other such contests were as hard as they sound, and Shankly learned the fine and dark arts of football playing on a street affectionately known as Monkey Row. On the rare occasions he was sitting still, merely being in the company of his four older brothers was an education in itself.

Alec Shankly, twenty years Bill's senior, played for Ayr before the First World War. Jimmy played for Carlisle before moving to Sheffield United for an impressive £1,000, before a move to Southend. John had been at Portsmouth, Luton and Alloa before a heart attack took his life while attending the otherwise life-affirming 1960 European Cup final at Hampden Park between Real Madrid and Eintracht Frankfurt. Bob was a Falkirk player for seventeen years and went on to have a fine managerial career, most notably with Dundee, who he took into the European Cup in 1962.

Shankly would play (and talk) football with his brothers. A young sponge taking it all in. Don't bother arguing with the referee. To get on in football, a man had to be able to look after himself and his teammates, in play offering a pass and space, or at times under darker circumstances. 'You would be playing against lions,' Shankly remarked years later about his early days learning the trade, 'but there would be lions on your side as well.' On one occasion, when Shankly was a boy, a visiting team brought a crowd of supporters on the train, hooligans hell-bent on disrupting the match, and when the inevitable fight broke out it was like a brawl in a western – one in which Alec Shankly held his own. 'There were a few broken noses that day,' said Shankly.

Playing the game was key. The mini-leagues within the village itself were taken seriously and getting out of the pit and into the fresh air to play was a morale booster few could do without. Football itself was there to be mined, and Shankly and his sort used it to fuel their very lives, and when they weren't playing it, watching was a worthy substitute.

Glenbuck being a prominently Protestant place, Rangers were often (although it was never set in stone) the locals' team of choice, and improved rail links meant journeys to Glasgow were easy. Once working, Shankly would pay the 1s 6d return train fare, but being of the opinion that football was his true religion, one week he'd go to Ibrox, the next Celtic Park.

Back in the village, standing with other men young and old by the old co-operative shop, games and players seen would be dissected. Other events would come up; some older men would proudly show off medals won in the Boer War; one man would brag that he had pushed three hundred trucks of coal that day when they all knew it was closer to six. A neighbour who had got himself a coat was chastized as a snob, while the English were regularly put down with Robert Burns-like tenacity. Shankly read the Scottish bard with a passion matched by an inherited love of cinema from his father, and he and his siblings would walk for miles through the elements to Muirkirk to see silent movies before marvelling at the 'talkies' and early film heroes such as W. C. Fields and James Cagney.

Invariably though, everything would turn back to football, and the sport was becoming more than a way to fill spare time. Shankly had become a fine player, tenacious and keen. The local side who had put a roof over the head of so many early careers was called the Glenbuck Cherrypickers. Shankly had a trial there aged sixteen, but the club was close to extinction. Mines were closing and the population again falling, so Shankly took his talents to nearby Cronberry.

By now he was signing on as unemployed, but his absolute confidence that football was to be his career meant his nights were far from sleepless. The twelve miles a day he used to run underground were replaced with twenty-four-mile round trips on his bicycle to play, but this was energy more than well spent to a teenager desperate to learn from the men he was thrown in with. 'It was hard, but if you survived it, you were a player ready for anything.'

At Cronberry his enthusiasm and talent stood out. A game at Sanquhar in Dumfriesshire was particularly enthused by his energy, and a scout by the name of Peter Carruthers saw enough to recommend him to Carlisle. After a trial game he was offered a contract.

It was 1932 and Shankly was packed and heading for a border he had never before crossed. Excitement filled his bones, but as the place he'd later teasingly liken to Outer Mongolia became a small speck behind him, he felt nothing but huge affection for home. There he had learned a world's worth of knowledge. At home and underground he had seen how work, both the hard and team variety, can impact lives. He had observed people. People talking, joking and fighting. He had learned how to start and how to finish an argument. He had observed his mother and father's kindness and his village's capacity, even in the face of life's harshest treatment, to laugh and give. Now though he was off. The towns of northern England beckoned, and eventually one football-mad city would call him.

Born a decade after Shankly, Jock Stein would have to wait a while before he could explore football's frontiers, and even when he came of age, the wanderlust shown emphatically by Shankly and perhaps reluctantly by Busby was never as keenly felt. Stein was a good player but not exceptional, but if his feet paled in comparison to those of others, his heart and mind were becoming finely tuned to the game he loved.

Not that those charged with picking school teams could see the potential in him. Well built and physical, Stein was noticeable on the field for more than merely his head of black curly hair, but his abilities with the ball didn't stand him out from a crowd that as ever in these parts, was full of talented young players. John Gibson picked the Greenfield School team. 'John [Jock] played left half for me,' he said in Archie Macpherson's *Definitive Biography of Jock Stein*. 'He wasn't the most outstanding player by a mile, but he was a lanky lad and good enough. I never thought he would get so far.'

What teachers may miss, fathers never do, and so it was with Jock's dad George, who had a clear plan of the path his son's footballing life would take. George was a Protestant who took such matters seriously. His son would join Blantyre Victoria (the Vics), the local team who played in red, white and blue, and then he would move to Rangers who of course did the same.

Burnbank was a typical west Scotland town in as much as religious divides mapped its streets, if not its soul. Matt Busby had grown up knowing sectarianism, and Bellshill – like Burnbank – on a Saturday night at closing time would speak violently of Protestant and Catholic angst. Nellie and Alex Busby were practising Catholics, and Matt himself would keep his religion closely to his heart all his life, but he had been brought up to keep such matters at home. Not that it was always easy. Eastern European Catholics had also migrated to Scotland's west coast and worked in the mines often for less money, their presence often fuelling further anger among Protestant locals. For Shankly in his more rural setting, religion of course was present but less intense. Shankly would say that his mum was a religious woman but had too much work to do preparing lunch for twelve people to attend the Presbyterian church on a Sunday.

Busby and Shankly both moved through life with a give-and-take attitude but (and perhaps given his family's strict protestant background, more impressively) so did Stein. In his football career Stein would have to stare down the malevolent gaze of sectarianism, but from a young age it was clear to those around him that division was never going to shape his thoughts on life or the game. Harry Steele, a schoolfriend of Stein and a fellow ex-miner, admits that when it came to settling a religious dispute on a Saturday night, he was never shy of using his fists, but not Stein. 'There was plenty between Catholics and Protestants,' recalled Steele in Macpherson's biography. 'Saturday nights coming out of pubs you had to watch yourself. There was a lot of drink taken. You should have seen the fights then.

'Now, I was in the Orange Lodge myself and played the flute in the local band, but all the time I was with Jock I never heard him saying anything against Catholics, and by God there was plenty said about that, for all his pals were Orange. Aye, he and his father were Rangers men, of course, but that was all.'

It may have been for football rather than religious reasons that George Stein opposed his son's early moves within the game. On hearing that the almost-seventeen-year-old Stein had been signed by Burnbank Athletic, his dad was less than pleased by what he saw as a diversion from the Vics/Rangers path he had always envisaged. Athletic played in black and white, not the British national colours of both the Vics and his beloved Rangers. The club's officials had signed Stein on the bus home from his trial, an opportunist act akin to treachery. 'You'll never kick a ball for that team,' George told his son on hearing the news. Even the arrival at his home of two Burnbank Athletic officials with offerings of whisky couldn't placate his ire. 'They thought they would be able to talk my father round with the drink they brought,' said Stein's sister, Margaret McDade. They were wrong. 'They hadn't offered John a signing-on fee or anything, and my father thought they should have at least given him the price of a suit. He was angry and determined that John would not play for them – and he never did. The form was torn up and the next thing we knew he was playing for the Vics.'

A Burnbank father's ambitions for his son may well have centred around football, but a mother's often came in gentler guises. Jane Stein, the long-time wife of a miner, like so many wanted her son to avoid the clank, clank, clank of the pit cage. Jane had also lost two daughters, and John (never Jock), her only son, was always the apple of her eye. 'My mother was always very protective of him,' said Jessie McNeill, Stein's sister. 'She loved every hair on his head.'

In Burnbank and beyond the boys become men, the men invariably headed into that cage, and too often a mother's fears of harm or loss came true. The inter-war years had seen changes, with coal-cutting machines and conveyors, and the number of serious accidents rose, while the dust created by the machines brought a greater likelihood of lung disease. Stein's father had had his own health problems including a cerebral haemorrhage, and with the death of his sister, Stein wanted to get out of education and into work. He had been working in a carpet factory, but the pits offered more work and more money for the family. His mother tried to talk him out of it, but she was dealing with a strong-minded teenager and his mind was made up.

> Howkin' awa' 'neath a mountain o' stane
> Gaspin' for want o' air
> The sweat makin' streams doon my bare back-bane
> And my knees a hauckit and sair

This verse from the Bowhill miner and poet Joe Corrie speaks of the dank, cramped conditions in which men worked, and Stein, on the pitch a large centre half, was by no means designed for such graft. His mother's woes deepened each time she saw the cuts on his back, caused by him sliding along the rocky floors to get to the coal seams, but the money supplied by Stein's work all went on the family table, and in return his mother and sisters spoilt him.

'Everything was done for him,' recalled his sister Margaret McDade. 'When he was in the pits he didn't have a lot of time between finishing a shift and then heading off to training with the Rovers. When he arrived home he would be black because there were no pithead baths then. So I would have his shoes cleaned for him and Jessie would have his razors ready for him.

Mind you, he would always give us some money for doing these wee jobs. He looked after us that way.'

Stein had his routine. He didn't drink and tried to keep out of those Saturday-night fights, but he liked to play bowls with his parents and gambling became an early and lifelong vice. Illegal punts with the street bookies at Burnbank Cross was part of the town's male culture, and Stein was prone to bet on the horses and, even when he became a part-time pro, football. He also liked to go dancing, when local girls would join him and his friends, but it was his passion for football – more than a tangible talent for the game – that occupied most of Stein's thoughts. 'I tell you,' his friend Harry Steele later recalled, 'Jock liked a night out with his pals at the dancing. But sometimes when you went looking for him he would be up the football park teaching the kids how to kick a ball. He would spend hours with them.'

Stein had gained a reputation as a tough centre half. Nothing exceptional to the casual eye, but what was brewing below the surface – coupled with a passion for the game he had gained with walking – was a desire to understand and control football's technicalities. Economics and reality forced his body to mine for coal, but his love of football had his mind digging for sporting answers.

Years earlier, Busby had sat in his Manchester digs digging for answers to his own sporting queries. 'You can still make it.' Phil McLoy's words rang true, and his bags were unpacked. Busby had impressed in training, but pinning down a position was proving difficult. Proficient in attacking roles, Busby's debut had been at inside left, but Tommy Johnson, a star of the First Division, played there. He tried the wing, where he was decent but lacked the pace to be anything more. Being seemingly a jack of all trades but master of none was causing confusion among his coaches and insecurities within himself. As his fellow pros got on with making their own way in the game, the young man felt a keen loneliness that almost had him packing it in. Life on the right wing wasn't working and centre forward wouldn't do either. A place in the first team seemed a long way off, but those making the decisions saw enough in him to keep him on, and with the Great Depression digging in its sharp heels, Busby could take solace from a wage packet and summers off spent back home with Jean.

In 1930 Manchester United showed an interest in taking him from their neighbours but could not afford the £150 City asked for, and Busby was becoming resigned to a life away from professional football. It was a thought that, while saddening him, no longer caused the agony he had felt when he first arrived. Perhaps at the end of the season, going home and re-examining things might not be so bad.

On a November afternoon in 1930, Busby was called by Alex Bell, a trainer at Manchester City who needed a player to fill in for a Northern Midweek League fixture designed to give game time to eager trialists and professionals returning from injury. Spectators were scarce and interest less, but it turned out to be a game that arguably changed the fortunes of football in Manchester and beyond. Busby brought his boots, and was told by Bell that he would fill in at right half, a deeper role that he had never tried before. From the off, it suited him. He could tackle and he could pass. Assessing the game from the midfield suited his cerebral approach, and his manager, Peter Hodge had been sitting in the otherwise empty stand. The boss wanted a word.

'That was a right good game you played,' he told his young player. Busby walked away buoyed. He was twenty-one. Had he at last found the key to the game he longed to play? Suddenly Manchester and Moss Side seemed homelier, his future less foggy. Having found his position, Matt Busby could now settle in the city that one day he would call his heaven.

Chapter 3:

Sacrifice

A Spring Saturday in 1939. Bolton.

Serpent-like streams of people move towards the football stadium. Industry goes on around them filling the air with cloudy plumes reminiscent of the dark skies gathering over Europe. Germany has invaded Czechoslovakia, the Munich Agreement is nothing but useless pulp, thoughts of peace in this time are disappearing in the fog. Today though is Saturday. Burnden Park looms in the distance. Time for the match.

Harry Goslin is Bolton's captain. Brylcreemed hair and piercing blue eyes. Straight backed and tall. A right half with a taste for the defensive side of the game. The mood in the ground is nervous. Football, for so long the pill taken by the masses to numb the hardships of everyday life, now has its work cut out. War looms.

Prior to kick-off, Goslin takes a microphone and addresses the crowd. 'We are facing a national emergency,' he says. 'But this danger can be met if everybody keeps a cool head and knows what to do. This is something you can't leave to the other fellow, everybody has a share to do.' After the game Goslin and his teammates join the Territorial Army.

A September Saturday in 1939. Liverpool.

Supporters await their teams. Chelsea have come to Anfield from London, but the day before so did the news that Adolf Hitler's liking for Czechoslovakia had extended to Poland. It's only the third game of the fledgling season and no one knows how long it will last. People though have come. Time for the match.

Matt Busby is Liverpool's captain. Number 4 on his back, he leads the team from dressing room to pitch. He and many of those behind him are already signed up and have been on military duty until the early hours of that morning. There's a band on the pitch, it starts to play 'It's a Long Way to Tipperary'. Chelsea are beaten 1–0, but the following day Prime Minister Neville Chamberlain takes to the airwaves and war is declared. The season is over.

Later that day, while families gathered once more around the living-room wireless, this time to hear the King and hoping that his voice will hold out, footballers could be forgiven for pondering the fate of their now stuttering careers.

Not far from Anfield, Tommy Lawton, the First Division's top goal-getter, a swashbuckling centre forward whose thirty-five goals the season before had won the league for Everton, sits at home wondering. Lawton was every English schoolboy's cigarette-card hero. He had somehow filled Dixie Dean's boots, but now war had come once more, and those boots were to be – for the foreseeable future – of the army variety.

'Then came the war and, with it, the end of my career or so I felt,' Lawton later wrote. 'Surely there couldn't be room for a professional footballer in a world gone crazy? I, of course, being a young, fit man approaching twenty would go into the services.

Meanwhile, in the leisure time I had left I wound up my personal affairs, cursed Hitler and all his rats and occasionally sat down to think of what had been and what might have been.'

Lawton wasn't alone: Matt Busby, thirty and captain of Liverpool; Bill Shankly, his twenty-sixth birthday the day before war was declared, and a mainstay in Preston's midfield. Both were Scotland internationals, both FA Cup winners and both were left wondering if hostilities would finish their playing careers just when they were reaching their prime. Jock Stein was a teenager but also a miner – a reserved profession – so he remained at home fighting the usual battle underground while wondering if his prime would ever come.

Busby would initially join the 9th Battalion of the King's Regiment in Liverpool before accepting an offer to move to Aldershot to learn how to be a physical training instructor. His days as a soldier had brought back some old insecurities. Never comfortable with life as a miner, Busby now doubted his military prowess, even questioning why his boots didn't shine as much as his fellow servicemen's. Worrying about the finish on his boots paled into insignificance beside what he had felt in his early days at Manchester City, but with that fine performance at half back in the Northern Midweek League, Busby's fortunes and mood had turned. As so often in these cases, one teammate's bad luck is another's launch pad, and when Matt Barrass was ruled out of a match at Huddersfield, the right-half spot needed filling, and suddenly there was a natural among City's ranks. Busby had played, once again performed very well, and the position was his.

In January 1931 Busby went home to Orbiston to marry Jean in a Catholic (Jean had converted) church in nearby Bothwell. Earlier in their courtship Jean might have shared Busby's mother's concerns about his future in the professional game, but now she shared a name and a home with a young player who was turning heads in the English First Division. 'I hope you do well at wing half,' said Bob Smith, a director at Maine Road; 'you were a wash-out as a forward.' It had been a blunt appraisal by Smith, but Busby didn't take it to heart. Instead he took heart from it.

Later in his life, when it came to communicating with players, he would never shy away from brutal honesty. However, Busby had also learned not to be too quick to judge. A good footballer, he realized, is a good footballer, and a manager's job often entails the polishing of a rough diamond. Fate might have given him his place in Manchester City's side but Busby would take more deliberate steps when his time came to mould careers. Busby Babe and inside forward Jackie Blanchflower for one would benefit from a manager who saw in him a title-winning centre half.

Back in the 1930s, lacking the pace to affect a match from the wing, and by no means a finisher, Busby at right half was influencing games with his passing. Intelligent and forward thinking, Manchester City's new find was growing in confidence and constantly feeding the forwards ahead of him, even though those in defence knew they might have to work a bit harder. 'He wasn't too sound a defensive player,' recalled Sid Cann, Manchester City's right back, 'and his recovery when beaten was a bit slow, as I knew from playing behind him. But he was a fine player to watch, and he would have revelled in a modern midfield role with freedom to move about and plenty of cover behind him.' Meanwhile, in London, Herbert Chapman's Arsenal were redesigning the map of football that for years had seen northern clubs in the ascendancy. Chapman indeed was using tactics and formations that would change the game as a whole. Wing halves were given more attacking freedom, an innovation that more than suited Busby.

Bill Shankly would also ply his trade from that position but with a more conservative, ball-winning approach. For Busby, intelligently switching play and getting the ball forward was everything. Manchester City would reap the rewards. In 1933 they reached Wembley for an FA Cup final against Everton. Despite the Merseysiders and Dixie Dean winning the title the year before, City travelled to the capital as favourites, but injury and bad preparation would scupper Busby's hopes of a winner's medal.

One reason was cruel luck. An injury to centre forward Fred Tilson meant Alec Herd moved from inside forward to his central role. 'It knocked the stuffing out of most of us,' said Sid Cann. The other reason annoyed Busby and taught him that small details can influence big days. City left their Hertfordshire base early, and arrived at the famous old ground nearly two hours before kick-off. The players strolled around the pitch, bickered nervously among themselves, and by 2.15 they were changed. All dressed up and nowhere to go. Busby would admit that by the time he met the Duke of York his nervous energy was merely nerves, and he and his teammates played badly in a 3–0 defeat. Absentee Fred Tilson's importance to the side was underlined the following season when he scored four goals in the FA Cup semi-final against Aston Villa. Frank Swift, a giant Lancastrian teenager, had taken the team's goalkeeping position and become a firm friend of Busby, who himself had become a firm fixture not only at City but within the English game.

Joe Mercer of Everton played against Busby and would wax lyrical in later years about his opponent's craft on the ball. 'What made Matt noticeable was the silkiness in possession, the way he drifted inside from the wing and then switched the ball back over the head of the fullback for his winger,' recalled the future Manchester City manager. 'He had this calm influence on events around him. He always had this, the ability to influence.'

It's not clear if Busby's influence spread to organizational matters, but learning from the year before, City's plans changed prior to the 1934 Cup final, and the dressing room was a far calmer place thanks largely to their arrival just an hour before kick-off. This time Portsmouth stood between Busby and a winner's medal. Frank Swift had been visibly nervous in the dressing room (he'd received a slap in the face and a shot of whisky from trainer Alex Bell), and as the game started Busby was still aware of the young man's self-doubt. Just minutes in, Busby received the ball in his penalty area, and in an era when passing back to your keeper wasn't really the done thing played it to Swift, hoping an early touch would ease his anxiety. It didn't work, because Swift soon let an innocuous shot slip under him, and Busby must have headed to the dressing room at half-time, fearing another loser's medal for the mantelpiece. He needn't have worried. Storm clouds were raging over north London, but City, inspired by Tilson, dominated the second half, and two goals from the centre forward won the cup.

In all the excitement at the final whistle Swift fainted. Then when he came round and met the King to collect his medal, his mother fainted. Busby kept his head. He had his hands on a winner's medal, and if he read the *Daily Telegraph*, the words 'Busby, the finest right half ever seen at Wembley' must have warmed the young man, but not as much as the pride on the faces of his family and neighbours when he brought the trophy up to Bellshill, filling it with wine in the Angus Bar. The Depression had set in hard, but smiles followed the famous trophy around, and Busby with Jean alongside him was more than happy to spread some joy.

But behind the smiles Busby's home life was difficult. Jean had given birth to a daughter, Sheena, but the labour had been difficult and had affected her health. Since they had been married Jean had suffered four miscarriages, all boys, and concerns about his wife's health were regularly on Busby's mind. He would have a son, Sandy, a rare moment of pure happiness for the family during Busby's last days as a Manchester City player.

After the cup triumph Busby was dogged by injury, and with his ongoing concerns about Jean, his morale was low. 'I was dwelling morbidly on a run of bad luck,' he later would lament. He also felt his employers weren't as supportive as he'd have liked. Busby would later prove himself the most approachable of managers, there to look after the well-being of his players and staff as well as coax performances from them, but City's directors were in line with the more detached attitudes of the time, and so when they spent £10,000 on the Irish inside forward Peter Doherty, Busby took it as his cue to leave.

He wouldn't have to go far. Liverpool were struggling towards the foot of the table and needed reinforcements, and while the club's board would call £8,000 an 'extremely high figure', they agreed that in Busby they had 'laid something in for the future' of the club. That future for now would be in the top flight as Busby's arrival coincided with an upturn in form and relegation was avoided. Busby though had some reservations about his new place of work.

Liverpool's was an ageing squad, and in the summer of 1936 the club advertised for a new manager, someone who understood the changing, modern game. The fact that the board were only just building a manager's office at the club perhaps spoke of a club slow to look ahead, but when they chose George Kay from the fifty-two applicants, they had at least appointed a man who understood the game and those who played it, and who would have a considerable effect on Busby.

If Busby had grown disillusioned with the emotionally sterile club he felt City had become, in Kay he had a players' manager, a man willing to get close to those he worked with, willing to see more than a player. Busby liked him immediately. Kay, a Mancunian, had been a fine player – he captained West Ham at the first ever FA Cup final at Wembley in 1923 – before going into management at Luton Town and Southampton. Seen as a visionary, although not quite the 'tracksuit manager' Busby would become, Kay had more to say on both transfers and tactics than his predecessors. Busby was impressed.

By now, Busby, like so many in the game, was also impressed with a gritty footballer at Preston. Bill Shankly was proving a fiery competitor. Once after a win over Liverpool at Deepdale, Busby approached Shankly and a few of his teammates as he was leaving the ground. 'That's the way to play, fellows,' he sportingly said. 'Strength plus ability.'

The strength part of the game was very much at the heart of Shankly's approach to life at wing half. Tackle hard, win the ball. And while Busby was a keen passer with a different take on things, Shankly appreciated his style too. 'If as a boy at that time you wanted to model yourself on anyone,' he later said, 'there was nobody better to go and watch than Matt.' He would preface this though with his usual mischief: 'Mind you, I'm not sure that I'd have had him in my team: he was a bit too gentle.'

The *Liverpool Echo* saw Busby as anything but gentle and instead drooled over his attacking abilities. 'Busby goes far up, if so inclined and when he starts his upward trend, one knows his command of the ball will be such he will not be dispossessed,' they wrote in September 1936. 'He is the richest and most practised passer the game has ever known. Hence he appears in a blinding light when compared with some other half backs.'

Busby's good form was one thing, but the club's fortunes only rose to mid-table levels. Kay was trying hard to impose himself at Liverpool but money was tight. Arsenal, Manchester City, Everton, all could spend five-figure sums on players. In 1937 Kay even touted the idea of selling Busby to fund future signings. That enticed a local to write to the *Echo* calling for the entire board to resign. But Kay's hands were tied. Another letter in the *Echo* likened his task to that of a chauffeur asked to drive a car without petrol.

If the club at board level was running on fumes, its captain's footballing brain was developing into something akin to premium unleaded. He was approaching thirty, and while the nation wondered about Herr Hitler's intentions, Busby was still focused on playing the game he loved, but there had always been something in him, something that drew him to guiding others. A future in coaching was developing in his keen mind. From taking his half-brother Jimmy under his wing to the teacher he may well have become, pushing others was very much part of Busby's character. Even the way he played reflected this. Get the ball under control. Look up, look at others. What do they need? Play the ball forward into space that they can exploit.

Busby could learn from others too. For any player with managerial ambitions in those pre-war years, having Herbert Chapman in the game was something like Shakespeare being around to offer aspiring playwrights friendly advice. Busby looked admiringly at Chapman's tactical nous and his absolute demand to be the man in charge. At Wolves Frank Buckley's determination to build a team around youth and trust them to carry out his plans would also catch his eye, while at Liverpool his own manager's energy for the game and for those who called him boss was another trait he warmed to. 'George was a familiar figure on the trainers' bench,' Busby later said of Kay. 'Shouting, beseeching, wringing his hands, holding his head in apparent anguish, and making an excellent attempt to kick and head every ball . . . but a fanatical enthusiasm for his job . . . should never be condemned. He was a very fine man and manager.'

Busby was showing his own enthusiasm for the club's fortunes off the pitch. Still good friends with Alec Herd from his City days, they were regular golfing partners, and in the summer of 1938 when one day Herd stood Busby up at the first tee, the Liverpool captain discovered that Herd was watching a brilliant young player hoping to sign for Hamilton Academical. The youngster was sixteen years old and called Billy Liddell. He played for a junior team called Lochgelly Violet, but the step up to the professional game was proving tricky due to his parents' need for assurance that their bright son (he was also training to be an accountant) was right for a life in football. Liddell's father was looking for a part-time start in the game, and talks with the Hamilton club stalled. Busby saw an opportunity, called Kay, arranged a meeting and £200 was paid for a player who would go on to be in any conversation about Liverpool Football Club's finest of all time.

Busby's captaining responsibilities stretched further when he took a new recruit from Bishop Auckland under his wing. Bob Paisley had arrived from the amateur club in May 1939. A young left half who had worked in the mines of County Durham, Paisley was tenacious on the field but a little shy off it, and Busby, never forgetting how lonely he had felt when he took the leap from his warm mining community to the sometimes colder world of professional football, was first to welcome him to a club he too would one day so meteorically influence. The two would remain firm friends for life.

While two future giants of the game were familiarizing themselves with one another, Bill Shankly had become the player he always knew he would. Those early hardships at Carlisle wouldn't leave scars. He had appreciated the kindness of people there, notably the club trainer Tommy Curry, who would go on to take that same role at Manchester United and would lose his life at Munich. Curry had given Shankly a few shillings when he learned the young player had been cleaned out at cards. The manager too, Billy Hampson, who would go on to manage Leeds, eased the youngster in, fully aware of just how industrial some games in the Third Division (North) could be. 'The team wasn't great,' said Shankly later, 'so [Hampson] thought, *You're not going to get mangled in there.* He would take me to one side and say, "We're playing away to Rotherham. That's not for you."'

At Carlisle he won the North Eastern League Cup with the reserves, a medal he kept proudly among the more glittery ones he would later acquire. One season at Carlisle and he was where – career-wise if not geographically – he wanted to be, but there was an itch. 'I think if you're ambitious, the place you go to doesn't make any difference,' he later said. 'I was ambitious – impatient, if you like, because ambition is a form of impatience. You want to get at something before it's there. You want to burst the balloon before it's blown up.'

At the end of the 1932/3 season Shankly was impatient to get home, eager to get back to games of cards with friends and family less inclined to clean him out. Half an hour after the last whistle had blown on the campaign, Shankly was showered, packed and off up the road. Those friends and brothers who worked in the pits were finished by 2.30 p.m., and once they'd eaten, the cards could commence. Brag was the game of choice, sometimes pontoon, and with the summer in front of him, Shankly sat playing cards on the football pitch opposite his family home with his brother Bob, content among the green fields upon which his ambitions had been born. Taking some money from his brother was the only thing on his mind that afternoon.

His sister's arrival on the field wouldn't have attracted much attention from the card players, but when she told her brother he had a telegram from England, his ears pricked up. It was from Carlisle: TRAVEL TO CARLISLE TOMORROW STOP CARLISLE UNITED.

Contact was made, trains boarded and the news was heard that Preston North End of the Second Division wanted to take the eighteen-year-old to Lancashire. For all Shankly's talk of stepping stones, he wasn't at first sure. He felt he would be a regular in the Carlisle first team the next season and was on good money. Four pounds, ten shillings a week. 'I was much better off than a coal miner and for doing something in the fresh air that I would have done for nothing,' he'd say, and Preston weren't offering much more. And anyway, Second Division? He wanted his next move to be to the top.

It was his brother Alec, so often there with professional advice, who told him that this wasn't about where he was now and what he was earning but how this move could affect his future. 'Preston's a bigger club,' Alec told him. 'They used to be a great club, they might be again.' The young man listened and not for the last time headed to a north-west footballing institution down on its luck but, with his presence, would soon be back among the stars.

The town of Preston that Shankly found must have reminded him of home. The small groups of men gathered on street corners, warming themselves around fires, playing cards, talking. Yet the laughter was not as robust as Shankly had remembered it back in Glenbuck. Preston in 1933, like great swathes of England, was suffering from the crippling Depression, which saw nearly half a million cotton workers unemployed and their mills closed. Most of the six pounds a week now earned by the club's new wing half was sent home to his family, but Shankly never forgot the privileged position his talent for football had afforded him.

Shankly started in the Central League reserves team, but such was the desire and application of the new shaven-headed right half, it wasn't long before a first-team debut was granted. Shankly never had Busby's problem of finding a position to suit him. Low centre of gravity, granite-like attitude, wing half was perfect for him. Always had been. If he hadn't been a footballer, Shankly might have boxed such was his passion for the sport. A natural middleweight in the ring, instead his domain was as a natural in midfield.

For his debut Hull City were the opponents at Deepdale, and by chance Shankly had faced them the year before in the Third Division. Hull were a good side and had won 6–1 that day, but Shankly – already able to think about a team's tactics and how to counter them – recalled the high line the Humberside team liked to play and burst through to set up the first goal in a 5–0 win. Shankly was a hit, and in his first season Preston won promotion to the First Division.

First Division football came naturally to both player and club. Like Busby earlier in the decade, Shankly would reach two FA Cup finals and like his fellow Scot would have to wait until the second occasion to claim a winner's medal. In the 1937 final Sunderland, armed with Raich Carter at inside forward, were formidable foes and won 3–1. Preston were on the up. They might have won the league the following season but instead made do with another trip to the Empire Stadium, where this time Huddersfield were the team to beat. The game was a stalemate until deep into extra time. The BBC commentator Thomas Woodrooffe told a listening nation that should a goal be scored, he'd eat his hat. Moments later, Preston won a penalty, George Mutch dispatched it, and Woodrooffe was soon tucking into a hat, albeit made from marzipan and icing sugar.

'Of all the things that can happen in the game, when the whistle blows at Wembley and you've won, that's the greatest thrill of your life as a player.' Shankly was an FA Cup winner. Not the first boy from Glenbuck to boast that feat, but as the team headed north, his medal and the white silk shirt he had worn were safely and proudly packed and would always be kept.

The journey to and from Wembley was becoming familiar. Just weeks earlier he had made his debut for Scotland there, a 1–0 win over the auld enemy. Shankly relished the occasion. Playing for Scotland was so much more than merely a game. It unleashed a passion ingrained in him from those hours spent listening to men and women talk of people and days gone by. Alex James, a hero of Busby and so many others, was among many to see what it meant. 'Bill Shankly is a *real* Scotland player who will fight until he drops,' said the Lanarkshire superstar.

In 1940 Company Sergeant Major Instructor Busby found himself on the English Channel heading towards France. The monotonous swell wasn't agreeing with Busby, who was never at home on the sea, his spirits only raised by sharing the trip with the likes of Stan Cullis and Joe Mercer. They were teammates in an all-star team put together by the FA secretary Stanley Rous, who had asked Busby to be its player/manager.

The Liverpool captain was delighted to get a chance to play, but the manager part of the deal especially appealed to him and he relished the chance to develop 'the involved technique of handling men'. Those wobbly sea legs though would have to return to the waves, as Busby became a regular on convoys around the Cape of Good Hope. Ten weeks at sea conducting PT sessions with men being transported to the desert conflicts in North Africa was the closest he would get to the war. The firm ground of wartime football pitches was an easier place to be. Busby turned out for Liverpool when possible but also guested for other clubs including Chelsea, Reading and Hibernian, for whom in 1942 he faced a young Jock Stein, by now playing for Albion Rovers. He also captained Scotland, where he played alongside Bill Shankly.

Shankly had turned twenty-six the day before Britain declared war. The young man had options. He might have returned to the pits but instead took another reserved occupation when he joined English Electric as a riveter helping to make Hampden Bombers. Opting for a reserved occupation, however helpful to the war effort, came with problems. The great Raich Carter of Sunderland and England had immediately joined the fire brigade, but although he regularly helped extinguish the fires started in Sunderland's shipyards by a marauding Luftwaffe, he experienced booing from supporters who normally worshipped his every move. Carter soon joined the RAF.

Shankly followed suit, not because he had been vilified by supporters, but being asked to work inside all day didn't suit this most outdoors of men. Not interested in any sort of military advancement he nevertheless wanted to do his bit, stating that even if he was cleaning the latrines, he would work hard to do it better than anyone else. Shankly was posted to Manchester and, surrounded by other sportsmen, was happy, crying when it was time to leave. One day a low-flying plane dropped a couple of bombs into his camp, but that was to be the closest he got to any battlefield. Moving around the country, Shankly played for Norwich, Luton Town and even Liverpool, where a touch on the shoulder from George Kay, a manager he immediately took to, stayed with him for a long time. Matt Busby had a similar encounter with someone who in terms of the war effort was slightly more prominent than Kay.

General Sir Bernard Montgomery was a keen football fan, and on a rare day off from planning the invasion of Normandy in 1944 was a guest at Wembley for England's match against Scotland. As skipper, Busby introduced Monty to the likes of Shankly before talking to the man himself. 'I've never been to Scotland,' admitted the general.

'Shame on you,' came Busby's patriotic reply. 'You've missed the grandest country in the world.'

Two months later, the countries met again, this time at Hampden Park, and Montgomery was part of the 133,000 crowd. Busby was again introduced to him, and this time the general smiled and said, 'You see, Sergeant Major, I have managed to get to Scotland.'

Montgomery, in even these most busy of times, recalled the briefest of conversations. It was a moment that always stayed with Busby, a man and manager who for so long had the human touch. 'Just as Busby could take pride in a familiarity with Montgomery,' wrote Patrick Barclay in his biography, 'many a soul in or around the game would come to believe that somehow he had caught the eye of Busby.'

Bolton's Harry Goslin had also encountered Montgomery. His 43rd Field Regiment was part of the general's command, firstly during the El Alamein campaign in North Africa and then in Italy, where crossing the River Sangro he and his regiment encountered some of the fiercest fighting of the whole war. Eleven days before Christmas 1943 Lieutenant Harry Goslin was struck in the back by shrapnel. A writer for the *Bolton Evening News* took to his typewriter just days later to tell locals who had adored Goslin the footballer that Goslin the man had been killed. 'I regret his life has been sacrificed in the cause of war.'

In 1945 the war ended. Matt Busby's footballing career had been cut short and now he was wondering what would happen next. Bill Shankly's career had also been severely disrupted. There would be no self-pity though. These were men after all who knew the meaning of real sacrifice. Their careers had stalled, but that was nothing compared to what others had lost. Matt Busby and Bill Shankly still had their lives, and now it was time to live them.

Chapter 4:

Jock's on the Road

Jock Stein returns from a hard day's work. His legs are weary, his muscles sore. He walks through the front door and into the kitchen, where the lady of the house is busy with her own daily toil but greets him with a smile. 'Can I have a bath?' he asks. The lady points him to the tub below the kitchen table. Stein grins. This feels like home.

In 1950 Stein found himself in the South Wales town of Llanelli, where the chance had arisen to play professional football. The town's side may have played in the Southern League, but they were a club with ambitions above that station and for a man keen to not only get away from the mines he had worked in for so long but to also call football his profession, the chance and the move had been one worth taking. The bath was to warm himself after his sporting efforts, not to wash away the black soot from underground that used to cover him every day or the sweat that used to sting the cuts across his back; both these things belonged to his past. For ever, he hoped.

This is Stein's first night away and the lady who greets him in the kitchen is Lizzie Williams, the landlady in his new digs. The bath she points him to is a familiar sight. The step into professional football and the twelve pounds a week he gets paid is something like dreamland, but even at twenty-seven Stein could be forgiven for missing his wife and his family.

The home life Stein left behind had been quite regular, the monotony of working the mines broken only by family life and from 1942 football at Albion Rovers. It was, though, merely the part-time version of the sport, and while the extra money earned from playing at Cliftonhill in the Scottish Second Division was more than welcome to his family, ensuring a more comfortable way of life than for many of their neighbours, Stein would still daydream about playing the game at its higher levels.

Aged just seventeen when war broke out, Stein stayed at home, but any idea that mining meant an easier war than being in military uniform should be set aside. For years Stein worked the pits and the coalface itself, a working routine that those charged with doing it day in and day out might get used to, but whose grind and hardships never subsided. Death, or the constant threat of it, was always in the background for these men. In the three months straddling 1942 and 1943 seven men were killed in the Bothwell Castle pit Stein worked. He had started with the ponies at Earnock but moved when the coal seams there were worked out. Bothwell Castle was across the river, and in 1948 there was another move, this time to the Priory pit in Blantyre.

This last pit was especially damp, offering additional challenges to those working there. Lanarkshire was notorious for wet pits, and while conditions improved slightly by the time Stein arrived at the Priory, it was still gruelling work. Bob Smith, a long-time miner who worked in similar conditions at nearby Ferniegair described life at a fourteen-inch seam where water had to be bailed out before its level was low enough for men to get down to take the coal: 'The gum [small coal] from the bottom of the seam was wet, and stuck to the shovel as you tried to turn it out into the roadhead. As you lay on your side stripping coal, water was constantly dripping from the roof on top of you. It was ice-cold water and you felt pretty miserable. There was no oilskins or any other sort of protection: we simply worked in our trousers and singlets, lying in the wet mud and wielding shovels.'

Ferniegair and the Priory were two of the very few pits with baths and drying rooms; for so many miners the mud, water, and sweat were carried home. Rheumatic pains and boils were constant companions, but with a surplus of miners, opting out was a risky option. In Newtongrange over in Midlothian one disgruntled miner working the wet conditions for only a shilling extra one day cracked and walked out. His manager, a notoriously tough man called Mungo Mackay, kept him idle for over three months just to teach him a lesson.

Managers wielded enormous power, but Stein was learning that the men with whom he worked and for whom his respect and warmth would last a lifetime, were more than capable of fighting back. Underground there was no religious divide, there was only teamwork, and above ground looking out for each other was just as necessary. Where Stein worked in the Shotts and Blantyre-Hamilton districts, strike action was especially common. In fact, between 1936 and 1940 its forty-seven disputes were the highest in the country.

Wartime efforts in the mines were of course heightened, but the pit owners only upped their levels of exploitation. Despite the national feeling of togetherness that hostilities in Europe and beyond were supposed to ingrain in the nation, issues of safety, working hours, and discipline were still very real. Strikes and disputes continued in Scottish pits. Stein, his mind often on his possible sporting future, had nothing but respect for those who took action and those who led them – so much so that early into his career at Albion Rovers, and early into a dispute, Stein handed a week's football wages to Mick McGahey, a young communist who would go on to lead Scotland's miners. This showed Stein's belief in those he worked with and his passion for not only the camaraderie they shared but also their resistance to those who would try to ride roughshod over them. As manager, years later, all of these traits would govern his work.

While the ideals of Scotland's Keir Hardie, founder of the Labour Party, were engraved on Stein's heart, it was his feet that continued to take most of his attention. Even an early passion for bowls (the love for which he had inherited from his parents and a sport that he became more than just good at, once winning the Lanarkshire championship) would subside, and playing for Rovers was perfect in the wartime years because so many of their players were serving in the forces, meaning more openings for a young man spending his war in the pits.

In the early winter of 1942 Stein had been taken to Cliftonhill Park by their manager, Webber Lees, a dominating man who could spot young talent. When he saw Stein play for the Vics, Lees was perhaps drawn to his domineering way of playing at centre half. Invited to train, Stein continued to impress Lees and was given a first start against, of all teams, Celtic. Oh, how his father must have swollen with pride at the idea of his boy leaving the family mark on more than a few of the visiting enemy.

A cold November wind blew through the ground, the crowd unaware that the following day the nation would rejoice at the news of victory at the Battle of El Alamein, and Celtic took an early 3–0 lead. Years later Stein himself would admit that he remembered very little of the match, amazing considering his Rovers team somehow fought back to draw 4–4. At least the *Sunday Post* was on hand to record the new defender's contribution, laying the blame for the goalfest at the door of Celtic regulars when they noted that while, 'Rovers had a trialist in their raw, lanky junior centre half, the ponderousness of his counterpart John McPhail cost Celtic two goals.'

McPhail would go on to win Scotland caps, but to return to Stein's early brushes with Scotland's football hierarchy, that had already happened, and on a far grander scale. At the end of July 1942 Blantyre Victoria hosted a five-a-side tournament. Such competitions were commonplace, but with the war dominating everything, getting the required number of teams was an issue. On hand to help out was a local boy. 'The difficulty was overcome,' wrote the *Gazette*, 'with Matt Busby (Hibs and Scotland) raising an Army five, bringing the contestants back to the original six teams ... The Vics obligingly decided to play the Army five, beating them 2 goals to nil.' It is said that Stein played that day, and it is hoped that he did and on that summer wartime afternoon played against Matt Busby. Or as Archie Macpherson so eloquently put it, 'That Blantyre pitch could perhaps make a modest claim that the playing fields of Eton had no exclusive boast to inspiring men to future European triumphs.'

Whether two titans of the game did indeed lock horns that day we may never know. For now, getting into the Rovers team and staying there dominated Stein's mind. Even facing his and his father's beloved Rangers, Stein wouldn't hold back. His foe might be a granite centre forward such as Jimmy Smith, but there was no way the boy from Burnbank was going to cower, never mind his boyhood allegiances, especially when Smith was giving out kicks like a lover gives roses.

Stein kept his head. Tackles were returned, as were words. 'You're only a boy,' said Smith. 'Behave yourself.' Maybe it was the 'boy' bit, but Stein dug in and carried on until Smith, fed up with the upstart, the ball and the rules, butted his marker's face. *Crack!* Days later, Stein took his broken nose down to the pit and proudly paraded it to suitably impressed workmates, most of which, being Rangers men, were on Smith's side.

Stein's tenacity and willingness to put his nose on the line quickly endeared himself to the Cliftonhill locals. His reserved profession meant he was always available to play in front of them, and his stubbornness was enough to make him a crowd favourite. His right foot aside, a tool he found useful only when walking, Stein was strong and consistent. Nothing fancy of course, but he knew a centre half's job and like he did every day at the coalface, he just got on with it.

'I don't think any of the Rovers fans could have imagined the levels of grandeur he would rise to,' said lifelong Rovers fan John Smith, who was there in the 1940s. 'He may not have been the best player on the park at that time, but the players all respected him.' Vocal and putting his natural understanding of the game's tactics to those around him, Stein's ability to guide a team was starting to shine. 'You could tell even then that he was a leader,' recalled Smith. 'I believe that he was born with those management skills and you could see he had them at Rovers. He was the key to that team and would encourage all the players around him.'

Stein's words were not only reserved for those with which he shared a football pitch. One day at East Fife, Stein and his team were having the sort of torrid afternoon that inspires opposing fans to mock. Stein, beaten again by a tricky forward, had heard enough when one fan shouted, 'Away you go, ya mug!' Stein got hold of the ball, smashed it into the loud-mouthed section of terracing and shouted, 'I'm a mug? You're the mugs for payin' to watch me!' Quick-witted and able to shout down anyone stupid enough to cross him, Stein's character was on show long before his name was of the household variety.

Away from the pitch and even at work, Stein's personality and charm were beginning to win friends. 'Jock's main job was to send the empty hutches along the coalface where we were working,' recalled his workmate and friend Harry Steele. 'We would send them back full and he would organize emptying them out and send them back. He had his wee benefits. Where he was he didn't have to move to get his food. The canteen would send down his rolls and ham to him in the lift. He got warm rolls, we got none.' The same workmates also had to watch enviously as their pal was dropped off at the back of his home. 'He knew all the train drivers, because he was playing with Albion Rovers at the time,' recalled Steele, who like others had a long walk. 'When we were on the wee puffer that took us back to Burnbank, it went past his row of houses at Earnock. Well, they used to slow down to let him off there while we had to sit and get off when it stopped at Burnbank station further on. He seemed to have this knack of talking people into helping him out.'

Aged nineteen, and in the local chip shop ordering a fish supper, Stein talked a fifteen-year-old girl named Jean into going out with him. She agreed, and for five years did just that, and then he talked her into marrying him. In October 1946 they became man and wife in Hamilton.

If Stein had shown his physical toughness in his dealings with Scotland's hardest strikers, it was nothing compared to the bloody noses he might have had to endure courting and marrying a Catholic girl, as Jean was. Such things mattered little to Stein himself, and while his father's eyebrows might have been raised, the family as a whole were not perturbed by the young girl Stein was bringing home for tea. 'As long as people are happy,' Stein's mother would always say, 'that's all that matters.' Stein's family was immersed in the community, as was typical of mining families, where hardships could be shared and hopefully halved. The harshness of life in these communities meant that wasn't always possible, but for Stein, getting by meant getting on, and the question of religious difference was, amid all of life's other struggles, not one worth answering.

It was an example of Stein's freedom of thought, one that would greatly aid his life as a football manager, but there were plenty of people where he did his growing up who would have frowned upon his relationship with Jean. 'If you wanted to go out with a girl or a boy from the other side,' recalled Harry Steele, 'you couldn't be seen walking down the main street with her.'

You would have to walk her home round the back streets even if it was a really long way round, just to be safe. That happened to both sides. If you were going regular with somebody from a different religion, most parents would end up saying, 'Get rid of them. I don't want you to be seen with them again.' That was the common response. It took some nerve for most people to mix. And of course if you 'turned' and left your own religion and went over to the other side, you were out in the cold. You were finished with your own community.

The phrase 'some nerve' stands out. Stein was single-minded and wouldn't be dictated to, however big the fuss. As we have seen, Matt Busby's wife (also called Jean) had converted to Catholicism before marrying, underlining the strength of character that these men and their wives showed so early in their lives.

Stein's abilities as a comfortable part-time Albion Rovers player were rarely stretched, but his thoughts were very much so. He wanted so much more. His wife would later say that in those early years she didn't really understand how much the game meant to him. He was still working in the pits, and his focus was on earning money for his family, but the desire to become something more within football was burning bright.

Rovers' striker at the time Adam McLean had an inkling that his young teammate was desperate to be more and keen to know more. 'There I was sitting after training on the first day and this lad starts to quiz me about certain players in the league and in the juniors he had seen and whether a certain player kicked with his right or left foot. And I don't mean in the religious sense, I mean he would sit and analyse. It was Jock.'

Stein had taken his boots as far as Dundee United during the war, where he enjoyed a brief loan spell, but now disillusionment with his everyday life of mining and training and mining and playing was eating away at him. 'Stein was obviously spellbound by a game he wished he could have played better than he actually did,' said Archie Macpherson, and while the challenge of First Division football was accepted (if not met – Rovers were relegated with Stein's defence allowing 105 goals to appear in the goals-against column) he wanted more.

One day in 1950 his teammate Dougie Wallace, a South African, told Stein about an ambitious club in Wales looking for Scottish players to aid their project. Stein was immediately interested. The money on offer was generous, the challenge tempting, and despite Jean opting to stay at home with their brand new daughter Ray, Stein was leaving the mines, leaving Cliftonhill and leaving Burnbank.

Baths under his landlady's table would of course remind him of home, as would the community itself, a town that, along with tin and steel, had been influenced by coal. His new salary of twelve pounds a week (similar to those of Old Firm players) might have lifted him above local average earnings, but he felt an immediate kinship with the Carmarthenshire people who were now his neighbours and fans.

An array of other Scottish players would also make the same journey south. The Llanelli manager Jack Goldsborough had taken Neilly Fleck from Dundee United, David Mathie from Motherwell, Bobby Jeffreys from Aberdeen and Lachie McInnes also from Albion Rovers. Despite an initial dispute regarding the legality of his move, Stein settled in, impressed in a 7–1 win in his first game, and was quickly made captain. A strong headed goal in the FA Cup against Merthyr Tydfil further endeared him to the locals but ultimately disappointment lay ahead.

In 1951 Llanelli had their application for Football League membership rejected; the club's finances were stretched, and when Stein discovered his bosses had turned down an offer for him from Wolverhampton Wanderers, his mood once again slipped into disillusionment. Jean and Ray had joined him in Wales, but then one day while Stein was playing an away fixture in Hastings, his wife took a call telling her their council house in Hamilton had been burgled.

Stein returned to a distressed wife, worried about what might become of the house. She wanted to go home, and she wanted her husband to come with her. His desire to play football at a higher and more regular level had got him this far, but maybe this was all there was. Maybe it was time to get back to what for so many others was normality. He went to Goldsborough, who understood but asked what he would do next. 'Pack in football and go back to the pits' was Stein's response, his heart surely breaking. Goldsborough then told him some news.

Jean and Ray were waiting for Stein, ready to pack their bags.

He walked through the door, gave his daughter a hug and sat his wife down. 'How did Jack take the news?' she asked.

'He understands,' said Stein.

'So we're going home?'

'Yes,' said Stein.

A smile formed on Jean's face.

'There is one more thing though,' Stein said. 'And you're not going to be believe it.'

Chapter 5:

Round the Back

The darkness of a March morning is disturbed by fire. Flames rage as black smoke mingles with the night sky. Fire engines rush to the scene, and volunteers do all they can to quell the orange storm. Among them is Walter Crickmer, a police reservist. Others buzz around doing their best but Crickmer stops and looks on in disbelief. The flames rage on. Crickmer is the secretary of Manchester United Football Club, and he is watching Old Trafford burn.

The stadium's Main Stand wouldn't have been high on the Luftwaffe's list of targets; however the nearby munitions factories at Trafford Park, helping to construct both Lancaster bombers and Spitfires were, and on the night of 11 March 1941 German planes filled the Manchester sky, dropping their incendiaries to destroy a stand that had stood for over thirty years.

Crickmer, who had also been managing the team since before the war, looked on and thought of his stadium. The dressing rooms. They were in that stand. The kits and the boots, could they be saved? As the hoses aimed their desperate loads into the carnage, he tried to reach them but the flames, smoke and heat thwarted him. As night turned to day, the flames settled, the smoke lifted to expose rubble and charred wood, revealing the true cost of the raid. Crickmer remained among the ruins. 'It was heartbreaking to see our Main Stand ablaze,' he told gathering reporters. 'I tried to reach the dressing room to save our kit but could not get near.'

Days later, Bill Shankly, stationed in Manchester, visited his old friend and trainer at Carlisle, Tom Curry, now at Manchester United and manfully trying to make sense of the damage caused. 'Yes, I was there when the blitz came to the city,' he would later say. 'I saw Old Trafford a few days after, and when I looked at it, I thought, *That's the end. There will never be another football team here again.*'

A late summer's evening in 1949. Thousands gather to watch their team. They've never stopped of course, but now Old Trafford is once again open for business. From those flames and from that rubble a new stand houses Manchester United's public. There is little in the way of cover yet, but as the August sun goes down over their heads, roofs can wait. The people are happy, the people are home. Bolton Wanderers are beaten 3–0. The side that they cheer on are the league's great entertainers and the manager they are beginning to adore is Matt Busby.

A year after the Luftwaffe's visit to Manchester, Crickmer's chairman at Old Trafford, James Gibson, was visiting friends in Dorset. His host, Captain Bill Williams, happened to be the officer in charge of sport for the army's Southern Command, and conversation turned to the adjustments Gibson wanted to make at his club and how a young forward-thinking manager was vital to implement such changes.

Over the three years of war Captain Williams had come across plenty of footballing men, PT instructors proving themselves natural leaders. One name he mentioned stayed with Gibson:

Matt Busby. The chairman returned home and mentioned it to Crickmer's assistant Louis Rocca, a friend of Busby's and his long-term admirer. War was on everyone's mind, but the name of Busby was on Manchester United's radar.

Christmas 1944, and Busby received a letter while posted at Sandhurst. It was signed, 'Your Old Pal, Louis Rocca'.

Dear Matt,

No doubt you will be surprised to get this letter from your old pal Louis. Well Matt I have been trying for the past month to find you and not having your reg. address I could not trust a letter going to Liverpool, as what I have to say is so important. I don't know if you have considered about what you are going to do when the war is over, but I have a great job if you are willing to take it on. Will you get in touch with me at the above address and when you do I can explain things to you better, when I know there will be no danger of interception. Now Matt I hope this is plain to you. You see I have not forgotten my old friend either in my prayers or in your future welfare. I hope your good wife and family are all well and please God you will be home to join the happy circle.

Rocca had made his fortune selling ice cream, and now Busby, with the Allies closing on Berlin, had an apparent job offer as tempting as any 99 sprinkled with strawberry sauce and pistachios. Manchester United? He'd hoped to go into management once the war was over, of course he had, but Manchester United? So soon? Liverpool had of course also wondered about their captain's future. He was their registered player, in his mid-thirties, obviously fit and capable of resuming his career, but they also understood he had ambitions beyond pulling on a red shirt. A role as player/coach was offered.

Busby was torn. The chance to learn under Kay, a man he deeply admired, was tempting, but being some sort of assistant? His itch to manage footballers wasn't going to be so easily satisfied. Surely he could wait, thought the Anfield board, but Kay was only fifty-three and eager to take his team on to greater things and Busby liked him too much to be the vulture hovering over the carcass of a career. He would talk to United.

Having played an international in Birmingham, Busby was heading home to Scotland, but went via Manchester, where he and Gibson met. They talked and they talked some more. An interview turned into a meeting of minds. Gibson had a firm idea of how he wanted the club to look, how he wanted them to play, and how he wanted youth to be given a chance, a local team entertaining Manchester people. Music to Busby's ears.

In turn Busby, still in uniform, set out his vision for how he saw management. He wanted absolute control. He wanted to coach, appoint coaches, recruit and select players. Gibson wanted a forward-thinking manager, but he was talking to a revolutionary. 'Even the great Herbert Chapman had needed to win a power struggle with the first Arsenal chairman, Sir Henry Norris, to achieve that,' wrote Busby's biographer Patrick Barclay. 'But something about Busby and the harmonic chiming of their ideas convinced Gibson.' A five-year contract was agreed. Once this war was done with and he was demobilized, the job was Busby's. A one-time resident of the city and stalwart of its blue football club's midfield, a manager's job across town beckoned.

Manchester United, formerly Newton Heath, title winners in 1908 and 1911, FA Cup winners in 1909. Billy Meredith had made the step from Manchester blue to red, and inspired that run of success. Busby could too. They had long been the city's second team, he knew that first hand, but in those last twelve months before the war, the club's potential had been awakened. Manchester United reserves had won the Central League in 1939, and an A team of under-18s were champions of the Manchester League. In 1938 Louis Rocca with Crickmer had set up the Manchester United Junior Athletic Club (MUJAC), and a policy of championing youth had been born. Rocca may have sold ice cream, but he had an eye for local footballing talent, and Charlie Mitten, John Aston, Stan Pearson and Johnny Carey were all products of his and Crickmer's desire to develop players.

Prior to the war, the first team had been less stellar. Promoted from the Second Division, they had in the 1938/9 season only found lower-middle-class status, their fourteenth-place finish only slightly redeemed by a 2–0 win over Liverpool at Old Trafford in the last game of the season. A game in which their visitors' right half caught the eye. 'Hardly a Liverpool attack that mattered did not owe its origins to one of those beautiful passes of Busby's,' wrote the *Manchester Guardian* correspondent. 'Every one made with strokes that seemed to belong to cricket rather than to football – drives up the centre, square cuts to his right wing, mighty hooks and pulls to the left.' Those playing days now over for Busby, he had taken the long walk back to the pavilion and was eager to get his men into the nets.

Having secretly agreed his future at Manchester United, Busby celebrated with a whisky at his mother's house.

'You shouldn't be drinking that,' she said.

'But Maw,' he replied, 'I'm thirty-six years old.'

A grown man perhaps, but still in an almost teenage love triangle with two major football clubs. On hearing Busby's decision, Liverpool wanted some sort of transfer fee for the loss of their registered player, while Busby had retired but wanted a farewell appearance. United wanted to announce the happy news, but Liverpool rejected any notion of a farewell match, although there would be no fee. That was that. On 19 February 1945 United told the world they had a new manager. Walter Crickmer, no longer the team manager but very much the club secretary, stood in front of the press, a smile on his face, the new man beside him. 'He will build up the team and put it right where it belongs, at the top,' gushed a prophetic Crickmer.

At this point, however, Busby was still in the army. As a nation and a continent rejoiced at the impending demise of Adolf Hitler, Busby and a group of 'all-star' footballers found themselves dining in the Great Western Hotel in Paddington, adjacent to Brunel's great train station. As the team sat down to eat before their flight to Naples, where they would begin a tour of Italy and then Greece entertaining the troops, Busby must have been impatient to start the construction of a football club he believed could become Brunel-like in its magnificence.

Stanley Rous at the FA had chosen Busby to player/manage this band of brothers for the tour that ultimately – despite the distant sound of last-gasp gunfire – celebrated victory in Europe. With him were, among others, that superstar Joe Mercer, his mate from Manchester City Joe Swift, the brilliant Tommy Lawton, Cliff Britton of Everton and a tank driver who had seen more action than most called Tom Finney.

Busby played, but it was managing that was so appealing, and his understanding that the individual can do more than merely play for the team was immediately evident. 'Each player had his responsibility, allocated by Busby,' wrote Patrick Barclay. 'He reasoned that Mercer, whose wife's family were in the grocery business, would know a little about the procurement of food, so he became "messing officer" in charge of scrounging from villagers, while the teetotal technician Cliff Britton took charge of the truck. Swift, who had forgotten to bring his boots, might have seemed a surprising selection as baggage man.'

Matches were played across Italy, and visits made to Pompeii and Rome, where the devout Catholic Busby enjoyed an audience with Pope Pius XII. A blessing for his impending managerial career perhaps? It was in the east-coast port city of Bari that Busby had another meeting, seen by many as a quasi-religious moment akin to something like Michelangelo's *Creation of Adam*. For it was here that Busby met Jimmy Murphy. They had played against each other before and Busby had appreciated the ferocity of his fellow wing half, but it was by the shimmering Adriatic that the Manchester United manager-elect realized he was in the presence of a footballing man who could aid his new work. Busby promised to make a phone call when he returned home.

In the summer of 1945 a version of First Division football also returned home, albeit a regional one. On a warm afternoon nearly half a million fans each paid one shilling and sixpence to stand on their terrace of choice. Stan Mortensen scored a hat-trick for Blackpool; 35,000 watched Newcastle beat Sheffield United 6–0; Manchester City won 2–1 in front of 25,000 at Maine Road, while their tenants (City had shared their ground with United after the blitz) lost 3–2 at Huddersfield. Due to so many players still to make it back from the armed forces, Crickmer and Curry were forced to pick a ramshackle eleven that day, and despite the club's promising left half Allenby Chilton defying the army and going 'absent without leave' to play a cup game, the start of the season's results were very much affected by the club's players (and new manager) wearing khaki rather than red.

Busby watched United draw with Barnsley in late September

1945, and then on 3 October he was demobbed. 'United have a first-class side,' he would say, 'if only I could get them together in one place.' He was talking as a manager though. That was something. He was there. Work could begin.

He managed from a small office owned by his chairman in Cornbrook Cold Storage, a space he would share with Crickmer and a helpful young typist called Les Olive who would one day become a club director. 'In that small office, there was not much room for dreaming, or time,' Busby recalled. 'But dream I did.' Thirty-six years old, still scolded by his mother for drinking whisky, a dreamer and by his own admission a 'very raw' manager, but that former self-doubt was gone. Early in his tenure Busby was sitting in the directors' box when a director called Harold Hardman behind him voiced some concern and questioned why the manager hadn't taken more action. Busby stayed quiet, took his own counsel and asked himself whether he should turn and 'give him a blast'. His inner voice said no. Instead he waited until he was alone with the vociferous director (the men's toilet was a conveniently discreet location) before letting him have it. 'Never dare to say anything like that to me when other people can hear you,' the young manager said, a keenness in his eyes underlining the point. At the next board meeting, there on the agenda was 'Interference by Directors'.

A raw manager maybe, but just as he had grown up quickly after the tragic death of his father, Busby was growing up as a manager, imposing his own personality on the club, not for reasons of vanity but to implement his ideas on how a football club could and should be run. His own personality was one thing; as a manager he had to deal with others. His experiences training and to some degree managing men during the war was one thing; young footballers might be another.

There was Billy Wrigglesworth, a Yorkshireman and former miner but only three years his junior; Stan Pearson, a Salford boy still away on military duty but a huge presence at the club, who had shown great promise before the war; young John Aston and John Anderson, two locals keen to get on, and of course Charlie Mitten, a confident product of United's early desire to foster young talent. Men in their twenties, eager to get going, but post-war men. Busby was not long a player himself of course, but he would have to get used to directing a newer generation of footballer.

Mitten was cocksure. Full of potential and skill but vocal in the dressing room. John Carey was a man who impressed Busby. Mitten though wasn't shy and called the Irishman 'a bloody terrible inside forward'. Other players would complain that Carey was aloof and mean with his money, but this was the man Busby had earmarked to captain his side. Dressing rooms and training grounds were more opinionated than in his time; players' personalities and ambitions would need managing.

Busby could handle it. He'd been raised among wilful characters, men in Orbiston and Bellshill with fiery opinions and actions to match. Like his own best friend growing up, Frank Rodgers, a good footballer who had joined Busby on his journey to Manchester City. Large and up for a fight, be it the verbal or the bone-on-bone variety (legend has it he once punched an offending horse square on its whiskers, knocking it to its haunches), Rodgers was the yin to Busby's yang, especially when it came to a sectarian scrap, from which Busby could usually talk his friend down, an early indication that this was a man capable of managing the rowdiest of personalities.

Busby was soon among his players. A photographer was on hand to catch the moment players met manager. Behind the smiles and the handshakes there must have been surprise because Busby was dressed in full tracksuit and studs, just like the playing staff. He wasn't going to wear a suit and manage from a distance; his hands (and boots) were going to get dirty.

Busby was bringing change, but change was also coming from further afield. Football's tactics could be manipulated and improved. At the end of 1945 and to the delight of the thousands of fans who came to see them, Russian champions Dynamo Moscow played an undefeated tour of Britain that opened myopic local eyes to how teamwork, quick and short passing, and running off the ball could open up defences. Busby's eyes were already open.

As his squad returned from wartime service, and calling on his own experiences as a young player when he was literally finding his place in the game, Busby set about looking closely at his players, studying their strengths but more importantly evaluating their weaknesses. Not because he wanted to clear the dressing room out; no, he knew that players could be cured of their faults. As a player at City, luck had changed his fortunes and dropped him in at wing half, but Busby the manager was in no mood to rely on chance again.

Allenby Chilton, a Normandy veteran, was moved from half back to centre half; and John Aston and John Carey, both inside forwards, were shifted to fullback. Some managers might have listened to Charlie Mitten – 'a bloody terrible inside forward' – and simply moved them on. Busby instead looked and saw good footballers; they just weren't forwards. 'I used to play at inside forward before the war against Matt Busby,' recalled Carey. 'When he became manager I can remember him saying, "You know, I've never pictured you as an inside forward, but as a wing half or even fullback." I said, "That's probably because I never got up into the opposition penalty area!" Certainly it was an inspiration on Matt's part to convert myself and Johnny Aston to fullbacks. As fullbacks we were ball players and supplied the finesse ... It was contrary to the general pattern of the way defences operated at the time.'

Quietly changing the way the game was being played, Busby went about his business in those early months, the supporters and wider footballing public unaware of the work going on in his mind and in training. A 5–0 win at Anfield in February 1946 might have aroused Schadenfreude in Busby, but he had too many friends at Liverpool and too much respect for his time there to head back to Manchester with anything close to smugness. But what he was starting to see was that he had a collection of players – no, a collection of men in their prime – that he could very much work with. Very much win with.

The major clubs were on manoeuvres. Squads were being added to and hopes raised for the following season, when the Football League would properly start up again. Busby liked what he had, but prior to that win over Liverpool he had spent £4,000 on Jim Delaney from Celtic. Many in the game doubted the sturdiness of his bones ('brittle' they said, due to a long-standing broken arm issue) but Busby saw something in the energetic thirty-year-old winger, and despite the collective raising of eyebrows at board-room level, Busby got his way.

A team was taking shape, and not only on the pitch. Jimmy Murphy had got that call, and going into the new season Busby had him by his side. They made quite a duo. The similarities were pronounced. Both from Irish stock, both from mining communities. Welshman Murphy too had been a good student, and it had been hoped that both would avoid a life in the mines by teaching. Then there was their shared deep understanding for football. They were also different. Murphy had a way with words, a way of talking to players. Sure, Busby's man management was knowing and wise, but Murphy could get down and dirty when it mattered. He spoke their language, swearing like a sailor, and while Busby might advise a player to keep his head in the face of intimidation, Murphy – in his deep Welsh accent – could give counsel on the game's darker arts.

Murphy had been a respected and tenacious half back for West Bromwich Albion and Wales, but his knowledge and even more importantly the skills he possessed in passing that knowledge on were immediately vital to Busby and the club. He would look after the first team but also coach the reserves and look after the youth players, the latter being at the forefront of Busby's plans.

The first team certainly reaped immediate benefits from the duo's arrival. The first five games of the Football League's post-war era were won by United, with their front five running amok. Liverpool were once again beaten 5–0, but over a long, wintry season that overflowed into June it was the Anfield team (aided markedly by both Billy Liddell and Bob Paisley, two men welcomed to Anfield by Busby before the war) who took the league title, pipping Busby's men to it with a final-game win at Wolves.

Busby wouldn't settle for second best, although those early years would give him plenty of practice, but there was a contentment in his team's style. Brave, free-flowing and fit, the work being done at the Cliff, the club's impressive training ground, and 'round the back' was sticking. Round the back was what they called the cinder pitch behind Old Trafford's damaged main stand. There, after some running up and down the unused stadium's terraces, ball work (more than many had ever been used to) was followed by matches. Busby would join in, always critiquing, always guiding, the teacher that so many of his own had seen in him coming to the fore.

He had players willing to listen and improve and a collective started to form. Busby and Murphy worked off each other, passing on knowledge, allowing the players to contribute and even debate. The duo could take turns being good cop and bad cop, but this was far from a police state. Busby was never going to allow total liberty or even democracy, but he was absolutely adamant that the job of being a professional footballer should be fun, and that a happy player was a better one. 'Just go out and play,' he'd say. It was a line that invited freedom, but don't be fooled; the work round the back was precise and demanding, but if adhered to, the players and the team would see results. '[Busby] wanted football to be a matter of educated instinct,' wrote Patrick Barclay, and that education was being carried out daily.

The togetherness and unity that Busby would always desire from his football teams was aided by simple gestures. A Manchester United blazer and flannels were issued to each player; there were golfing days followed by mix-grill dinners, visits to the theatre and the always popular cinema. On 24 April 1948, the very few with no interest in the FA Cup final being played that day at Wembley might have taken themselves to the cinema to see Frank Capra's *The State of the Union*. There they would have been enthralled by the enduring partnership of Spencer Tracy and Katharine Hepburn, the couple's crackling chemistry illuminating the silver screen.

Those with football on their minds that spring day had no time for mere partnerships. Manchester United were in town with a front five that was the talk of the nation. Delaney, Morris, Rowley, Pearson, Mitten. Names to entice the crowds, and now playing with 'educated instinct', they were box office. Aston Villa had been overwhelmed 6–4 in a remarkable third-round thriller at Villa Park, and then Blackpool and Stanley Matthews were beaten 4–2 with a second-half display at Wembley that dazzled the nation. Geoffrey Green of *The Times* had already compared the shapes this Manchester United team could create to those of Picasso or Matisse, and 300 miles away in England's northeast a young boy listening to the match on the radio, unable to curtail his excitement, picked up a ball at half-time to play on the street, where of course he would represent the team he had chosen to be his that afternoon. The boy's name? Bobby Charlton.

United had missed out on the league, finishing runners-up yet again, but the FA Cup was won, and it was perfect. Yes, the title was sought after, but because Busby so wanted to entertain with this team, the FA Cup, the showpiece event of the season, televised for a fortunate few, listened to by the masses, was the trophy the team needed to win. What was happening round the back was getting a national audience.

Busby's vision of what a football team could do for the public was being realized. A club identity, one by which managers would be judged for decades to come, was being born. Here was a manager who by sheer weight of personality was shaping a football club, while also abiding by a philosophy. Here was a man who had always known what football when played a certain way could do for those whose everyday hardships might be forgotten when they were under its spell. He had seen men's overworked leathery features suddenly lifted, smiles appearing on their faces just by watching the merest of feints from Alex James on a Saturday. Their tired eyes, so often dimmed by the darkness in which they worked, suddenly open and sparkling at the ferocity of a shot at goal from Hughie Gallacher.

The season after Manchester United's cup triumph, record

attendances were enjoyed at Football League grounds, forty-one million people making their way to stadiums, with L. S. Lowry moved enough to capture the sheer artistry of a Saturday at the match. The wonderful Frank Keating on observing a Pathé News clip of the season, later wrote of 'the serried monochrome banks of pinched but smiling faces under flat caps, a squashed up multitude stretching distantly back to the raked heights of infinity through the warming fug of Woodbine smoke'. All so reminiscent of Nottingham Forest fan J. B. Priestley, who in his 1929 novel *The Good Companions* wrote of football supporters, 'To say that these men paid their shillings to watch twenty-two hirelings kick a ball is merely to say that a violin is wood and catgut, that Hamlet is so much paper and ink,' and,

All brothers together for an hour and a half, for not only had you escaped from the clanking machinery of this lesser life, from work, wages, rent, doles, sick-pay, insurance cards, nagging wives, ailing children, bad bosses, idle workmen, but you had escaped with most of your mates and your neighbours, with half the town, and there you were, cheering together, thumping one another on the shoulders, swapping judgments like lords of the earth, having pushed your way through a turnstile into another and altogether more splendid kind of life.

Life as normal wasn't easy for those Busby had grown up with, or now for a country picking itself up from the ravages of war. Football was life-affirming. Busby knew that and was determined to give the people its release. In February 1949 he took his side to non-league Yeovil, where over 80,000 people gathered to witness an 8–0 United win. After the game Busby went to speak to his opposite number, Alex Stock, offering an apology for the size of the defeat.

'Don't worry, m' dear,' said Stock in his deep Somerset tones. 'At least we've all lived a little.' Busby would certainly have smiled.

Chapter 6:

Natural Enthusiasm

The manager leaves the ground. His team has won. Away from home. He does the buttons up on his mac and walks into the Cumbrian air. He thinks about the match. His team played well. Did what he said. Took his words and his passion on to the pitch, outplayed and out-battled the opposition. Yes, that was a good one.

A woman approaches. She's elderly but has a purpose in her stride, her walking stick struggling to keep pace. Their eyes meet and he starts to offer a polite salutation. 'Good evening–' He's cut short. The woman is beside him, her burning eyes telling him this is no time for pleasantries. The walking stick is raised, as the woman prepares to strike. 'Go back to Workington!' she screams. The manager ducks. She strikes again. He weaves, his love of boxing coming to the fore. She aims a kick, but once again he avoids her ire. 'Get back to Workington!' she cries. 'Get out of Cleaton Moor! You're not welcome here!'

Bill Shankly loved telling this story. His elderly attacker had accosted him after his Workington side had won easily at Cleaton Moor Celtic. A supporter of the hosts, she had taken umbrage at Shankly's team's audacity. He had managed to dodge her blows, but her passion, her sheer disgust at the thought of defeat always stayed with him. This was football in its rawest form, what he fell in love with as a boy. Today a statue of Shankly stands outside Liverpool's famous Kop end. Inscribed underneath his bronze likeness are the words, HE MADE THE PEOPLE HAPPY. True enough, but in football to make people happy, you also have to make other people unhappy. That's the pay-off, and therein lies the passion.

This was football and he was now living it as a manager. This was the game fought over on Monkey Row back in Glenbuck, the game that could make or destroy someone's weekend. Natural enthusiasm, he'd later call it, arguing there's nothing without it, and there, not where the millions flock, not at Celtic Park or Molineux or Goodison Park, but in a Cleaton Moor car park, he's right at the heart of it. That'll do him. For now.

Bill Shankly's first steps into the world of football management were taken in the same manner as everything he approached, with verve. Starting at Carlisle, a club in the lower echelons of English football, a club where the manager had to answer the phone as well as pick the teams, right down to the enthusiasm he showed towards the new washing machine he had installed at his new home to wash the new kit, Shankly was immersed in life as a manager, and while he worked at less than fashionable clubs in those early years, he had utter belief in what he was doing and how he was doing it. 'I never felt that Matt Busby or Stan Cullis at Wolves were better managers than me,' he'd say of those formative years. 'Not for one minute. I don't mean to brag or boast. Matt and Stan are brilliant men, but I knew I had a system of playing and a system of training, and I was clever enough to go on with it.'

During the war, those years when Shankly, a man chomping at the bit to build his life in football, was moving around Britain with the RAF, his thoughts were very much on the game, on his body, on staying fit. He worked hard. To him, no one could clean the latrines any better, but the game, it was there at the front of his mind. Always.

He'd run. 'When I die, I'll be the fittest man in the cemetery,' he'd boast. He boxed too. Everything was done to the nth degree. If he boxed, he'd box with a champion. While Shankly was stationed in Scotland he trained and ran with Jack Porter, Scottish heavyweight champion. It was while training with Porter that a young member of the WRAF called Agnes spotted the sparkling Shankly running and lifting weights and running some more. 'She thought Jack and I were nutcases,' Shankly would later say, but he also noticed her noticing him, and soon he and Ness, as he would call her, would be married.

A serious knee injury had hampered his football, even prompting an MO to state he would never play again. Medical school might have taught that particular doctor a thing or two, but no book will have told him that his patient wasn't the sort to let a piece of floating cartilage prevent him from playing football. *Thanks, Doc, now where are my boots?*

After demobilization, Shankly returned to play for Preston. Thirty-three years of age but now a family man with a daughter, football was still approached with all of his giddy zeal, but futures were starting to form in his mind too. Money was tight for the whole country – the long winter of 1947, the rationing of food, the lack of coal with families huddled around sparse fireplaces. He had worked hard to make it in football, to not live the life of a miner, but still things were tough. 'Everyone was out for themselves,' he'd say of this time.

The game still gave him such a buzz, aided further at Preston by playing alongside Tom Finney. The local boy had been at the club prior to hostilities, but now, in his prime and mesmerizing, he played with a skill that breathed extra life into Shankly's game.

Playing behind him at half back afforded Shankly not only the best view in English football but also kept his own professional fires burning bright.

'How Shankly keeps it up game after game,' asked the *Sporting Chronicle*, 'year after year, I don't know.' Playing with and even protecting Finney ('You'll be the one leaving with a broken leg,' he once told an opposing half back who was threatening Finney with a fracture) kept him going, but in early 1949, despite being captain and playing, he thought, his best football ever, wasn't enough, so when a job came up at Carlisle – first as coach but then having met the board, the full manager's role – he took it.

Leaving Preston wasn't done on the best of terms. Finney, his lifelong pal, had begged him to stay (Who'd look after his ankles?), and the club pulled the plug on a benefit match. Shankly and his family had to make the journey up through Lancashire into Cumbria with very little money, and start work at a club off the game's beaten track.

'Gie me a spark o' Nature's fire, That's a' tha learning I desire.' Shankly might have had Robert Burns' words in his mind as he drove closer to his beloved Scotland. Money at Carlisle was tight, and prospects seemingly tighter, but how fitting that he should start his managerial career at the club that had offered his playing days the flint on which to spark his life in football. And so, as he had as a player, Bill Shankly threw himself head first into his dream. At home, alone, he tried to take on the washing (Ness was in a nursing home having their second child) using his new Bendix machine. The miniature clothes that came out suggested domestic work was not his forte but no such incompetence hindered his sporting life.

With all his playing experience and having studied to be a masseur, Shankly obviously had a handle on the anatomy of the game. Now what he proved was how brilliant he could be with people. He understood them; they responded to his positivity. He would talk to them, and they hung on every word. Managers could get a few thoughts over to the public via short messages to the supporters in the match-day programmes – snippets about the team and the match. Shankly had other ideas. Microphone in hand, his voice (a tool whose power he was beginning to utilize) boomed over the Brunton Park tannoy: 'This is your manager speaking!'

The players certainly got the message. Still young, Shankly knew how to be one of the lads, but he was also sure that success lay with discipline. Players might be tempted to stray from the path of clean living, but now they had a boss watching any misstep. 'He was always up to date on any player's misbehaviour,' recalled Geoff Twentyman, Carlisle's centre half. 'If he heard that players were womanizing or drinking, he'd be down on them like a ton of bricks. He'd be very angry. He was a good masseur, and while he was giving a player a massage, he'd also be giving him a bit of advice about his private life and how he should be looking after himself.'

Shankly, like Busby, knew the value of a happy player. Everything from training methods (more ball work than monotonous running) to clearing out a player's flat so he could get in his own furniture was centred around a player's well-being. Shankly would pay out of his own pocket for group trips to the cinema; he jumped off the team bus one day and ran into a sport shop to buy new kit for the team, and even got in touch with the war office to demand that Gunner Twentyman be made available to play a fixture while he was still serving. And it worked. Everything was done with passion. Everything mattered.

Then there was diet. During the war Shankly had developed

the knack of sourcing good food, making friends with people that knew people who could provide rare treats. Rationing was still in force for everyone, including needy athletes, but at Carlisle Shankly knew a farmer who late in the week would bring in a few dozen eggs and some butter. With a reserve team and a large squad, Shankly had to implement his own rationing system, and should a player be politely refused his share, he knew that he was out of the team. For all his people skills, Shankly never quite got the hang of the straight talking required when it came to dropping players. 'The pitch won't suit you, today, son.' For a man who so loved to play football, perhaps the thought of telling someone they weren't up to it was just too much.

Dropping players aside, Shankly took to management with gusto. With steel caps on his shoes, his team could hear him coming. Soon the world would too. The club itself wasn't as ambitious. At the bottom of the Third Division (North), Carlisle's single objective was to stay up and avoid the uncertainty of re-election. The team's future depended on their new manager's success but so too did Shankly's. Get this wrong, fail to make an impression, and life back down the mines beckoned. That would not do.

Methods and philosophy in place, results followed. Youngsters were trained, the reserves flourished, crowds of 8,000 weren't rare, the team even gaining the nickname Shankly's Babes. It wouldn't stick, but it underlined the man's mission, and the success he was having realizing it. That success was pretty much confined to Cumbria and the supporters who called Brunton Park home, but in 1951 the FA Cup brought Shankly and his team to Arsenal. The Gunners. The holders. Serial visitors to Wembley. Packed with internationals. No one gave Carlisle a chance. Well, almost no one.

Having given his players a tour of Arsenal's marble halls, the pleasantries came to an end. Tactically, Shankly asked centre forward Jack Billingham to play as a deeper-lying threat. Prior to the kick-off, he lined his team up against the dressing-room wall, telling them to tuck their kits in and pull up their socks. 'Whatever happens on the field today,' he shouted, 'you are going to go out of this dressing room a credit to the city of Carlisle.' It was not a rallying call, more a statement of fact. He was proved right.

Carlisle battled to a more than creditable goalless draw, and might have even won it. Shankly stepped from the dugout at full time, striding on to the pitch. His players had given everything, and rightly the 58,000 crowd applauded. Shankly lifted his arms towards the north London sky. The Arsenal fans watched, wondered and walked home, unaware that they were witnessing the arrival of a man they would one day all know. The replay was lost 4–1 but a reputation had emerged. Shankly applied for the job at Liverpool after George Kay's departure. No one gave him a chance but he got an interview, ruining his chances when he vehemently told the directors that he would stop their practice of picking the team with the manager on a Friday. The directors smiled and put his application on file.

Shankly's eye was roving, and in the spring of 1951 he moved to Grimsby Town. Carlisle's lack of ambition and funds had frustrated him for too long. Going to Blundell Park, a club in the Third Division, was a sideways move but a move worth taking. The club had long been famous for giving a bag of fish to visiting players, but Shankly wanted to make their style of play every bit as appetizing.

He was working on football's lower rungs, but there was no inferiority complex. Shankly, whatever club he was at, however small in the national scheme of things, had a bigger outlook. The men he worked with at Carlisle, now Grimsby and later Workington, were of a certain level, but he worked with them as if they were the best. In many ways, he thought they were. In his time there, Grimsby, despite amassing an impressive sixty-six points, missed out on promotion. 'It was sad because that Grimsby team was, pound for pound and class for class, the best football team I have seen in England since the war,' Shankly said years later. 'In the league they were in they played football nobody else could play. Everything was measured, planned and perfected, and you could not wish to see more entertaining football.'

The best since the war? Hyperbole? For sure, but Shankly had total enthusiasm and respect for that stage of his career. Grimsby finished fifth in 1952/3, and again the manager was faced with a board unable or unwilling to write cheques. Nessie was feeling homesick, Shankly too, a move closer to Scotland at Workington back in Cumbria presented itself, and once again the Shanklys were packing their bags. Workington were in the Third Division but facing relegation. Shankly acknowledged this one was a risk, but his wife's need to be close to home and a tempting bonus should the club survive was enough to convince him that this was the right move. On his first night there that decision might have seemed a tad hasty.

On walking into the ground, in darkness, Shankly felt around the wall for a light switch. 'What are you doing?' asked a club official.

'I'm putting on the light.'

'There's gas in here.'

No electricity, a ground shared with a rugby league club, life on a shoestring. This was raw, but it was real and once again Shankly was going all in. He scraped together £3,200 to buy

Ernie Whittle from Lincoln. Whittle was a tricky forward from the north-east, only five feet four inches, but he could jink his way around a defence. His fourteen goals kept Workington in the league, and his presence was an indication of Shankly's eye for a player and ability to get the absolute best from people.

Shankly became very much part of the club. The town itself, population 25,000, was famous for little. Mining disasters had warranted some national attention but in Shankly's grand scheme of things, this was a hamlet, a place that even Carlisle and Barrow thought of as small. Nessie, although her wish to be closer to Scotland had been answered, might have been forgiven for wondering about her husband's career choices. 'It was bleak,' she recalled. 'We moved into a big old club house which was nice, but Workington just seemed to be miles from anywhere. We didn't have a car there either. And that made things difficult. There was always this film of dirt everywhere. I think it must have been from a chemical plant or something. Every time I put the washing out it was always dirty when I brought it back in.'

Domestic gripes and perceived professional cul-de-sacs didn't deter Shankly. He could be found answering the phones at the ground, opening mail, walking to the bank and back to get the wages. He'd also sit in on directors' meetings. Many of those present were rugby league men. To Shankly this game was played with a wrong-shaped ball and churned up the pitch. Small frustrations, but never enough to swerve the manager from his passion.

What Shankly liked about the place was the total lack of pretension. In Bill Watson, the club's groundsman at Borough Park, there was a fellow football man, someone to talk to. The boiler room, warm and sparse, was where they would meet. Sitting on crates, the two of them would discuss the game. It was like a

Glenbuck street corner, the conversation a simple but valuable pleasure. Shankly loved to talk and Watson was happy to listen.

'I can still hear his steel-tipped heels as he walked down the tunnel,' recalled Watson. 'He would pull up a lemonade crate to sit on and I would say to myself in anticipation, 'What will he reminisce about today? Would it be Tom Finney, or even West Brom's Ronnie Simpson with his emerald-green overcoat?' Shankly had grown up with men like that, talking about the game for the sheer love of the topic, and some years later he would come across another cubbyhole within the bowels of a football ground.

Mixing with football's footmen was a pleasure, but now and then the opportunity arose to meet the game's royalty. On the train from Carlisle to London with his team in tow, Shankly was told that the Hungarian national side were in first class. It was the Flying Scotsman, but so was Shankly as he darted along the carriages to get some time with the likes of Puskás, Kocsis and Hidegkuti, the team who the year before had changed a country's perception of how football might be played when they beat England 6–3 at Wembley.

Autographs were obtained (for now it was Shankly asking rather than signing) and stories swapped of footballing der-ring-do. Shankly dashed back to ensure his team met these giants of the game. 'Some of their magic rubbed off on us,' Shankly told the newspapers after a win over Leyton Orient that weekend, and a letter of congratulations arrived from the Hungarian FA. Arguably the best team in the world had acknowledged his small achievements at a club like Workington. How long until others would?

Shankly was thinking big. He tried to sign Stan Mortensen from Blackpool, but to no avail. Times were not getting easier at Workington, and Shankly's itch for a bigger stage wasn't going away, but no matter; that itch was nothing compared to the sheer love and enthusiasm that tickled his skin every day. Up early, Shankly would walk the mile to work, the mile back for lunch, then back to work and home again. Like the teenager in Glenbuck riding his bike twenty-four miles to play, the same expectations of what the day might bring, despite its problems, remained with Shankly. While he worked in football, it always would.

Word of this fireball raging in the lower reaches of the English game was spreading. This was a man who would play a ninety-minute game in training with his players at Workington, get himself to Manchester for a meeting, and then get another train back and play an evening game under the floodlights. Who wouldn't want that sort of effervescence at their club? In 1955 someone who certainly did was Andy Beattie, manager at Huddersfield and former fullback at Preston, who knew all about Shankly from their playing days. Beattie, lacking the sheer natural giddiness possessed by his countryman, was struggling at Leeds Road. He wanted out, had been persuaded to stay but had demanded another pair of hands. A phone call was made, and Shankly was reacquainted with an old mate.

The match day programme introduced the new arrival by writing, 'Mr Shankly is a man with a reputation for living football,' and it wasn't long before those working at the club had an idea what that was about. Shankly took to his new surroundings with his usual fervour. He was to work with the reserves with the brief of developing younger players and very much liked the group he had. He also liked the town – quiet, surrounded by beautiful moors, similar to where he grew up, its wool and cloth industries also offering a reminder of home.

Beattie was immediately reminded about the force of nature he'd brought back into his life when Shankly called Eddie Boot, Beattie's other coach, and advised them both to leave the first team alone and work with the youngsters. 'Eddie,' Beattie said to Boot. 'I've just made the biggest mistake of my life bringing Bill Shankly here. I should never have hired him. We never agreed at Preston. I can see it's going to be the same here.'

Shankly would later say that, given time, their partnership might have been as fruitful as Matt Busby and Jimmy Murphy's, but while the Manchester United duo's differences were also their strength, at Huddersfield there could be no similar long-term bonding. On a Friday at Huddersfield, the first team would go up on the noticeboard. The popular Shankly would stand with the players, and as a face dropped at the omission of his name an arm would appear around his shoulder. 'Oh, I see you've been promoted, son,' he'd quip. 'You're coming to play for my team.'

Shankly would argue this was merely a boost for a dropped player, but Beattie felt undermined. Either way, Shankly's devilish side was taking shape, as was his belief in brave, attacking football, shown in his reserve side but not displayed within Beattie's more conservative first team.

Results had been poor, relegation suffered, and in 1956 Beattie, feeling the pressure of the modern game in which bucks were starting to stop with managers and with the news that Arsenal boss Tom Whittaker had died of a heart attack, took the decision to step away from the game. He recommended Shankly for the job, but their relations were strained. Shankly, on a night out with Nessie and oblivious to the news, was called and told that the chairman wanted to see him. He left his wife and friends to be asked if he'd like the job. Yes. Would he like to sleep on it? No. That night Shankly drove to Beattie's home but couldn't muster the bravery to face him. He drove up to the gate, stopped and drove off again, before finally plucking up the courage and going in to sit in an awkward silence with the man he'd replaced.

Now as a manager in the Second Division, a step up, Shankly had some of the best talent around. By the time Shankly's name adorned the Huddersfield manager's door, both Denis Law and Ramon 'Ray' Wilson, two young men he had worked with in the reserves, were recognized as real talents. Shanks could work with them, mould them and learn from the attention their talents attracted. Wilson was already showing the sort of drive that would make him a Rolls-Royce of a fullback. Shankly immediately took to him. The eventual World Cup winner described his own upbringing in a small Derbyshire mining town as 'Backstreet football, a paper round, a punch on the nose, that was my heritage.' No wonder his new manager liked him. Then there was Denis Law, a modest-looking, slight and bespectacled forward from Aberdeen. Prior to Shankly's promotion to first-team manager, Matt Busby had spotted Law in a FA Youth Cup tie between Huddersfield and Manchester United. He'd run at United's gilded youngsters, and run some more.

Busby took Shankly by the arm. Old friends from Scotland internationals, but now direct opponents in the manufacturing of great football sides. 'That's a promising young lad you've got,' he said, before offering Huddersfield £10,000 for the sixteen-year-old. The offer was turned down flat, but still they came, and not only for Law. Shankly, now manager, had to fend off bids for Wilson. Shankly loved to turn opposing managers and their offers down while telling directors with pound signs in their eyes that his players weren't going anywhere.

'Listen, get your diaries out,' Shankly once told his board, pondering a £45,000 bid for Law. 'If you think this is a lot of brass for Law, you have a commodity and you don't know its value, which is a bad job. Put it in your diary that one day Law will be transferred for £100,000.'

Stan Cullis of Wolves, Johnny Carey at Everton, Ted Drake at Chelsea, all offered very tempting sums for both players. Jimmy Thompson, a renowned scout at Chelsea who discovered Jimmy Greaves, once came to Shankly at half-time during a game at Sheffield Wednesday. 'What about this fellow, Wilson?' Thompson said.

'We don't usually transfer them at half-time,' Shankly said as he walked away.

Shankly was moulding the young reserves he had worked with into first-team regulars. Results were good. The likes of Kevin McHale, Gordon Low and Jack Connor were complementing Law and Wilson, and a good team was taking shape. The cafe over the road was instructed to feed them all steak and milk. One of his protégés was in need of both. Denis Law was a nine-stone ball of talent, a young skeleton with a skill set that, in Shankly's mind, merely needed meat added to its bones. At the cinema Shankly loved the likes of Cagney and Bogart – diminutive but tough. Law had to be the same. Chinese tea, and milk and steak, and the odd quiet beer. That would do it, and it was over a beer on a Saturday night that Bill took the teenage Law to one side. 'You're all over the field at the moment,' he said to the winger. 'It's no good for you. If you're going to do anything in this game, you have to be up front scoring goals. That's where you'll be better.'

It would take a while for Law to both listen and bulk up enough to lead a forward line, but the young Scot was taken with his manager and his ability to look after young men miles away from home. 'Shanks was always there for us,' Law would later say. 'Making sure we were healthy in mind and body, even making sure that our parents were all right.' The team and its youngsters were beginning to play in its manager's image. Fiery and passionate. 'All he ever talked about was football,' recalled Law, 'and I mean all the time. Shanks taught us all a lot. He would say, "Don't work on your strengths, work on your weaknesses. Get your left foot going and get your heading going." His greatest strength was his enthusiasm. He loved playing football. He gave you confidence and made you feel a bit cocky. He made his players think they were the best in the world.'

One day Law would be regarded by many as just that, but here at Leeds Road, Huddersfield careers were only beginning to blossom. Promotion was a hope rather than a certainty, but on some Saturday afternoons opponents were blown away and the directors would take note. A 5–0 win against Liverpool was noteworthy, especially for the Merseyside club's directors, who left in single file 'with their shoulders slumped, like a funeral procession', Shankly later observed. Results such as that weren't uncommon, but they weren't common enough. His young team were good but, added to, they could be the best. That's what Shankly would tell the board. Two footballers north of the border had grabbed his attention but the board decreed their combined fees were just too much. Ian St John and Ron Yeats would have to wait. Huddersfield were close to something big, but the purse strings were too tight, constricting Shankly's ambitions, although . another club, recently made aware of his winning ways, was about to request his services. A club down on its luck, but a club with a big name, a city club. Shankly was going to Liverpool.

Chapter 7:

Making it in Paradise

These are football men we are dealing with. Kings yes, and they would build kingdoms, but Matt Busby, Bill Shankly and Jock Stein never felt their crowns made them taller than others. All three valued the men they worked with, the quiet men who on a Saturday evening after a game would walk from the stadium, hunch their shoulders, flip up the lapels on their jackets and slip into the river of people without causing a ripple in its waters.

Lear, that most troubled of kings, was wrong when he told his less vociferous and more erudite daughter Cordelia, 'Nothing will come from nothing,' for it is the quiet, thoughtful advisers that a good leader seeks, and all three managers would appreciate these still men who worked the shadows. Jimmy Murphy, Bob Paisley and Sean Fallon were there beside them, but managers and clubs also relied on coaches, trainers, scouts. Shankly had had Bill Watson at Workington, the groundsman who he would share conversation and thoughts with in the boiler room. At Liverpool, that became a boot room, where men like Reuben Bennett and Joe Fagan talked football and plotted victories over bottles of stout. Matt Busby had, among others, Bert Whalley and Tom Curry, men who loved the club and shared his vision. Stein had trainer Neilly Mochan and later coach Willie Fernie, employees of a football club but so, so much more.

Jimmy Gribben was a football man. Decades later Stein would call him one of the great Celts, adding, 'Jimmy was one of the real backroom boys, a good player in his day, an able coach. Never in the public eye, he did a remarkable job at Celtic Park. No one knew more about football than Jimmy Gribben. He was my friend and my mentor.' Gribben helped Jock Stein and helped Celtic Football Club by getting Jock Stein. It would be folly to say that the hugely respected and shrewd coach who had become a Celtic scout in 1940 displayed some sort of magical foresight by recruiting the centre half from Llanelli, but that's the thing: the subtle decisions made by these knowledgeable men so often had seismic effects.

Reserve team coach Gribben had been sought out by Bob Kelly, a chairman presiding over a difficult period in Celtic's history, one in which trophies and goodwill were in short supply. At the end of 1951 the first-team squad was looking thin. Would Gribben know of a defender who might come and shore things up, more in terms of numbers than quality. Gribben had a think, and for some reason the name Jock Stein emerged from a memory.

Maybe it was an image of the solid but unspectacular centre half who had done a decent job against Celtic reserves two years before; maybe it was the fact that Gribben lived near the Albion Rovers ground in Coatbridge that had kept Stein in the back of his mind. Football men have a habit of remembering the small things, the less obvious things about a match, and so there was the name Jock Stein for the first time in a Celtic conversation, and once they tracked him down to Wales, requests were made and decisions made. It was to be the best £1,200 Celtic ever spent.

Not that the move initially shook football's foundations. Supporters of the club greeted the signing with incredulous disappointment. Nothing against Stein, although his Burnbank heritage will have caused some to disapprove, but this was another sign that the club's board lacked any ambition. These were fans who came to Celtic Park in their tens of thousands, but the odd cup win aside, they were following a team who couldn't even boast of being Scotland's second best. Rangers and Hibernian were battling it out for the league title, and now, as Christmas 1951 approached, this was far from the gift the Celtic faithful had hoped for.

As he travelled up from South Wales, Stein might also have given a passing thought to what those who drank and fought and drank some more at Burnbank Cross might have to say. Their prejudices wouldn't have swayed or dampened his journey up – this was Celtic after all, a massive opportunity for a man who thought such opportunities had passed – but the religious divide and the opinions that it invited would greet him on his return.

'He lost a lot of pals overnight when he signed for Celtic,' recalled his old friend and workmate Harry Steele. '"Turncoat" was about the kindest thing they said about him. After a wee while his name just wasn't mentioned at the Cross. And although he was in and around Burnbank for a long while he never came back down among us to stand and have a blether.'

One old friend from his childhood turned and walked out of Stein's mother's house on seeing the new Celtic player was also visiting, but his wife Jean, having got over the shock, saw that side of things as secondary, especially to her husband. 'The religious question didn't bother him – I don't think he gave it a moment's thought,' she said. 'But maybe his father would have liked him, at one time, to see him become a Rangers player. I can well remember when we went up to see his mother and father on a Saturday morning before a game. If they were playing Rangers that day his mother used to wish him good luck as usual. But all his father would say was, "I hope it's a draw," because he was that wee bit Rangers-minded.'

The religious question might not have outwardly affected Stein, and it certainly wouldn't influence his career, but the reaction from those with whom he had grown up and even worked underground must have had some sort of lasting effect. Archie Macpherson, who once sat and listened to Stein's tale about the old friend turning and walking away from his mother's, was in no doubt.

'To watch Stein deliver that anecdote,' Macpherson wrote,

in an almost languid manner as he lay back against a leathered couch late at night in a small hotel in Elgin, was to appreciate that for all his apparent hardness, for all that he was trying to recount a story in a deceptively casual way, the incident had pained him deeply. But life socially would never be the same again, and it is not difficult to conclude that one of the driving forces for the rest of his life in club football at Parkhead, and especially when he became manager, was to wreak revenge on those who had turned their backs on him by making Celtic great.

Making Celtic great again might have been a flickering fantasy in Stein's mind on joining the club, but the immediate reality was that he was there merely as back-up. 'A steady chap' was how Jimmy Gribben had described him to the club's hierarchy, someone able to fill in when needed and a journeyman who might pass on some knowledge to the younger players in Gribben's reserves.

As Stein walked through Parkhead's corridors, heads hardly turned. Anyway, it was the reserve-team dressing room that beckoned, and so first-team bigwigs such as Charlie Tulley and John McPhail were hardly bothered, while Sean Fallon, an old teammate at Rovers, didn't even recall him from those Coatbridge days. This was an inconspicuous start to life at Celtic, but anonymity wasn't to last.

Four days after signing his sixteen-pound-a-week contract, injuries took Stein from the reservests to a bigger stage, St Mirren at home with the first-team. 'Jock Stein made a quiet debut, attempting nothing spectacular,' reported the *Sunday Post*. Whistles from a frustrated crowd had greeted the announcement of his name, but, steady and brave and organized, his performances soon started to win the doubters over. Those in the crowd anyway.

Celtic's amiable manager Jim McGrory and the chairman, Bob Kelly, who had a big say in team affairs, had heard from senior players that Stein was unpopular, his Protestant background counting against him with some, his age and self-confidence counting against him with others, but Fallon, an Irishman from Sligo, argued that the Protestant players were invaluable to the team, and in Stein he saw a resolute individual with an air about him that wouldn't allow the dressing-room establishment to dictate his mood.

'It's not easy to walk into a club,' Fallon said.

In any club, well established players can make it difficult for a new boy . . . There were one or two of the long-serving players that you were lucky to get a 'good morning' from. At the time it was annoying, but then you realized what it was all about. Everyone is there for the same reason basically, to make Celtic a better side, a successful side. But there is that selfish thing too – that you want to be in the first team yourself. You are there to prove that you are a better player than someone else, and so there is always a chance of animosity. If you take the place of a player who has been in the team for a long time, then he won't be happy and some of his mates won't be happy. Jock had a bit of that kind of backlash, but he didn't let it worry him. He just got on with the game.

By the start of the 1952/3 season, Stein was an integral part of the team, the organizer of a sturdier back line in a team showing improvement. McPhail, the captain and a grand doubter of the new arrival, might have taken to comfort eating at Stein's resolute displays because a weight issue saw him start the season at a health farm. A new skipper was needed, and it was Fallon, who in turn opted for Stein as his deputy, drawn to the centre half's hard work and thoughtful thirst for improvement – both the team's and his own.

Players then were very much left to their own devices when it came to motivation and even tactics. In McGrory, they had a manager not prone to *Braveheart* William-Wallace-at-Sterling-type pre-match rants. 'It's going to be a hard game today, lads' was about as chest thumping as it got, and despite the example of Matt Busby in Manchester, the notion of a manager in a tracksuit was still alien in Glasgow. 'The game was different then, and maybe that's why Jock stood out,' recalled Fallon. 'He thought seriously about the game.'

Fallon then broke his arm, and so in 1953, just months after being signed as some sort of stopgap and reserve, Jock Stein was the club captain. As footballing coronations went, it was pretty impressive (a fairy tale was how one fan put it), but this being 1953, when it came to coronations even Stein couldn't compete with a certain young princess turned monarch. Queen Elizabeth's coronation did bring Celtic some glory. The Coronation Cup was a tournament arranged that spring in Glasgow and played out between Rangers, Hibs, Manchester United, Newcastle, Arsenal and Celtic. There Stein faced Busby's United and won, going on to underline their vast improvement with a 2–0 win over Hibs in the final.

The following season only pushed the point further. Stein was the leader in a team paving the way. Celtic were winning games; the crowds were massive, and respect for their uncomplicated centre half, known for clearing danger with his big knee and with a knack for calm leadership even during the most frantic of Scottish League games, was being slowly noticed and more than appreciated. Fortunes were turning, Stein's luck was clearly benefiting the club, or as his pal Tony Queen quipped to him, 'If you fell intae the Clyde you'd come up with a trout in your mouth.'

With said trouts in their mouths, Celtic played and won their way to a triumphant league (the club's first since 1938) and cup double in the 1953/4 season, with Stein learning that planning and thoughtful discussion can garner such results. Stein, Fallon and Bertie Peacock would have lunch at Ferrari's restaurant on Sauchiehall Street in Glasgow, where they would work out their own ways of combining. Like Shankly in his boiler room at Workington, Stein had Ferrari's in which to talk with football men, and there his footballing brain was becoming the finest of machines.

Further fine tuning would occur that summer. The reward Celtic's squad gained from their double was a trip to Switzerland for the World Cup. Stein had been at Wembley to see the Hungarians dismantle not only England's team but British perceptions about their place in the game. Scotland, after a 7–0 defeat to Uruguay in Switzerland, were also reminded of football's global reach, but Stein came home further enamoured by the Hungarians, convinced that the game he so loved could be played in a way that made hearts soar. Archie Macpherson noted a sea change. 'Puskás, Hidegkuti and company put a gleam in Stein's eye and an ideal in his sights that stirred his imagination, and that in itself was to rub off on anyone who put on boots for him at any stage.'

There was immense pride in pulling on the green and white hoops the following season, but this time the club finished runners-up in both league and cup. The cup final was lost to Clyde after a replay, a result which Stein put down to boardroom interference. Much to the disbelief of fans, opponents and the Celtic captain, Bobby Collins was dropped, as was Neilly Mochan, seemingly against the wishes of manager McGrory. If the deft skills of Puskás and his teammates had shaken a kaleidoscope within Stein's mind about how football might be played, then that day and that defeat and those decisions from up high at Hampden Park would stay with him too. If he ever managed, he'd do it his way.

The fans, very much won over, voted Stein their player of the year. This prompted him to write to the supporters' association, 'I cannot, like other Celts, claim that Celtic was my first love, but I know it will be my last and most enduring.' Around the corner though was an ankle injury, sustained against Rangers at Celtic Park in the August of 1955, which was to prove irreversible. He would have treatment, but an operation went wrong, with dirty stitches causing a septic reaction. He'd try to play, but the ankle was weakened beyond repair, and as fast and as far as his fairy tale had taken him, in 1957 his playing days were over.

The affection for Stein among the club's fans endured, but that wouldn't pay the bills. Stein was understandably concerned about what would happen next, but Bob Kelly, mindful of the reasons Stein had been initially sought out, had an offer. For all his meddling in team affairs, the chairman was a popular figure and had both Stein's respect and friendship, and when the reserve-team coaching job was offered, Stein jumped at it.

Bob Kelly's decision to have Stein look after the club's reserves was by no means a carriage clock to thank a good player for services rendered. Kelly put huge stock in the club's development of young players. With a nod to Matt Busby's exploits south of the border, 'Kelly's Kids' was how some in the press would label a hugely promising group of youngsters clearly ready to be nurtured by the right person. Kelly had seen Stein lead on the pitch; he'd seen a footballing mind grow; he'd noticed the innovations. This was a young man who could help his project, and these were the first steps – for the young players, for the new coach, for the club – the first steps to something truly spectacular.

Stein's enthusiasm was immediate and helped by a pool of talent that included Billy McNeill, Tommy Gemmell, Bobby Murdoch and Paddy Crerand. Quickly added was a seventeen-year-old wing half from Lanarkshire called John Clark. Clark would later go on gloriously to partner McNeill in the centre of Celtic's first-team defence, but having signed for five pounds a week, the teenager was immediately struck by the man who had brought him there.

'He had this personality about him,' said Clark. 'As a player you sensed what he was about. I was only seventeen, but straight away we all trusted him, and if you put that trust in him you were rewarded. When you're young, you're just delighted to be at Celtic, and you got on with things, but what was happening was bigger than that, and with Jock there it was the start of real youth development at Celtic that would last a long time.'

What struck the young players about Stein was multi-layered. His presence, his grasp and love for the game, his enthusiasm and his ability to make them feel special were all there. So was the coaching – methods on the training pitch a world away from what they were used to. 'What we noticed immediately was how much we used the ball,' said Clark, a spark still in his voice when reminiscing about those early days at Celtic. 'It had always been a lot of running with a wee game of football to finish. Now don't get me wrong, we ran. We ran a lot. Jock was a great man for believing in leg power and stamina, but what stood out was the amount of ball work. We'd work on technique and us players responded to it.'

Stein might have been looking after the second string, but to him this was a club within a club. Training would be intense but fun, and it would be educational. First-team players would stop what they were doing and glance enviously at what Stein was doing with his youngsters. Paddy Crerand laughed at the difference in enthusiasm. 'The first team were doing boring old stuff. Laps, maybe a game at the end of the session. It was a joke really, but for us training every day with Jock was a pure pleasure.'

The young reserves would often play their games on Friday nights so as to attract bigger crowds. In the spring of 1958, just weeks before a seventeen-year-old called Pelé was showing the world his boyish brilliance, Stein's young team won a two-legged reserve final against Rangers in front of 40,000 fans. For Stein it was a victory that gave him a taste for blood, and shark-like he would hunt for more success. For the youngsters playing, it was a taste of the big time.

'It was so exciting,' said Clark. 'Those Friday night games especially. You'd get big crowds coming and there was always a good atmosphere. Those days helped push us, and when it did come to playing for the first team, you were that much more comfortable. All the boys that played at that time got used to occasions, and the crowds wouldn't put you off. That was clever.'

Stein took time to get to know his team. Before he got his driving licence, after training he would accompany Billy McNeill and Clark to catch the bus home to Lanarkshire. 'He was a great man for not letting us on a bus if ours came first,' said Clark. 'He'd say, "I'm no' waiting here on my own; you boys can get the next one." His would then come along five minutes later and we had to wait another forty-five minutes in the rain!' When he got his licence, he would drive them (always a hair-raising experience with Stein) back to Bellshill, talking football, describing the great Hungarian team he had seen. 'He'd tell us to keep working on our game,' said Clark. 'He'd tell us to work on our ball control, the basics. He was our gaffer, and his enthusiasm was amazing.'

Stein's zest for his new life extended to his approach to tactics and teaching. His way of coaching was fresh and innovative. Sure, he'd work on repetition, cross after cross sent in for McNeill to head goalwards; midfielders such as Crerand would fire long pass after long pass at benches set up along the perimeter of the pitch, but there was more. Stein was working on a player's second nature, and he also wanted to nurture their talent.

He would talk to them as equals. He may have come to the professional game late, but he knew what it took to make it. He had his past of course, and while he didn't use his days working the pits as some sort of romanticized motivational tool, he could now and then use it to nudge a young player in the right direction. Someone might come to him and say, 'Boss, I feel a wee bit sore.' They'd be greeted with a knowing stare and the words, 'See the people down below working? They're sore 'n' all, but they have to get on with it. So do you.' And the players responded.

As a four-year-old, Stein's son George would have his father encouraging him to kick a ball with his weaker left foot against a wall. Stein would stand watching him until he could do it all on his own. It was a method he took beyond his family. 'He wanted to have your game developed in your head so when you're on the field you knew exactly what you were doing,' said Clark.

He would tell you what to do, but you had to grasp that. He made you think. Nine times out of ten, what he had said on the tactics board was spot on, and you just carried out his demands.

He could express through his team talk and coaching methods what he wanted from you but ultimately he wanted you to think for yourself. He was one of those guys, he didn't like repeating himself. 'I'm not going to keep telling you and keep telling you,' he'd say. 'If you can't do it, I'll get someone in who can.' It got a response and brought a zip to training.

His presence was the thing. He was a powerful guy. Soon, what he said was gospel. The senior players had respect for him then too. He'd played with some of them and so his respect at the club was huge.

Respect for Stein at the club was one thing, but there was the matter of a career. Stein was keen to manage at a higher level, and clubs in Scotland had seen with interest the strides he and his reserve team had taken and would soon want to talk. The first-team job at Celtic was of course the prize, but it became apparent that Stein wasn't on a fast track to that particular role. In 1960 the job at Dunfermline came up, and after careful consideration on Stein's side, was his. While Clark and the other Celtic youngsters were sorry to see him go, it was football and he had his own ambitions to realize, while Jean felt that promotion at Celtic was out of her husband's hands and there was a definite if unspoken sense that his Protestant background would hinder him at the club.

'He was more or less told by the chairman that he had gone as far as he could ever go with Celtic, and that therefore he should take the chance of the Dunfermline job,' she said. 'I know the old chairman used to suggest that he simply let John go out for experience and that it was always the case that he would go back to Celtic, but I don't think that was right. John didn't think so either.'

Stein would leave to become a first-team manager knowing he had helped shape young footballers' lives, but neither he nor they guessed that they would one day work together again. 'This is football, anything can happen,' said Clark. 'We just felt Jock was leaving to gain experience and make other clubs better. That's what he did.' He'd drive the forty miles across to Fife with nothing but thanks and admiration for Bob Kelly and the Celtic supporters who had so taken to him. At Celtic he had become the football man he'd always wanted to be. There he had learned so much more about the game, and now it was time to pass that knowledge on.

Dunfermline was now his place of work and work he would.

Chapter 8:

His Babes

An early evening in February, 1958. A car drives through the darkening streets of Huddersfield. Bill Shankly is at the wheel, the club's assistant secretary, Eddie Brennan, sits in the passenger seat. The only sound is the windscreen wipers moving back and forth, clearing the glass of the incessant rain and sleet that falls on the Pennine Hills. An hour or so earlier Shankly had received a phone call in his office from a local journalist. 'Good God,' he'd said ashen-faced, turning to Brennan. 'Manchester United. They've been killed. I think we'd better get home.'

They drive in silence, thoughts of friends and footballers, of young lives and disaster filling their minds. Matt Busby had long been a hero of Shankly's. Born and reared just miles from his own home, a fellow miner, a footballer who had come to England and achieved so much. A Scottish teammate and wartime skipper. Matt Busby, the man who had turned Manchester United from a club reduced to rubble by war into a flowing blur of youthful brilliance, and one that refused to be limited to only domestic adventure. Matt Busby, his friend.

Shankly pulls up at the George Hotel to let Brennan out. 'You're a Catholic, aren't you, Eddie?' he says.

'You know I am, Bill,' Brennan replies.

'You say a prayer for them,' says Shankly. 'Say a prayer for them.'

*

It had become obvious to those on the plane that things were badly wrong. As the engines failed and it rolled further along the runway without finding sufficient power to take off, Busby's thoughts turned to panic. 'We sped on and on and on, and my thoughts sounded just like that – "On and on and on and on" – until they changed to "Too long, too long, too long, too long!" We were not going up.' Busby, in what he would call a pathetic attempt at self-protection, threw out his arms. And then darkness.

He now lies in a Bavarian hospital bed drifting in and out of consciousness. Thoughts and dreams blur into one; pain is the only constant. A room full of covered bodies. A doctor looks down at one. 'This one is dead,' he pronounces. Busby thinks this is Frank Swift, his old mate from Manchester City, who had travelled with the team as a journalist.

His old friend Jimmy McGuire, president of the United States Football Association, has been by his bed, talking, reassuring. Busby cannot talk, but he knows he is there and he nods. Doctors come and go, their concerned faces shattering hope. Clergymen are frequent guests, his last rites are even read. Darkness and pain.

Jean is by his bedside. A clergyman is talking and Busby overhears him saying, 'Duncan Edwards is dead.' Busby is seriously injured, and ignorant of the scale of the tragedy that has visited his football team, the true horror of what had happened on that runway kept from him for his own good. 'And then, for the first time, it really dawned on me,' he later said on hearing of Edwards' death. 'I really knew, though had no idea what, that something even more than I could imagine had struck, and that they were keeping it from me.'

He asked his wife to tell him everything. 'Don't worry,' came the reply. 'Don't talk. I'm supposed to do the talking.' Busby though was in turmoil. Physical pain was one thing, but he would later say the mental pain of knowing something beyond his nightmares had happened to his team, to the group they called his Babes, was 'a new torture'. Unable to sit up and demand to know, he simply said, 'Jean, I want to know. I want to know the worst. For my peace of mind.'

Jean gave in. Busby would say a name, and she would simply nod or shake her head. He had talked of peace of mind, but what followed the terrible revelations from his heartbroken wife was more akin to hell. Unable to move, but more importantly and more punishingly unable to control his thoughts, Busby was left to wonder and to grieve and to despair as the disaster sank further and further in. 'I was spared,' he'd later say. 'But even if I survived how could I face the loved ones of the lads who were not spared? Was I to blame? Was I to blame? Why can't I die?' Busby, a devout Catholic, had his own grievances with his god, but no longer wanted to have them as a living man.

The fans wouldn't know the depths to which Busby's morale sank. The thought that the man who had created such a life-affirming football team no longer wanted to be alive, let alone remain in football, would have affected them deeply. In those post-war years, amid rationing, austerity and the death of a wartime monarch, football had offered solace, and Busby's brilliant young team especially. Lowry painted flocking crowds with almost featureless faces, but Busby and the young men who played with such individuality within his team had created smiles.

As 1951 turned to 1952, John Arlott, that wonderfully mellifluous cricket commentator, wrote a book about another passion of his. In *Concerning Soccer* he dedicated some pages to Manchester United: 'Under their new manager, they have proved that class football and consistent success are more closely related than some

The tiny mining village of Glenbuck, where Bill Shankly grew up. Stein and Busby were raised in similar nearby communities.

A Celt at last. Jock Stein in the green and white of Celtic.

Matt Busby, after a few early doubts, finds his feet at Manchester City.

Always a proud Scot, Bill Shankly prepares to make his debut for his country in 1938.

Shankly loved his playing days at Preston as a hard tackling half-back.

Matt Busby, now in the red of Liverpool. He was a hugely popular figure at Anfield and might even have managed the club.

Bill Shankly, at Preston's Deep Dale.

Jock Stein (second from right) enjoys training with Albion Rovers in 1948.

Shankly's early decision to keep his Liverpool back room staff was one of the best he ever made. *From left to right*: Shankly, Bob Paisley, Joe Fagan, Ronnie Moran, Rueben Bennett and Tom Saunders, at Melwood in July 1971.

Above: The best of friends. Jock Stein (centre) with Bill Shankly (left) and Shankly's brother Bob, the manager at Dundee.

Left: Jock built a second team after the break up of his Lisbon Lions. At its heart was Kenny Dalglish.

Left: Jock Stein makes his frustrations clear to Internazionale's manager, Helenio Herrera, at half time during the 1967 European Cup Final in Lisbon.

Below: Home! Matt Busby returns from hospital in Munich to a warm welcome.

Above: In his hands at last! Matt Busby with Paddy Crerand (left) and George Best, and the beloved European Cup.

Matt Busby with his customary pipe, proudly stands at Old Trafford, a ground that had been reduced to rubble by German air raids when he arrived.

Left: Making his way up the ladder. Bill Shankly at the helm at Huddersfield Town in 1956.

Above: 'He made the people happy!' Bill Shankly in front of his people on the Kop after the league championship has been won in 1973.

Left: Bill Shankly rarely thought about anything else other than football. Here he is enjoying a game of Subbuteo at home.

Bill Shankly puts his troops through their paces at Melwood, the training ground he totally redeveloped after his arrival in 1959.

'I'm privileged to have followed', Sir Alex Ferguson once said.

'Manchester is my heaven.' Busby at Old Trafford.

Left: Liverpool legends Emlyn Hughes, Ray Clemence and Ian St John are among the pallbearers at Bill Shankly's funeral in 1981.

Below: Alex Ferguson looks on anxiously as Jock Stein suffers what would be his fatal heart attack in Cardiff in September 1985.

contemporary judges have suggested. The club is not a young one; but it has never enjoyed such success as its record since 1946 – four times runners-up and once fourth in the league; with a cup win, a semi-final and two sixth-round appearances – all in five seasons.'

With only one trophy Busby would have been less inclined to celebrate, but it must have heartened him that what he was trying to do at Old Trafford was bearing fruit. Arlott continued:

Matt Busby was himself an artistic footballer – but an artist whose play always had a point, every subtlety he produced had its aim. The team he has created plays good football all the time. Even when Blackpool had gone ahead of them in the FA Cup final of 1948, Manchester United continued to play skilful football. A rapidly taken free kick took instant advantage of a momentary Blackpool slackness, and Rowley scored the equalizing goal.

When Morris, one of the finest inside forwards in post-war football, was sold to Derby County; when Mitten, the outside left, went to Bogota; when Delaney – ageing a little by football standards – returned to Scotland, some critics thought that Manchester United would begin to fall off. Each time, however, the gap was filled and Busby's young players – appearing only infrequently, for he is not prepared to ruin them by attempting to hurry their development – promise that the illustrious first team of the moment can be replaced from home resources when the need arises.

Other sides may achieve their success over brief periods; Manchester United, under their present management, may well continue at the top of our football for many years. It will be for the good of the game if they do, for their perpetual sermon of class football, perpetually switching from defence into combined and controlled attack, is one which all football will do well to mark.

By the time Arlott's book was published, Busby's 1951/2 team were very much charging towards that elusive championship and their manager very much becoming an all-round boss. Results and performance were one thing, but here was a man now totally at ease with life on the touchlines.

He could be cunning. In 1948, during the team's victorious cup run, the club drew Liverpool at home. The problem was City had also been drawn at home, so a new venue had to be found. Busby pushed for Goodison Park. Many scoffed at the geographical advantage this would hand Liverpool, but Busby had other ideas. Not only did Everton's wide pitch suit his side's expansive way of playing, but the shrewd young manager saw Liverpool's split loyalties as playing into his hands. 'He knew it would be a full house,' John Aston later said. 'A third of the ticket allocation would be going to Everton, and they'd be bound to shout for us, so we would actually have two thirds of the crowd on our side. Busby was always very cute at thinking about things like that.' Liverpool were beaten 3–0.

He could also be tough. Busby's approach in 1950 to the Charlie Mitten affair, which saw the brilliant winger succumb to the temptation of the huge wages and luxury on offer in Colombia, was one of belligerence. When the South American bubble burst, Mitten returned wanting to resume his career at Manchester United. Fines and bans were handed out, while a meeting with Busby at which Mitten argued he had merely gone to better himself and had come back better for it went badly. 'It was like talking to a wall,' Patrick Barclay declared. Mitten was sold to Fulham.

The attributes of everything a successful modern manager should be were now present in Busby, but it was his and the club's determination to develop young men that was most important to him. Both Roger Byrne and Jackie Blanchflower were given their first-team debuts in the 1951/2 season, slotting in when necessary, seamlessly adding to a fine team. 'Do you need a good young wing half?' John Arlott heard a rival manager ask Busby prior to the season.

'No,' came the reply. 'I have got all the good young players I need in my reserve side.'

The old guard of John Carey, Henry Cockburn, Jack Rowley, Stan Pearson, John Aston and Allen Chilton were brilliantly understudied by the newcomers, most notably Byrne, whose seven league goals in twenty-four appearances went a long way towards bringing the title to Old Trafford for the first time in forty-one years.

Nearly 54,000 people made their way to Old Trafford for the last game of the season, which saw their team officially crowned champions. A 6–1 rout of their title rivals Arsenal spoke volumes for the sheer moxie this team had for the game of football. Enterprising and brave, Busby's team had long been seen as the country's best, but now the league table agreed. The *Manchester Guardian* certainly did. 'M. Busby has shown himself as great a coach as he was a player, with an uncannily brilliant eye for young local players' possibilities, whether it's in their usual or in other positions; a believer in the certainty of good football's eventual reward, and a kindly yet, when necessary, firm father of his family of players,' wrote the paper's correspondent Donny Davies.

'Between them they have built up a club spirit which is too rare in these days, a spirit which enables men to bear cheerfully

personal and team disappointments and to ignore personal opportunities to shine for the good of the whole.' Davies went on to
laud Busby's skill at 'eschewing the dangerous policy of going
into the transfer market whenever a weakness develops and giving
their chances instead to many local citizens on the club's books'
and write that the relationship between manager and board must
be 'the envy of many other officials in all parts of the country'.
He was right, but it had been Busby's sheer resilience and refusal
to panic when the chips were down that had reaped rewards for
the club and the careers of so many local boys.

Early in his tenure Busby was accosted by the club chairman,
Jimmy Gibson. Gibson had previously hoped that the club's
coffers wouldn't be emptied for new players, but with success
tantalizingly close and a good player at Newcastle reportedly
available, he suggested Busby sign him.

'No, he is not good for us,' was Busby's answer.

'You are always telling me no,' Gibson barked, before saying
menacingly, 'Well I'm telling you now, go and sign him!' Busby
understood the missing end to this instruction was 'Or else!'

'No,' said Busby, 'and I will remind you of two things, Mr
Gibson. I am here to manage the club, and part of management
is giving you advice, and the second is that I lived long before
I saw you.'

Red faced, Gibson walked from the room, only to return fifteen minutes later, slightly calmer and now clear his employee
was a manager not to be trifled with. 'Mr Busby, you are a very
strong-minded person. I have come back and I want to say I
am sorry this has happened. We will carry on as we were.' This
was a green light. Manchester United would be a place where
youth was promoted and where the manager had the final say
on all matters relating to the team. Gibson died prior to the title

triumph, but so adamant was he that Busby's autonomy should be safeguarded that he placed his son Alan on the board.

Harold Hardman took over as chairman, but if he thought his chequebook would gather dust, he was wrong. Transfers weren't completely outlawed. The summer before the title win, a skilful right-winger called Johnny Berry joined from Birmingham City for £25,000. Berry had been spotted giving Manchester United's left side a torrid time in a cup tie the previous season and his brilliance noted. Promoting youth players from within the club wasn't some sort of vanity project. Busby, like Rocca before him, truly believed that by mining the local area (and beyond) you would unearth genuine quality at a far cheaper rate and with a stronger link to the club and its fans. You could also mould a way of playing from a young age, but should quality become available, should players who would add to the team come up for sale, then a visit to the chairman and his board would be made.

Six of the team who called themselves champions of England also had 1948 FA Cup winners' medals on their mantelpieces. Four of them – Johnny Carey, Allenby Chilton, Stan Pearson and Jack Rowley – had been signed before Hitler had made his dangerous intentions clear. They had played brilliantly, captured the imagination of supporters everywhere, but ageing is as constant as the kit a player wears, and a manager has to eye the future. Busby, Bill Shankly and Jock Stein would all have to face the reality of breaking up football teams that had served them well. After his title win in 1952, Busby had his eye on improvements, and going into the 1952–3 season, with Jack Rowley, that most prolific of his forwards, clearly entering the latter stages of his career, thoughts of evolution were uppermost in his mind.

Busby would of course look at his youngsters. The reserves included Eddie Lewis, a talented eighteen-year-old who had played in the first team but was deemed not ready. At Barnsley though, Tommy Taylor was scoring goals for his hometown club, and with many predicting elevation to Nat Lofthouse's throne, Busby swooped. A fee in the region of £30,000 was mooted, but the United manager was concerned the twenty-one-year-old would find it difficult to live up to such a sum so he offered Barnsley's tea lady a tip of one pound and the club's board £29,999. It was accepted and Taylor, soon to be capped by England, was a Manchester United player.

His arrival was timely in as much as United had been finding the season tough. As low as second from bottom in October and out of the cup, their fortunes improved only slightly. This was a season bereft of tangible success but one that hindsight would judge as vital to later greatness. Nineteen-year-old forward Dennis Viollet made his debut that April, while twenty-year-old Bill Foulkes had made his first appearance before Christmas. Foulkes, from St Helens, was still working underground as a miner at the Lea Green colliery when he started his career at Old Trafford. He would train on Tuesdays and Thursdays, but receive detailed letters from Bert Whalley – Busby's hard-working reserve-team coach and a great help to many coming through the gilded ranks – explaining the strengths and weaknesses of the forwards the defender would face in the next match.

And then there was Duncan Edwards, a sixteen-year-old in a man's body who commanded football pitches like most his age did sweet shops. At Easter 1953 that boy took the club's number 6 shirt and despite a 4–1 defeat to Cardiff looked every bit the First Division footballer. Edwards, from Dudley in England's Black Country, had been very much on the top clubs' radar. Playing under-15 football aged just eleven, and captaining England schoolboys, his signature was in demand.

Busby had feared Edwards' local team, Wolverhampton Wanderers, were the front runners, but a visit to see him play only further whetted his appetite. 'What everyone said about him was correct,' Busby would say. 'It was obvious he was going to be a player of exceptional talent. So easy on the ball, two-footed, perfect balance, legs like oak trees and a temperament to match.' Busby's chief scout, Joe Armstrong, had been charged with oiling the wheels of Edwards' signing and is thought to have discovered the schoolboy's affection for Manchester United, but Bolton were particularly keen and when Reg Priest, Armstrong's man in the Midlands, informed him that they were travelling down and that he feared the worst, Armstrong and Bert Whalley had jumped in a car with signing-on forms and smiles.

It was 2 a.m. when they arrived at Edwards' family home in Dudley. Greeted by the man of the house in his pyjamas, they were shown upstairs, where Edwards told them they needn't have made the trip: his heart had always been set on Old Trafford. A little over a week later, Bert Whalley greeted the young man at Manchester's London Road station to take him to the stadium. There, in the summer of 1951, while the first team and Busby were touring the United States and having their photos taken with Bing Crosby and Bob Hope, they signed a footballer who would take them on the road to glory.

Going the extra mile to get their man was not unusual. Busby and Murphy had lingered in Barnsley for days, staking out Tommy Taylor. Wilf McGuinness talked of Joe Armstrong insisting the young hopeful call him Uncle Joe, tricking rival scouts into thinking they were dealing with a relative. Bobby Charlton's family in Ashington, near Newcastle, was visited constantly and charmed by Armstrong. Again he was known as Uncle Joe, Charlton even calling his wife Auntie Cassie. Again it worked.

The title won in 1952, Busby set out on his next mission, the mission he had always envisaged being his life's work. Current form might be affected by the transition but that didn't matter. Players who had made the first team would be left out in order to play Youth Cup games, a tournament that Jimmy Murphy had achieved great success in. 'The future was more important than the present,' Busby would say, and so while finishes of eighth, fourth and fifth after the title win might have concerned the masses who flocked to the matches, for Busby, blooding Foulkes, Byrne (now moved to left back), Blanchflower, Viollet, Eddie Coleman, Liam Whelan, David Pegg, Mark Jones and later Bobby Charlton was the priority. These young footballers were gaining both experience and gelling in a team seemingly born to play together.

Prior to the 1955/6 season, the *Manchester Guardian* ran a preview in which the champions Chelsea and perennial hopefuls Wolves were touted as probable championship winners, with Portsmouth and West Bromwich Albion afforded honourable mentions. Busby's young team were seen as too callow, too inconsistent, to even warrant a mention.

Two draws, three wins and three losses in the first eight games suggested that the newspaper had it right, but after a defeat at Preston at the end of January, the team clicked, going unbeaten for the rest of the season and winning Busby his second championship. A cup final defeat to Aston Villa denied them the first double of the century, but no matter, The Busby Babes were the talk of football's chattering classes. The term itself had been created years before by a subeditor on the *Manchester Evening News* on the day Byrne and Blanchflower had made their debuts, but now it stuck to the whole team. Busby didn't like it, feeling it ignored the contributions others had made in the development of this most exciting of teams, a team that would retain the title in 1957.

By now Real Madrid, the powerhouse of the European game, had seen enough. Matt Busby, this innovator, this builder of empires, must be their manager. Busby and the Real president Santiago Bernabéu, by now friends, talked of such a marriage, but the United manager wasn't having any of it. 'Manchester is my heaven,' he famously said. He admired Real Madrid – who wouldn't – but the Orbiston boy had another idea. Instead of joining Real Madrid, he was going to take them on.

Busby had set up a team to support his boys, and while he provided the inspiration, he never forgot those who did the basics. 'Our whole world revolved round Jimmy Murphy, Bert Whalley and Tom Curry,' recalled Albert Scanlon, a locally born winger who came through the ranks to make appearances in both title-winning campaigns. 'The staff made it so happy – people like the laundry ladies. The older players were more reserved but they would still join in the fun, that was the secret, although it would take nothing for someone like Jack Rowley to snap at you. You had respect for the first-teamers, but the kids were really in a little world of their own.'

The football on offer was also in a world of its own, but now played by a group of young men who through time growing up with each other had become very close. Even those who joined from other clubs bought into it – men like Tommy Taylor and Johnny Berry, arriving from Barnsley and Birmingham respectively but now fully integrated and the best of pals.

Other clubs looked to youth. Bill Shankly at Huddersfield was promoting young reserve players such as Denis Law and Ray Wilson into his first team, and Jock Stein was revelling in the work he was doing with Celtic's youngsters, but Busby's

Manchester United were the beacon, and moving into the 1957/8 season, this brilliant side and their manager had even greater and brighter challenges in their sights.

Huddersfield and Arsenal had each won three titles in a row, both clubs hugely indebted to Herbert Chapman. Busby – his stock sky-high and a keen admirer of all Chapman had done for the game in general – wanted to emulate that. His young side winning the title for the third time in a row was paramount in his mind, but by now there was a new and exciting competition to take into consideration. Its name? The European Cup.

In January 1955 Gabriel Hanot, a former French international and now editor of the sports paper *L'Equipe*, had taken note of football's shifting sands. Wolverhampton had beaten plenty of good European sides at Molineux in high-profile friendlies, tempting their manager Stan Cullis into declaring his side world champions. 'Let them go to Moscow and Budapest,' Hanot wrote before calling a meeting at which fifteen clubs agreed to start a new competition the following season.

Invitations were sent out. The Spanish FA enthusiastically promised Real Madrid's involvement while Scotland agreed that Hibernian would take part. The English Football League were less open, and Chelsea, on their way to winning the title, wouldn't be playing. Alan Hardaker, the Football League's secretary, was making noises about a new cup competition to be played under floodlights, and that would take priority over some European love-in. Busby, that most forward-thinking men, looked on frustrated but had an influential ally, so when he received a letter from the FA secretary Stanley Rous, a man with whom he'd always got on, it became clear his ambitions could be realized.

Kindred spirits, Rous had seen Busby's managerial potential during the war, and now he saw the potential of this new European competition. Unlike Chelsea, Manchester United would be invited and they would accept. Busby was itching to get involved, and while United would have to rent Maine Road again (City had installed floodlights), the revenue gained would allow them to erect their own. Futures were being planned.

A preliminary-round 10–0 win at Maine Road over Anderlecht illuminated the possibilities of this brave new world, and Busby's team continued – like they did in any competition they played – to hurl themselves towards brilliance. They beat Borussia Dortmund, but in northern Spain were beaten 5–3 by Bilbao, meaning English football fans for the first time were about to see the sort of European night that they could file under 'G' – for 'Glory'.

In the second leg United took a 1–0 lead into the dressing room thanks to Viollet, a forward at the very top of his game. They still needed two goals against a top team, but Busby stood in front of his eager young team and was calmness personified. 'Boys,' he said, his fatherly persona filling the room, 'do not panic. Play the game as you know how. Make your passes and do your running, but, above all, keep your patience. If you can do that, we will get there.'

Tommy Taylor scored with eighteen minutes left and set up his pal Johnny Berry for the winner with only six remaining. It was an exhilarating win, and while the semi-final was lost to the all-conquering Real Madrid, the appetite for such drama and adventure was growing fast. Even fans of other clubs were enthralled. 'There was rarely a dull moment watching them,' wrote John Moynihan in his book *The Soccer Syndrome*. 'They attacked without mercy and scored goals without mercy. If they were behind they fought back and beat the opposition by sheer exuberance. If their lead was cut they came back and built up another lead which was this time insurmountable. They greeted their goals with outrageous enthusiasm throwing up their hands and leaping with delight.'

This was the late 1950s. Teenage culture was emerging from the grey skies of post-war austerity. Rock 'n' roll, quiffs, Brando's *The Wild One*. It was all there in a football team dressed strikingly in red shirts with white V-necks, but while rebellion was on so many teen minds, this group of young men were under the spell of their elders and all the better for it.

The 1957/8 season was another thriller. United went for it on all three fronts. The chase for a third title was going to be tough. Performance levels remained enthralling. A 2–1 win against Nottingham Forest moved Donny Davies to note, 'The splendour of the performance was enriched by the grace of sportsmanlike behaviour.' At the heart of it was Duncan Edwards. Bobby Charlton had by now broken into the team and was shining bright, but in his great friend Edwards the team had a supernova, a player threatening to be the best these shores had ever known. Less than six feet tall but huge, an all-rounder with thighs like power-station chimneys, he had skills unbefitting a man of such strength. 'He was so strong people could only see the power, but he had a most delicate touch,' said Tom Finney. Bobby Charlton later called him 'More than a great player – sometimes he seemed like a bright light in the sky.'

Strides were made in Europe and, after Christmas, the FA Cup too, but United's league form while good lacked consistency. In December 1957 Busby signed his first player since May 1953. Harry Gregg was brought in to replace the struggling Ray Wood in goal, and it seemed the team was complete. Wood would later be sold to Bill Shankly at Huddersfield.

On 1 February United went to Arsenal and won 5–4 in a game so thrilling that the 63,000-plus fans attending refused to leave. 'Everyone was cheering,' recalled Dennis Evans, the Arsenal fullback. 'Not because of Arsenal. Not because of United. Just cheering because of the game itself. No one left until five minutes after the game. They just stood cheering.' Afterwards, Busby, those cheers ringing in his ears, took his team to Red Star Belgrade for the second leg of their European Cup quarter-final.

Earlier that season Busby had visited Everton to see them play Burnley. There he bumped into Shankly, and they stood chatting. The Burnley chairman, Bob Lord, strolled over. 'Hello, Matt, would you care to come into the boardroom for a drink?' His eyes stuck on Busby, suggesting it wasn't an offer that stretched to Shankly.

'No, thanks,' replied Busby. 'I'm having a chat here with my old friend Bill.'

Driving home, Shankly turned to his club secretary Eddie Brennan with a smile. 'Matt, what a wonderful man,' he said. 'He wouldn't go off with Bob Lord because I had not been invited. What a man he is.' A few months later, on that cold February day, dropping Brennan off in Huddersfield, Busby was once again in their thoughts. 'You say a prayer for them.'

Manchester United had won through to another European Cup semi-final and this time would face AC Milan. As they left Belgrade, thoughts must have twinkled in their minds of a possible final against the holders, Real Madrid. The party – which included the team, management minus Jimmy Murphy, who had been looking after the Welsh national team, club officials, the travel agent and his wife and members of the press – landed in Munich in adverse weather, but despite the heavy snow the plane was prepared for the onward flight to Manchester.

Twice the plane attempted to make it up from the slush covering the runway. Twice the plane taxied back due to a problem in the left engine. An overnight stay in Germany was discussed but rejected. The players in their card schools, the other players choosing to sleep, the press men looking forward to a meal, all were in their seats as the plane started its third attempt.

'Suddenly, there was a thunderous roar as the engines burst into life,' wrote Frank Taylor of the *Daily Mirror*. 'I listened intently. Not a cough, or a splutter, as the motors throbbed louder and louder, until they had reached their familiar high pitched whine ... then we started to move. Slowly at first, then faster and faster.' There was, though, not enough power to lift the plane from the ground. Slush rising from its speeding wheels, the plane was running out of runway,

Captain Ken Rayment cried out, 'Christ ... we're not going to make it.' He braked desperately, trying to avoid the perimeter fence and a small house nearby.

'We're all going to get killed here,' said Johnny Berry.

Busby threw out his arms.

Johnny Berry lay in his hospital bed, the same hospital as his manager. Why hadn't his great pal Tommy Taylor been to see him? Jimmy Murphy, who had flown over, was sobbing in the hospital corridor. Two weeks later news of Duncan Edwards' death was met with national grief. Geoff Bent was dead, so was club captain Roger Byrne, Eddie Coleman, Mark Jones, David Pegg, Liam Whelan and Tommy Taylor. Walter Crickmer, the club secretary was also gone. Journalists had died, including Frank Swift. Berry would never play again because of his injuries. Neither would Jackie Blanchflower. Bert Whalley, so instrumental in getting Edwards to Old Trafford, and Tom Curry, the trainer who had looked after a young Bill Shankly at Carlisle, had both died. Busby lay in his bed, and with every piece of tragic news tears flowed, and with thoughts of facing the widows and parents of those gone guilt raged.

'I will never go back into football,' he told Jean.

Weeks passed, and that sentiment grew and then Jean had her say. 'I don't think you are being fair to the people who have lost their loved ones,' she said. 'And I am sure those who have gone too would have wanted you to carry on.'

Busby listened and took in his wife's words.

He would later write, 'This plea went straight to the crux of the matter. Jean's wisdom, common sense and logic won. And had I not some more foster sons to look after? I must not let them down. Or their parents. From that moment I wanted to live.'

Chapter 9:

Cleaning the Toilet

Arthur Hopcraft, that splendid observer of football, once wrote, 'The Kop is not the members' enclosure at Ascot, and nor does it regret it.' For years a sea of cloth caps – not top hats – had gathered behind the goal on Anfield's Walton Breck Road. As a gesture of thanks to an increasingly influential set of supporters, the terrace had been built using bricks and cinders in the title-winning year of 1906 and named after the Boer War battle of Spion Kop, in which local Lancashire regiments had suffered heavy losses.

People had always come. They'd come to watch Alex Raisbeck, their Edwardian centre half with the blond hair and 'tache; they'd come to cheer Elisha Scott, their Ulster goalkeeper with the bandaged knees and shovel-like hands; they'd come to see Matt Busby, their fine wing half with a flair for leadership; they'd come to see Albert Stubbins, the red-haired goal-scorer who helped them win the first post-war championship.

Bill Shankly had come as manager of Huddersfield. Sitting in the dugout he turned to his right and saw the people. While some might have seen only a mass, Shankly saw individuals, young and old, coming together as one. He had seen first hand that it was people, real people, who drive progress. That's what he saw at Anfield when he looked to his right at the Kop.

What those on the Kop were watching was less impressive.

Liverpool's post-war title win and FA Cup final appearance in 1950 had been only preludes to disappointment. The 1950s at Anfield were grey days. The board were apathetic and resigned to mediocrity, showing little concern and even less ambition to halt the decay that they presided over. The supporters came, but their grievances were many. 'I think the way the club has been run in the past couple of years has been scandalous,' stated an angry fan's letter to the *Daily Post* in early 1954.

While their old captain Matt Busby had a plan, winning the FA Cup with Manchester United in 1948 and then the title in 1952, Liverpool's faithful could only salivate enviously at the flowing football being feasted on down the East Lancs Road at Manchester United. At Liverpool, replacing Busby's old mentor George Kay, Don Welsh was at the helm, but the nagging feeling persisted that he was an unassuming manager willing to nod and smile as his directors pulled the strings.

As winter turned to spring in 1954, Welsh's Liverpool were facing relegation. With Everton already in the Second Division, Leslie Edwards in the *Daily Post* tried to put the region's foot-balling woes into context. 'In the hydrogen-bomb age,' he stated, 'should we worry about the prospects of no First Division club in the city next year?' Edwards' readers of the blue persuasion needn't have worried though, because while Liverpool went down, Everton came up, while at Anfield this was the start of a cata-clysmic winter. A record 9–0 defeat at Birmingham darkened the skies, an FA Cup humiliation at non-league Worcester poisoned the waters.

By the autumn of 1959, five seasons had passed in the Second Division. Promotion was flirted with, but to many of their suffering fans the team and club were merely going through the motions. Crowds dropped, and those who continued to make their way to the ground might have argued that they were only coming to see Billy Liddell, the player recommended by Matt Busby before the war. Liverpool's star winger in the championship-winning side of 1947, he was now the only bright spot in a dreary vista of decline.

Liddell's skills and goals kept some sort of spring in the steps of those making their way to Anfield, but the overriding cause of the dismay among Liverpool's support was the club's board and its unwillingness to embrace the changes inching their way into the game. Managers such as Busby were in full control, even donning tracksuits and coaching players. Youth was being developed, futures planned. European competition was developing. The World Cup was now fully recognized. At Liverpool a new manager was in place, but popular ex-player Phil Taylor was described by the board as a 'liaison man' in the club dressing room. The board and their set ways were still in control. The world may have been enthralled by the space race, but Liverpool Football Club was still sitting on a horse and cart.

Leslie Edwards in the *Daily Post* reported on the lack of forward thinking and noted change had to start in the manager's office. 'If a manager contracts to manage,' he wrote, 'he should be given absolute authority over the team, leaving directors to direct.' Not many at the club listened, but one director, Tom Williams, was at last seeing the bigger picture. He had talked the board into buying land in the West Derby area of the city, and a training ground, although basic, was built. Profits were up, and in the summer of 1959 the club tried to sign Brian Clough from Middlesbrough for £40,000. The offer was turned down. The board pointed to renewed ambition, the board's critics called it all talk and no action.

The 1959/60 season started with the usual inconsistency. Billy

Liddell's now ageing limbs couldn't even brighten the mood, and in November a 4–2 loss at Lincoln jolted even this most static of football clubs. Phil Taylor would stand down, telling the press that the strain of trying to win promotion had taken its toll and that he had 'never tried to cause anyone any trouble'. Tom Williams was about to approach a manager happy to do just that.

Matt Busby had taken a phone call from Liverpool's directors asking his advice on who might be the manager the club so desperately needed. Bill Shankly's name came up and Busby enthusiastically sang his friend's praises. On putting the phone down, Busby turned to Jimmy Murphy. 'You know what, Jimmy,' he said. 'I think I might regret that phone call one day.'

A year earlier Liverpool had travelled to Huddersfield and lost 5–0. Bill Shankly had remarked upon the Liverpool directors leaving their Leeds Road seats in single file, 'their shoulders slumped, like a funeral procession', but now, led once more by Williams, they would return to Yorkshire with a question for Shankly they hoped would turn a funeral into a wedding day.

'How would you like to manage the best club in the country?' asked Williams.

'Why, is Matt Busby packing up?' came the reply.

Shankly eventually got serious, but Williams left only with the promise that he would think about it. The Liverpool board were on tenterhooks, but for Shankly the idea of being the boss there was growing into something more than interesting. He had been to Anfield as a visiting manager but had also enjoyed boxing bouts at the stadium. Local flyweight Peter Kane had beaten Jimmy Warnock there before the war, and the passion of the people had caught Shankly's imagination. 'Liverpool was a city like the Scottish cities and the people were similar to Scottish people,' he'd say, and while in terms of current league positions a move from Huddersfield was a step down, the potential and the chance to manage in front of that crowd was too much. The Huddersfield board hoped their outgoing man might work a month's notice, but Shankly's head and heart were already over the Pennines and he would take the job with immediate effect.

The task was far greater than he had imagined. The ground itself was decaying at a faster rate than the team. Later Shankly would call it 'the biggest toilet in Liverpool'. There was no water to irrigate the pitch; dead light bulbs hung unchanged; the training ground had potential in terms of space but was as basic as the training on offer. The ground itself was too small for a club of Liverpool's stature, but the truth was, that stature was mere potential, and it was going to take hard work and sheer personality to bring the greatness back. Fortunately for those who cared, Shankly had an abundance of both.

Shankly went into Anfield to meet Williams and club secretary Jimmy McInnes. Dressed with his typical sharpness in a two-piece suit and polished shoes, he strolled in like he had been there for years. 'Shall we show you around the place?' asked Williams.

'That's hardly necessary,' came the reply. 'I was here on Saturday watching the reserves.' The tone was set.

In his first press conference Shankly spoke of his pride, of the Liverpool support being among the best in the game and deserving success. 'I make no promises,' he said, 'except that from the moment I take over I shall put everything I have into the job I so willingly undertake.' He sounded almost regal, and although only the new manager of a mid-table Second Division club, Shankly made some onlookers feel that something significant had happened.

The *Liverpool Echo* described him as 'an expert and an enthusiast rolled into one' and 'a one man combination that will not rest until Liverpool are in the First Division'. Shankly was indeed both expert and enthusiast, and yes, he was one man, but he knew about football management and how those by his side were key to a manager's success. Leaving Huddersfield he had wondered about who he would ask to come with him. Bill Watson, the groundsman and his footballing ear at Workington perhaps? He'd wait. See who was already there. Little did he know that in the dark and apathetic corridors of Anfield lay a treasure chest of knowledge waiting to be opened.

There was reserve-team trainer Joe Fagan, a Scouser who had played at Manchester City. 'You must have been a good player, Joe,' said Shankly when they met again, 'because I tried to sign you.' There was Reuben Bennett, a head coach with a fierce devotion to fitness and a man Shankly knew well. Bennett had played in goal for his hometown club Aberdeen and was a good friend of Shankly's brother Bob. Also quietly doing his job at Anfield was Bob Paisley. A similar player to Shankly in as much as he gave everything, the Durham-born former miner was from similar stock but very much his new manager's opposite. Unassuming and basic, the first-team trainer was a warm pair of slippers to Shankly's polished steel-capped brogues. But, and Shankly immediately got this, Paisley was the sort of football man he had always sought, and enjoyed being around.

'You fellows have been here, some of you, a long time,' Shankly said. 'I have my own training system and I will work in cooperation with you. I will lay down the plans and gradually we will be on the same wavelength. I want one thing – loyalty. I don't want anybody to carry stories about anyone else; the man with the story will get the sack. I don't care if he has been here fifty years.'

Shankly had come to a club lower down the table than

Huddersfield, but for all the hyperbole there was no ego – if there had been he'd have changed the staff – and had seen the potential among the football men there, the potential not only to help the players but him too. At Celtic Jock Stein would mine the resources on offer from Sean Fallon's vast knowledge, while in Manchester Matt Busby recognized that in Jimmy Murphy he had a man who quite simply was a better coach than him. He would often ask Murphy for advice, even about who should start that Saturday. Should that selection turn out badly, he never blamed his assistant. Stein and Shankly didn't either. They were the managers and knew where the buck stopped, but they would seek advice. All three men valued the reliability of their workmates. Football is no coal mine, but the ability to ask for and take help from colleagues is as important there as it is in the darkness of a pit.

Paisley had been warned by a friend at Huddersfield that his new boss was difficult to work with, that the strain he put on those around him was too much. Such fears were quickly discarded, and for all their superficial differences, the two men quickly hit it off. Both loved boxing and would spend hours discussing the greats, Shankly never tiring of telling his new assistant that he had seen both Joe Louis and Sugar Ray Robinson in the flesh, Paisley always wondering if his boasts were true. Both men would be found at the ground late at night painting toilets and dressing rooms. Sure, their presence there was often planned to coincide with that of the directors, but things were getting done and the club was becoming a brighter place. Melwood, the training ground, had been levelled and cultivated, and a smart new pavilion built with good changing facilities and even a sauna.

Shankly had settled into the city quickly. He liked its spark, the effervescence of its people. He felt at home but was still getting his bearings. After only a month, Shankly pulled up in his car and asked a young boy, 'Look, son, can you tell me where Anfield is, the Liverpool football ground.'

'Oh, it's Bill Shankly,' came the reply. In those pre-television days and bearing in mind the fact Shankly had only been there only a matter of weeks, this was proof that he was living in a place which shared his own fanaticism.

One Sunday at Huddersfield, Shankly had been with his secretary Eddie Brennan. There was a knock at the door and standing there was a ten-year-old, a ball under his arm and excitement in his eyes. 'Are you coming out to play, Bill?' he had asked.

'Oh hello, son,' said Shankly. 'Aye, I'll be out in a wee while. Go, get the goalposts set up.' Shankly closed the door and turned to Brennan. 'He's a dirty wee bugger, that lad.'

Even a kickabout with a schoolboy would prick Shankly's competitive edge, and the people of Liverpool would become used to the sight of him watching park football, those most basic of matches that for the rest of his life he found almost impossible to drive past or ignore.

Shankly's passion for the game of football lit the flames beneath the football club at which he now worked, and the potential that he saw was about to be realized. He had looked at the club as a whole, its very fabric, and seen what was possible, but he was under no illusions as to the work required, especially when it came to the playing staff. The squad was too big, and Shankly was quickly thinking about trimming it and constructing a new spine. 'A goalkeeper and a centre half who between them could stop goals, and somebody up front to create and score them,' he said.

There was talent. Winger Alan A'Court had travelled to Sweden with England for the 1958 World Cup, and inside forward Jimmy Melia was a Liverpudlian with a receding hairline but growing fanbase. Recently signed was a blond twenty-year-old striker spotted scoring goals in the Mid-Cheshire League for Stockton Heath, and the minute Shankly laid eyes on Roger Hunt, he declared, 'Christ, this one can play!'

Another player able to make fans and managers call on their god was Billy Liddell, although Shankly's first season at Anfield was Liddell's last. It was clear the great man was ageing and slowing up, so thoughts turned to what he might do next. Joining Shankly's backroom staff was mooted as was a place on the club's board. Liddell was keen on the latter but for reasons never adequately explained was never elected, and as for moving into coaching, the man who had originally brought him to Liverpool believed that was not for him. 'I've made my bed in management,' Matt Busby would say to Liddell. 'I'm lying on it and enjoying it. But you'd never make a manager.'

Phyllis Liddell told her husband's biographer John Keith that Busby felt he was too nice for life in the dugout, and she agreed, but nevertheless it was clear that Liddell shared Busby's eye for a young player. 'I was asked several times who would follow me in the Liverpool team,' Liddell said. 'I knew the club were scouting people around the country looking to sign someone, but I told people, "They've got someone at Anfield already, a youngster named Ian Callaghan."' Shankly shared Liddell's confidence in the local wing half, although he would take one look at him and convert him to a dynamic outside right, giving him the first of his record-setting 857 appearances in April 1960. Shankly would also promote from within when he later brought goalkeeper Tommy Lawrence from the reserves to the first team, but for now time was of the essence, and Shankly cast his eye for a player further afield and set it on two men north of the border who were very much on his radar.

Liverpool came third in Shankly's first season, missing out on promotion by a disappointing eight points. That 1959/60 campaign was also the first encounter between Shankly and Matt Busby as managers of Liverpool and Manchester United. In front of 57,000 fans and thanks to two goals from Bobby Charlton, United left Anfield with an FA Cup fourth-round victory, with Shankly keen to make the changes he needed in order to make his old pal's next visit a little less comfortable.

Shankly had enquired about signing Leeds United's big centre half Jack Charlton, but his new board wouldn't offer more than the £18,000 the Elland Road club had already turned down, and Shankly feared the stinginess of the Huddersfield board had followed him to Merseyside. He had demanded that everything Liverpool buy be the best, be it training footballs or a watering hose at Melwood, but the new manager's biggest phobia – a director with a rusty lock on his chequebook – looked like hampering the acquisition of what he desired most, quality footballers. His compatriots Ian St John and Ron Yeats of Motherwell and Dundee United respectively had been targets for Shankly at Huddersfield, only for him to be told to look in the transfer market, not expensive boutiques. Now he had to convince the money men at Liverpool to produce some cash.

Gordon Milne was bought for a record £16,000 from Preston in 1960, but St John and Yeats remained out of reach. The board liked the idea of the club promoting from within, and Shankly – knowing that the youth system had also been neglected and he needed new players *now* – grew more and more frustrated. When his team selection was tampered with, Shankly had had enough, and not for the last time it was Matt Busby he went to for advice.

'I'm going to resign,' he said.

'Do you have another job to go to?' asked Busby, taken aback at the suddenness of his friend's decision.

'No'.

'Bill, things are bound to break for you,' said Busby with calm authority, no doubt thinking about the conversation he himself had had when so close to leaving Manchester City years before.

The break Busby had talked of came in the shape of Eric Sawyer, a man high up in the Littlewoods organization and new to the Liverpool board. Sawyer had ambition, a trait seemingly hitherto absent from the boardroom, and immediately hit it off with the manager. In 1960/1 Liverpool once again finished a frustrating third in the Second Division. Over coffee the two men would discuss what was wrong and how they might improve things. 'Bill,' Sawyer said one evening, 'if you can get the players, I'll get the money.' A symphony to Shankly's ears.

Years earlier, Shankly had attended a match between the Scotland under-23s and an army team. Yeats was doing his national service, and St John, then working in the steel industry, was playing for the youngsters. 'It turned out to be a right struggle,' recalled St John. 'We had a little bit of a scrap. He always was bigger than anyone else and really fancied himself. He had long fingernails and scratched me down my chest.' Despite the difference in size and talons, St John gave as good as he got, and Shankly left vowing to follow both careers.

In the summer of 1961, Yeats, who had formerly worked in an abbatoir, stood next to Shankly resplendent in a suit which made him look more like James Bond than a Second Division defender. Shankly was at last armed with finance. 'Jesus, you must be seven feet tall, son?' said Shankly.

'Er, no, I'm six foot three,' came the rather sheepish reply.

'Well, that's near enough seven foot for me,' said the rapturous Shankly.

A few days later at Anfield, having agreed a £22,000 deal with Dundee United, Shankly gleefully introduced his new man to the press. 'Take a walk around my new centre half, gentlemen,' he said, smiling as some of them obeyed. 'He's a colossus.' Shankly was beginning to sparkle.

So was his team. Yeats had joined St John, who had been enticed to Anfield two months earlier. St John had been doing brilliantly at Motherwell, winning Scotland caps and interesting many clubs, and Newcastle's manager Charlie Mitten was particularly keen, but on seeing a newspaper headline that read ST JOHN WANTS TO GO, Shankly was on the phone to Eric Sawyer ('He's not just a good centre forward – he's the only centre forward in the game') and in the car to Lanarkshire.

'I'll be honest, I knew absolutely nothing about them,' admitted St John. 'I didn't know who played for them, I didn't even know what league they were in. The club was simply sold to me by this amazing man called Bill Shankly. He told me he was in charge of a club that had the best fans and would have the best team. No one else could have made me make that move. Shanks was so persuasive, so dynamic.'

Clever too. Shankly had Reuben Bennett, St John's old trainer at Motherwell, waiting for the car in Liverpool, a familiar face for a perhaps otherwise overawed young footballer. The deal was done, and while some of the old guard in the boardroom might have gulped at the £37,500 spent, Shankly could start planning with the handbrake off.

St John arrived at Melwood like a kid in a sweet shop. Shankly had noticed in his first week at Liverpool that Jimmy Melia had grinned like a schoolboy at the sight of so many footballs. St John came from the old school. His manager at Fir Park had been Bobby Ancell, a suit-and-tie man. There the players ran and ran some more. Ask for a football and the answer was, 'Why? If you don't use one today, you'll be hungry for it on Saturday.' St John had been lucky enough to see Real Madrid training in Glasgow prior to the 1960 European Cup final at Hampden Park, and had been awestruck. With five other young footballers St John sneaked in and sat mouth agape at Di Stéfano, Puskás, Kopa and the rest. They all moved (with the ball) around the pitch like white swans on a pond, graceful in everything they did, but under the surface furiously fit and willing to work.

Melwood then was heaven to St John and his new teammates. The ball was the king, but don't be fooled, there was work to be done. Hard work. Shankly had designed a 'Sweatbox'– four wooden walls, thirty yards apart. Inside, a player would play the ball against a wall, control it, play it against another wall, and so on, until his legs turned weak and his heart raced. It was all about ball work coupled with stamina. Pass, move, pass, move. From the first whistle to the last.

The work ethic extended to the staff. Shankly wanted every opponent scouted, reports made. It might be Shankly himself pounding the roads of England, but mainly it was Reuben Bennett. Bennett's dossiers became an invaluable part of a key season. Other campaigns would bring more glory, but with his players in place Shankly lit the fuse for take-off.

The football began to capture imaginations. Crowd numbers began to rise. Some 48,000 people flocked to the first home game of the 1961–2 campaign, and while that number wasn't always reached, the team had pulses pounding. Yeats, Moran, Milne, Callaghan, Hunt, Melia and St John: all were roared on as goals and flowing football worthy of the manager's own firecracker personality were lapped up.

The Second Division was won at home to Southampton in late April, and the next Saturday 42,000 turned up for another win, this time against Stoke. St John's name rang around the old ground to the tune of 'Let's Go' by the Routers. The striker was carried across the pitch. 'With me held above them,' recalled St John. 'I think [the fans] did the twist, the rock 'n' roll and any other dance you can think of, and provided their own music into the bargain.'

Four mop-headed local singers were yet to enthral the nation but they had turned local heads, and the youngsters now milling among old cloth caps upon the Kop were stepping out of the shadows of austerity. Liverpool Football Club had endured the darkest of decades – and while it would be a few months until the Beatles released 'Love Me Do', the club were back in the charts.

In the boardroom the players and staff were all given smart-looking cigarette boxes by way of thanks. Shankly watched as they were handed out and scoffed at the trinkets. Bigger presents awaited, he thought to himself. Like the First Division title. A telegram arrived. It was from his friend Matt Busby: A CLUB LIKE LIVERPOOL DESERVE TO BE PLAYING IN THE HIGHEST CLASS. Shankly agreed, but after thirteen years working the lower leagues – 'the outposts of the nation' as he called them – he was in no doubt he deserved that too.

'While I was there, I knew that one day I would get somewhere else,' he later said of his early managerial years. 'While I was there, Matt might have been at Manchester United, Stan Cullis at

Wolverhampton Wanderers, Billy Nicholson at somewhere else, but I didn't think they were better than me because they were with big clubs, oh no.'

Now, with his wonderful team, it was time to prove it . . .

Chapter 10:

Playing Cowboys with John Wayne

'I don't have a magic wand.'

It is 1960, and for the first time as a manager, Jock Stein sits in front of a dozen or so journalists and gives them a throwaway line that they dutifully scribble into their notepads. Five years later, and having witnessed Stein's magic at both Dunfermline and then Hibernian, the reporters at that press conference might have been excused for wishing they had rifled through the big man's famous white overcoat, wondering where he kept his wand.

Armed with hindsight, the Celtic hierarchy would continue to say that Stein's departure from the club's reserve post was merely to allow him to gain experience and that a turn at their helm was always awaiting his return. Stein would smirk at that suggestion, and had left Celtic knowing he had everything to do if he was to prove himself more than just a good coach. He did that and more. At Dunfermline he found a club looking at relegation. With only six games remaining of a struggling season, and just two points off bottom spot, Stein not only turned things around but in little over a year had his players, staff, board and supporters dusting off their passports. Then there was Hibernian, a club looking back at better times when their Famous Five had brought sunshine to Leith. In his short time there Stein didn't rekindle those post-war glories, but he lifted the gloom, won a trophy and turned the club towards the light.

On Stein's arrival, Dunfermline's future looked grim. At that same press conference he called their position 'precarious'. Those travelling to watch his first game against Celtic (of all teams) might have allowed themselves a wry smile at their manager's clear fondness for understatement, but the players in the dressing room were immediately made aware that they were now being led by a man unwilling to do mediocrity.

'He was bouncing about the place,' recalled the club captain George Miller. 'The enthusiasm was unbelievable. There was nothing much he said except how we had to keep in about them. It wasn't a time for too many tactics, but he told us about some of the Celtic players and what to watch for. But that wasn't the most important thing. The previous manager, Andy Dickson, was a perfect gentleman, but he was a mild man. This new figure among us was going about as if our lives depended on it.'

This was the first proper glimpse of Jock Stein, the great motivator, and his players took to the pitch like men possessed, scoring after just ten seconds. Ten seconds! The old line from Stein's pal – that should he fall in the Clyde he would come up with a trout in his mouth – would need to be revised because surely the catch would be that of a prize marlin. Celtic were beaten 3–2, a win that set the tone for the campaign (and a managerial career). The Pars were staying up. Stein was able to lift good players towards greatness, and he had his beady eye on the club's youth treasures, with Willie Callaghan and Jackie Sinclair both soon promoted to his first team. He also knew the British game and the men playing in it. Tommy McDonald and Willie Cunningham were sought out from Leicester – both experienced, both huge assets.

There were early indications of the wiliness of Stein's character. During the crucial last games of those first few weeks, Dunfermline's fixture with Kilmarnock had to be rearranged due to the latter's place in the cup semi-final. Stein met his counterpart at Kilmarnock to agree the details, opting for the Monday after the semi. 'Kilmarnock would either be high after winning, low after defeat or worried about a replay,' Stein later said. 'Anyway, we would play them on a Monday night while their concentration was low. I wasn't very popular with the Dunfermline officials for going for a Monday-night game, but my decision turned out to be right as we defeated the cup finalists 1–0.'

Archie Macpherson was clear that these were the initial steps of a manager destined for so much more than the mundane. 'That sort of thinking was far removed from the mere drilling of players on a training ground,' he wrote. 'This was the first basic, untutored and instinctive foray into the managerial mind games for which he would become famous – or, as his opponents might say, infamous.'

With Stein's blueprint for life as a manager drawn up in his mind, it was time to get on with things. In 1960/1 the heights of mid-table were a welcome respite after the previous season's woes, but in the cup Stein proved a match for anyone and everyone. The first three rounds that season took Dunfermline on the road. Berwick Rangers were beaten 4–1, and then Stranraer 3–1. The following round was at Aberdeen, and Pars fans fretted over BBC's *Grandstand* teleprinter as the final scores rolled in. 'Aberdeen 3 . . .' their hearts sank '. . . Dunfermline 6'. The dream was still alive.

Alloa were taken apart 4–0 in the quarter-final and St Mirren (after a replay) beaten 1–0 in the semi-final. Within a year Stein had taken the club to a final, where they would face – inevitably given his life's tendency for the dramatic – Celtic. Stein got to work straight away. The Seamill Hydro Hotel on the Ayrshire coast was quickly booked for the final, the significance of this being that it was the place Celtic always stayed. 'A bit like someone prebooking the Royal Box for the night of the Royal Command performance,' mused Macpherson. It was a brilliant move, giving his players the grandeur he wanted them to express come the first whistle.

Exactly 113,328 packed into Hampden for the final. Stein had been worried about how a crowd of Glaswegian heavies might affect his players, but he built them up and up until they felt able to cope with their foe – player or fan. For much of the final Celtic pressed their opponents back only to meet resilience in the form of a steadfast back line and an inspired goalkeeper called Eddie Connachan. The twenty-six-year-old miner's (he only gave up working the pits shortly after the final) heroics in keeping the score at 0–0 were nothing compared to what he achieved in the replay. Rain blanketed the old ground, meaning this time only 87,866 turned up, and with still no score after the hour mark, Dunfermline were frustrating their illustrious enemy. Injuries had limited Stein's options but he showed the sort of tactical acumen that would win many a battle, and with John Sweeney policing Celtic's Willie Fernie from left half, his team began to grow in stature. So much so that in the sixty-seventh minute Davie Thomson silenced vast swathes of the stadium with a fine goal.

Cue Celtic pressure that tempted the press box to use words such as siege and blitz. Connachan flung himself around his penalty area as if living his last day, making save after save, thwarting attack after attack. Celtic, weighed down by the rain and exhausted by their efforts, then began to run out of steam, so much so that in the eighty-eighth minute Charlie Dickson took advantage of a goalkeeping error and tapped the ball into a welcoming net for Dunfermline's second goal. The whistle followed shortly afterwards and Dunfermline had their first Scottish Cup. As did Stein.

In his white overcoat he stalked the pitch, a footballing Gandalf, embracing his team. Players he had lofted to unheralded heights. Connachan was given the tightest of squeezes as, miner to miner, they celebrated in the pouring rain. Macpherson noted that this was the moment, on the wet pitch of Hampden in front of all those admiring eyes, when Stein became someone of note. He was 'now both local hero, and almost overnight, a national figure of substance'.

At Dunfermline both Stein and his wife were now content. Jean got on very well with the directors and their wives and started to travel to away games. Ray, their daughter, had become a Dunfermline fan, and had sneaked into Hampden against his wishes. She, like the town her father had illuminated, was now thrilled at the prospect of European football. To think Dunfermline could boast of such a thing before even Celtic or Liverpool is testimony to the sheer pace of Stein's managerial rise. That the club should play six seasons of European football during the 1960s was testimony to his achievement. Stein twice took Dunfermline from Scotland's provinces to far-flung corners of Spain and, perhaps most excitingly for him, to Hungary, the home of those Magic Magyars.

The summer of 1961 cemented Stein's place at East End Park, when he rejected a lucrative offer to move to Newcastle. 'It's not the money that interests me,' he said. 'It is the advancement of football.' And advance they did. Wins in Ireland and Macedonia took Dunfermline to Hungary, where they would lose a quarter-final to Ujpesti Dozsa. Stein wasn't in Hungary on a pilgrimage – however fond he was of the side he had seen beat England in 1953 – and the manner of his side's 4–3 defeat spoke volumes of his determination to play the European game on the front foot. The second leg was lost 1–0 and so for now the adventure was over.

Dunfermline finished the 1961/2 campaign in fourth place, commendable but not high enough to warrant European competition. When a Greek club pulled out, though, it was they who were invited for another go, this time in the Inter-Cities Fairs Cup. The first city they would visit was Liverpool and the challenge of Everton, dubbed the Millionaires for their transfer budget and on their way to a league championship. Stein may have turned down the chance to manage in England, but now he had the opportunity to show them what they were missing down there. Everton, managed by Harry Catterick, were an emerging force. Also nicknamed the Bank of England side, due to the £250,000 given to the manager by Littlewoods owner and club chairman John Moores to spend on players, their internationals such as Scotsman Alex Young and Billy Bingham from Northern Ireland would test any team's mettle, and Stein's chest must have swelled at the thought of beating a side so far above his own in terms of resources.

The first leg was at Goodison Park, and once again was a game that showcased plenty of Stein's managerial attributes. Tactically, his opponents were confused by his decision to play Willie Cunningham in a deeper defensive role, on the lookout for breaks forward. This role would eventually be known as a sweeper, but going into the match the player himself had his doubts, Cunningham making it clear to Stein he wasn't comfortable, Stein making it clearer that he would be. The manager was right. Cunningham had a brilliant game, frustrating Evertonian ambitions again and again.

Then there was Stein's sheer bloody toughness. This was a bad-tempered night on Merseyside. The only goal of the game was a contentious one with the visitors adamant that the ball hadn't crossed the line. The mood soured, the crowd turned hostile, and Stein, already feeling patronized by Everton's officials, was having none of it. 'I think they thought that this was the arrival of the "country hicks",' Stein later noted. 'At half-time I made sure the players would let the Everton stars know they would be sorted out at Dunfermline.' At the final whistle, Stein and his players were showered with orange peels and rolled-up newspapers as they left the pitch.

Some 25,000 were ringside for the return fixture. Everton were top of the English First Division and massive favourites, but Stein's team outmanoeuvred them, playing around and through them, winning 2–0 and advancing to the second round. The English champions-elect had been very much 'sorted out'. And so to Valencia.

Valencia too were a fine side. Holders of the trophy and victors, over the years, over Manchester United, Celtic and Rangers, they would give Stein a clear indication of the sophistication of the European game by beating his team 4–0. But this was December 1962. Britain was about to be enveloped by a freeze that would last until March. As Stein's plane rose over the orange trees on Spain's eastern coast, he thought he might just be able to use a Fife winter to his advantage. Plenty of Pars fans doubted it. Under 15,000 braved the cold for the second leg, but those hearty souls were rewarded with one of the club's and Scottish football's greatest nights. Stein saw the match as a battle against brilliant opposition, the elements and the odds, and from kick-off on an icy pitch, his team set about the Spaniards like Arctic orcas hunting baby seals.

Stein had picked sixteen-year-old winger Alex Edwards, who tormented his fullback, crossing for Harry Melrose to score in the eleventh minute. Five minutes later another teenager, Jackie Sinclair, scored, and when the same player got another a minute later, a roar rose from the old ground that had drivers over the Forth Bridge fearing for their safety.

Valencia nicked a goal back, but with no away-goal rule, two more from Dunfermline in an extraordinary first half meant the aggregate scores were level at half-time. Stein addressed his team now fully aware that all out attack, especially in Europe, could bring rewards. The second half saw both teams score for a result on the night of 6–2, so the tie was drawn 6–6. Remarkably the fans left East End Park bemoaning the fact they hadn't won out-right, such was their dominance, but that win was the blueprint for their manager's approach in the future. Valencia won the play-off in Lisbon by a single goal, but Stein came home with a swagger and the knowledge that he could take on the best. The big man had just got bigger.

He had a way about him. 'We can't lose on Saturday,' he told the press about a forthcoming trip to dominating Rangers. His team drew 1–1. In America a young heavyweight called Cassius Clay was starting out on his professional fight journey and would soon be naming the rounds in which he finished his opponents. This though was Scotland, and the young manager of a provincial football club calmly stating his team wouldn't lose at Ibrox and then doing just that, well, that raised eyebrows.

Stein had become great pals with Bob Shankly, Bill's brother and also a club manager, who in 1961/2 won the title with a brilliant Dundee side, leading them to the European Cup semi-finals. Through Bob, Stein had become close to Bill Shankly, while meeting and becoming close to Matt Busby was a thrill for any young manager, especially one whose mining background was so intrinsically linked to the great man.

While there was no doubt that Stein was studying his profession keenly, even then other managers were taking notice of him too. In late 1963, Stein with his counterpart at Kilmarnock, Willie Waddell, went to Italy to study the Internazionale coach Helenio Herrera. Stein came home with new methods and tactics, but he had also caught the eye of this great of football thinking. Herrera couldn't help but notice this enthusiastic man, large in more ways than one, never stopping, be it during drills or away from the pitch discussing anything from the merits of the sweeper system to a horse race back at Kelso. Herrera nicknamed his visitor *la grande formica* – the big ant. Little did he know that in a matter of forty-two months this ant would be crawling all over him.

There was still much to learn, but what came naturally to Stein was the ability to be among his players, something he, Shankly and Busby had a natural talent for. Lives forged in communities where human relationships were key enabled all of them to relate to their players, and in management empathy was vital. At Liverpool Busby had noticed that George Kay was closer to his team than any man he had previously worked with. By immersing himself in the welfare of his players he had gained trust, respect and ultimately success.

Stein would do the same. 'He would never ask anyone to do a job unless he knew he could do it,' recalled George Miller. 'He got to know everything about us. He would know which players liked golf, which ones went to the dogs or the horses, and he would kid and joke about it. He would get to know all about your families and he would take a genuine interest in all of us. It was one big family for him.' But then he was gone.

Stein had always drilled into his players they were a match for anyone, whether at home, in England or Europe. In February 1964 it was announced that he would leave his post at East End Park at the end of the season, but then, a month later, it became known that he was taking the newly available post at Hibernian. Stein might have seen this job coming, but for the players he left behind the surprise lay in the destination. 'It was a blow,' admitted Miller. 'We thought that we were a bigger team than Hibs! That is the way he had educated us to think.'

But Stein had achieved all he could at Dunfermline, and this was a new challenge at a club bigger in stature (for all he had said to his players) and playing in Scotland's capital city, with more funds to support his ambitions. 'There comes a time when you know you can't get more out of yourself,' he told Willie Cunningham, and while his wife and family were shocked by the suddenness of his decision ('He could be impulsive that way,' his wife Jean later said), they understood his reasons.

Miller had a point though. Dunfermline had become bigger and better than Hibs, and so a move to Easter Road in Leith didn't suggest simple ambition; Stein saw something there that suited him, and while his tenure at Hibernian was short, it once again spoke of a man in total control of the profession he had chosen. 'He didn't walk in,' recalled Pat Stanton, a talented young footballer at the club, 'he blew in.' Stein was a force of nature. At Dunfermline it had taken him a mere ten seconds to make his mark; at Hibs he again set about whipping up a storm. It was exactly what the club needed. On Stein's arrival in March

1964 the club lay in twelfth position, indicative of the doldrums the club had been in since the heady days of the 1950s, but the players responded in no time to the new man's motivational skills and tactical nous. Stanton, a midfielder, was encouraged to play as a second centre half and results soon reflected the positivity Stein always brought with him.

Relegation was staved off, and that summer they won the Summer Cup, a tournament started during the war and continued for top-flight clubs. Among those to shine in the summer was another talented teenager, Peter Cormack, an elegant playmaker immediately pleased with the manager and the opportunities that were now coming his way. Cormack was friends with Alex Edwards, the teenage winger let loose by Stein at Dunfermline, and knew this was a manager only interested in talent.

'Jock had an aura about him,' Cormack recalled. 'All the young players called him Mr Stein, but the established pros got away with calling him Gaffer. I likened him to a strict but fair headmaster.' What the young Cormack was made aware of by older players who knew about such things was that Stein was also known as the father of the chapel, a title used in some trade unions for a shop steward. It was a term the manager would have enjoyed. 'At times he was one of the boys,' Cormack continued, 'but you always knew who was boss and woe betide anyone who got on the wrong side of him.'

Stein set about creating a team that relied on fluidity: wingers moving inside, fullbacks pushing up, centre forwards dropping deep, midfielders getting beyond them. 'He didn't want anyone holding fixed positions,' Cormack remembered. 'Both wingers were encouraged to roam across the forward line and switch wings during games. Inside forwards and wing backs would also interchange throughout the ninety minutes, and fullbacks were encouraged to venture forward, which was virtually unheard of in the early Sixties.'

Innovation was key, but so was a canny nod to theatre. In October 1964 Stein persuaded Real Madrid to come to Edinburgh for a prestigious friendly. It would cost the club £20,000, but suddenly all eyes were on East End Park. Di Stéfano, Puskás, Gento: they would all come, and Stein was going to make a fuss about it. 'To us all they're the greatest,' Stein wrote in his programme notes. He went on to rhapsodize about the 1960 European Cup final in Glasgow, but made it clear he and his side were up to the task. 'I know you will not be disappointed by such famous stars as Puskás and Gento, but we hope you will all be able to cheer a Hibs triumph. It would be an achievement, indeed, if we could inflict on Real their first defeat in Scotland.'

Which is what they did. A fine goal from young Cormack and an own goal from Zoco sealed a famous night. His players were thrilled about taking on footballers they had all idolized as doting teenagers, although Cormack, on being told by Stein he was playing, was simply advised to go out and enjoy himself. 'You're good enough,' Stein told him simply. Pat Stanton was in awe but played like a seasoned continental. 'Real Madrid,' he said. 'You had photographs of these chaps on your bedroom wall. It was like playing cowboys with John Wayne.'

The game shone a light on Stein's ability to take on the giants of the game, and Celtic were by now very much aware that their former reserve-team coach was becoming a national figure. Shortly after the Real Madrid victory, Wolves, having sacked Stan Cullis, approached Stein to be their new manager. Stein went to Bob Kelly, the chairman at Celtic, for advice. Wolves were a big club – huge in fact. They had struggled in recent years, but their history and the support the team enjoyed were appealing, but by telling Celtic of the offer, Stein was pushing them into making their own move. 'It was clearly an overture,' said Archie Macpherson.

An overture heard and acted upon. Stein met Kelly in a Glasgow hotel. The first offer was for Stein to be Sean Fallon's assistant. Rejected. Then a joint managership with Fallon was suggested. Kelly and the Celtic hierarchy were clearly concerned about Stein's Protestant background and were looking for a way to get him there without upsetting the more sectarian supporters of the club. Stein was having none of that either.

Stein had nothing but respect for Sean Fallon. He would want him involved, but there could be only one father of the chapel. Stein reiterated his interest in the Wolves job and waited. As Celtic reserve-team coach, then manager at Dunfermline, and now at Hibernian, his talents had been fine tuned. In matters of tactics his eye was sharp. As a motivator, players would walk through walls before building them up again for him. His trust in youth would benefit any club, and his canny eye for an opportunity had people as far away as Spain talking about his teams. This was a man and a manager ready. The question was, were Celtic?

Almost 300 miles south, and with still no offer from Parkhead, a Scottish footballer called Bertie Auld received a phone call. Auld had started his career at Celtic but for four years had been impressing in England with Birmingham. The call was from Dougie Hepburn, a friend of Stein and well known within football. 'How would you like to rejoin Celtic?'

Auld was keen, of course. 'Who's asked you to make the call, Doug?'

'Jock Stein.'

'But Jock is manager at Hibs.'

'Just you wait.'

Chapter 11:

The Swinging Sixties

1966 and all that, but not here, not now. This is Anfield, and in the cramped, dark confines of its old Main Stand there is anger. Celtic have been beaten in the European Cup Winners Cup semi-final amid controversy. Jock Stein is prowling the stadium's bowels, audibly disgusted that a late Bobby Lennox goal has been ruled offside, thus depriving his team of a final ... at Hampden Park. The Belgian referee and his linesman have been given a glimpse of his fury, and so has everyone else in those corridors, but the big man is about to be provoked even further.

Allan Herron, a popular journalist with Scotland's *Sunday Mail*, has removed himself from Stein's rage and takes time to talk to the – for now – more congenial Bill Shankly. But spies are listening.

'Congratulations, Bill,' the scribe says, shaking the hand of the Liverpool manager. 'Good luck in the final.'

Minutes later an onlooker is telling Stein of Herron's apparent treachery. Having said his goodbyes to Shankly, Herron is faced with a granite-faced Celtic manager, who ignores an offer of a handshake; instead his booming Burnbank tone fills the old stadium. 'You're nothing but a fucking traitor!' shouts Stein. 'What were you doing shaking his hand? Don't you ever come back to Celtic Park again!'

Herron would of course be welcomed back to Celtic, but Stein's disgust at the defeat to Liverpool spoke volumes not only of his desire to win trophy after trophy, but of a decade in which three kings were vying for the top throne. Three managers, three friends, three men from the same place, all wanting the same thing. Glory.

In the weeks after Munich, Liverpool, like other clubs, had offered Manchester United players to help them fulfil fixtures. Of the first game at Anfield after the crash, the *Daily Post* noted, 'Men's minds were still very much on the Munich tragedy, and the hush that descended on this so boisterous ground when the players lined up for the two minutes silence was almost uncanny.'

Jimmy Murphy had received news of the crash and had sat all night in an Old Trafford office with a bottle of whisky. He didn't sleep. The faces of the boys he had trained filled his thoughts. The plight of the men he worked with and for filled his prayers. He cried. The following day Murphy was in Munich, moving from bed to bed, holding the hands of the injured. A nurse approached him. In pidgin English she told him that, when conscious, Duncan Edwards was asking about his watch, fearing it had been stolen. The nurse had it and passed it to Murphy, who was soon sitting beside his young friend. The watch was broken beyond repair but he put it back on his wrist. Murphy looked at Edwards. This colossal young man, surely he would never, could never, stop ticking.

Edwards' eyes opened and he tried to talk. Murphy moved his face closer. 'It's you, Jimmy,' he said. Murphy nodded, squeezing his hand. 'What time's kick-off tomorrow?'

Minutes later, Murphy was alone in the hospital stairwell, more tears streaming down his face.

That Edwards should ask Murphy about a game of football he could never play tells of a man, a coach and the effect he had on so many young footballers. Later, with the hospital beds cleared, the funerals attended and convalescence begun, a football team still had to move forward, and in Murphy they had a man who knew the club and felt its grief profoundly.

In the hardest of circumstances Murphy would take the team to an FA Cup final, where they were defeated by Bolton. The European Cup semi-final was lost to AC Milan, but the way Murphy kept the club afloat – 'Superhuman,' as the surviving Bill Foulkes would later call it – and the way those charged with pulling on the red jerseys rallied, meant Manchester United won the love and support of the whole country.

The supporters who had long streamed to Old Trafford kept coming. Over 63,000 fans were there to see West Bromwich Albion visit for a First Division fixture just days after the same opposition were remarkably beaten in the quarter-finals of the cup, but all were silenced as a reassuringly familiar if under-standably jaded voice came over the PA system.

'Ladies and Gentlemen,' Busby said, 'I am speaking from my bed in the Isar hospital in Munich, where I have been for a month since the tragic accident.' Busby thanked the medical team at the hospital and, now deemed well enough to be told about football, talked of his delight that his team would play in a semi-final for a place at Wembley. It was a poignant moment but Busby was keen to get back. He had always known hard work; he was drawn to graft. So, while the clean Alpine air (Busby conva-lesced in Switzerland) must have soothed his damaged lungs, and thoughts of the more-than-capable Jimmy Murphy allayed his professional concerns, Busby was itching to get home.

So much so that he even took on more work. Busby had been appointed Scotland manager before the crash, and having missed the 1958 World Cup, took control of the national team for a couple of games in the autumn of that year. One of those matches saw him pit his wits against Murphy, who managed Wales in a game that saw Denis Law, Bill Shankly's young striker at Huddersfield, win his first international cap. Busby would soon conclude that the Scotland job was too much of a burden, but Law had long since caught his eye and would remain in his plans.

Planning was what it was all about. As the austere 1950s turned into the swinging Sixties, a young American senator was thinking of the White House. John F. Kennedy's slogan for his 1960 presidential campaign was 'Time for greatness', and two managers – at Old Trafford and Anfield – were inclined to agree.

At Liverpool Shankly set about adding tartan squares to his team's quilt, and while Ian St John and Ron Yeats – followed later by Willie Stevenson from Rangers – settled in, over in Manchester Busby made his own additions. The years after Munich had been hard in so many ways, and financially things got tight. Busby would later admit that his biggest regret, having lost Jackie Blanchflower because of the injuries he sustained in Munich, was not signing the much-admired Jack Charlton before Don Revie arrived at Leeds, but the £26,000 being asked for Bobby's big brother was far too much. The manager would instead have to use his tactical nous and convert Bill Foulkes to centre half, but how he would have loved to have had them both.

By the early 1960s funds had improved at Old Trafford but the team remained poor. Eyes had turned to London and Tottenham's double winners. In 1961 David Herd was bought for an impressive £40,000, but it was the eventual capture of Denis Law a year later that hinted at the ambitions Busby harboured for his new team. Law had expected to join Shankly at Liverpool, but the money quoted for his services made Anfield toes curl, and the £115,000 that United would eventually spend on the striker was too much for even Shankly to consider.

Law was no stranger to Manchester, having joined City from Huddersfield in 1960, but it was in 1958 that he had made his first visit to Old Trafford. Law would call it a pilgrimage. Less than two weeks after the Munich crash he paid a pound out of his small weekly wage packet for a ticket on the black market to join 60,000 supporters to show love and respect as well as cheer on a depleted team. By the summer of 1962 the team had been rebuilt, but the addition of Law was a step further in the direction Busby was so keen to go.

It wouldn't happen overnight though, for either Busby or Shankly. When Liverpool entertained United at Anfield in the November of 1962, an exciting 3–3 draw demonstrated attacking prowess on both sides, but with Liverpool twentieth in the table, two places below their visitors, onlookers spoke only of the work still to be done. That day the press wrote of the vociferous Anfield crowd, who despite the club's lowly position made their excitement known with chants of 'Liv-er-pool!' They could see that their team was moving forward, slowly but surely. For Busby, a man who had presided over a great team before the disaster at Munich, such patience was harder to come by. Relegation would have seemed as distant as a star in the sky to Busby and the team of 1958, but in the first few years of the 1960s his sides would struggle to keep their feet off the bottom rungs of the First Division – so much so, some in the press wondered if the manager was up to it.

Busby dismissed that sort of talk as idle. Years later Alex Ferguson came to Busby bemoaning newspaper criticism. 'Don't read them, then' was the simple reply. Journalists were summoned and growled at for 'stirring up trouble'. Harold Hardman, the

United chairman, publicly ridiculed the suggestion that Busby could be replaced, and Busby himself was never swayed by speculation. In fact it was he who had to calm the nerves of his friend Shankly, who would call Busby and regularly threaten to resign from Liverpool.

On one such occasion, still in the Second Division and frustrated with a board who wouldn't sanction the acquisition of Denis Law from Huddersfield, Shankly phoned Manchester, saying enough was enough. He was quitting.

'Bill,' said the calm Busby, perhaps mindful of the conversation he had had as a player wanting to leave Manchester City so many years before, 'have you got a job, some place to go?'

'No,' said Shankly.

'Don't do anything daft until you have.'

At the start of a freezing 1963 Busby was aware that the changes he was making needed to bear fruit. With Law settling in and Shankly's Liverpool improving so much so that they would finish a credible eighth, his team couldn't get itself up into the top half of the table. A cup run though, now that could underline the potential in what he was doing. And so the 3–1 win over Leicester at Wembley that spring eased fears, and once again greatness was in sight.

'That cup win was massive for us,' said Paddy Crerand, a brilliant addition from Celtic to Busby's midfield that February. 'Back then the cup was huge anyway, but for us as a squad it injected belief. Like Alex Ferguson winning it in 1990, we felt we could move up from that win and we did. It was actually the first time that Matt's new-look team really gelled.'

Down the road at Liverpool progress wouldn't need silverware to help it along. There was the hard-wired belief of a manager totally confident in his and his team's ability. Destiny was calling, but amid a shaky start to the 1963/4 campaign, it might have been only Shankly's ears who heard it. Liverpool lost their first three home games, but instead of the usual histrionics Shankly was calmness personified as he walked into the club boardroom to face some agitated-looking directors. 'I can assure you, gentlemen,' Shankly said, 'we will win at Anfield this season.' And he walked out.

Games were won, both home and away. The addition of Peter Thompson from Preston had given Liverpool an extra dimension, his mesmeric abilities on the left wing a bonus for a team already capable of superhuman energy. By spring, Shankly's team were in a race for the championship with Busby's United, and in April a 3–0 home win for Liverpool over a team they now could call their rivals effectively sealed their first title for nearly twenty years. And that was that. For the next three years the famous old championship wore the red ribbons of Liverpool and Manchester United. Two clubs, two teams and two managers swapping titles, chasing cups, pitting their wits and starting a rivalry that endures today.

That day in the spring of 1964, Liverpool's victory was clinched thanks largely to Shankly's defence nullifying Denis Law. The watching correspondent from the *Daily Express* noted the joyous Kop revelling in the striker's anonymity. 'The choir, as if mystically sounded off by some invisible baton, chorused: "Eee, Aye, Addio, Denis Law's a twerp," or words to the same devastating effect. You could see Law wince.'

Over the next few years words related to twerp accompanied by the odd V-sign directed by Nobby Stiles towards the Kop were sporadically joined by bouts of trouble, but the odd brick thrown at a stadium window by an overenthused fan was no reflection of how those charged with playing or managing the two teams felt about each other. 'Oh, there was no malice,' recalls Crerand. 'We all got on. At United we were very proud of what Liverpool were achieving. That sounds crazy today, doesn't it? If we were playing and Liverpool wasn't, Bill was at our game. Every time. I think he thought we were a bit of a threat.'

If he did, Shankly wasn't the type to let on. On one occasion before hosting United he ran through the day's game plan. Straight-faced, he said that even sharing a pitch with them was an insult to his side. 'In goal, Dunne is hopeless,' he said. 'At right back, Brennan is a straw – any gust of wind will blow him over. Foulkes at centre half kicks the ball anywhere. On the left Tony Dunne is fast but he only has one foot. Crerand couldn't beat a tortoise.'

The usually quiet Ian Callaghan took all this in before piping up, 'What about Best, Law and Charlton, boss?'

'What are you trying to say to me, Callaghan?' Shankly hissed. 'I hope you're not saying we cannot play three men.'

Away from the bolshiness of a First Division dressing room, Shankly had only respect for Manchester United and love for their manager. He would, once Busby retired, call the Lanarkshire man 'the greatest manager that ever lived'. Ever since playing wartime football with him, Shankly had looked up to Busby with a younger brother's intensity. Busby returned the affection with obvious pride in the younger man's achievements. 'They were thick as thieves,' recalls Paddy Crerand. It was a togetherness that transferred to their players. Of the shared success the two clubs enjoyed in the Sixties, Denis Law likened it to 'keeping it in the family,' stating that if he and United couldn't enjoy the tag of champions, 'There was no one else I'd rather see win it than my old boss Shankly.'

Players and their wives socialized. Shankly was a regular at Old

Trafford. Wearing his red tie, he'd greet the United players with a friendly handshake. 'How are you doin', sonny?' Busby would slip a Scotch into his usually teetotal visitor's tea, ensuring an even more entertaining conversation. Even the United tea lady (like most around the country) was greeted affectionately by Shankly. Bobby Charlton, by now England's world-class playmaker, was often at Anfield, calling the club to ask for tickets, especially for European nights. 'It is a long time now since anyone with Manchester United close to their heart has been able to say that a night in that ground was fun,' Charlton later wrote, 'but in those days no one with any feeling for the game, or working class humour, could say otherwise.'

In 1965 Liverpool went to Wembley to face Leeds United in the FA Cup final armed with a telegram from the players at Manchester United wishing them luck. 'Try telling younger fans that now,' laughed Crerand. By now, the friendship between the two north-western title-winning clubs had been intensified by the challenge from Yorkshire. Leeds United were a threat and a far from friendly one.

Liverpool and Manchester United. Manchester United and Liverpool. The teams and their supporters realized that if they wanted to win things, the other would have to be beaten. But now, dressed all in white but far from virginal, Leeds had arrived, and if Busby and Shankly were the English game's alpha lions, Don Revie was the hungry hyena stalking their pride.

'Leeds offered a nastier rivalry,' said Crerand. 'Whereas we'd socialize with Liverpool players and I had huge respect and a fondness for the likes of Ian St John and Big Ron [Yeats], there was mistrust about Leeds. We didn't like the way they dived or the way they tried to get at referees. They had great players but all you had to do was touch one of them and they went down like they'd been fucking shot.'

Even family ties couldn't gloss over the growing ill-feeling between Leeds and those they were trying to topple. Manchester United were especially prone to suffering the consequences, and when they clashed in the 1965 FA Cup semi-final, it was clear to Bobby Charlton that blood wasn't necessarily thicker than water. During the needly tie at Nottingham Forest's City Ground, United's Charlton went to contest a ball with Leeds' Norman Hunter. The odds were against him, but given the opposition and with his parents present, Charlton was going all out. And then he heard a familiar voice, that of his big brother Jack: 'Clatter the little bastard!'

A Leeds triumph that day (after the game Jack came into his brother's dressing room to tell him he'd been selected by England. 'Go away, I thought,' recalled Bobby) pitted them against Shankly's Liverpool on a day at Wembley that Shankly described as the greatest. The showpiece event of the English game, the day the nation watched and admired, for decades the cup had eluded Liverpool. Prior to the game, demand for tickets was unprecedented. Even Shankly manned the phones and took a call from a supporter with a Birmingham accent hoping to get lucky. 'I wouldn't give a drop of my blood to Birmingham,' said Shankly. 'I've got a hundred relatives and there's not one of those beggars getting a ticket. They're going to the boys on the Kop.'

The game started with the boys on the pop-up Wembley Kop singing over the national anthem, 'God save our gracious team,' and ended – after a 2–1 win – with, 'Eee, aye, addio, we've won the cup!' The winning goal epitomized Shankly's vision. Skill and pace on the wing from Callaghan and the neck-twisting will to win from St John. Perfection. Grown men cried, but four days later, before their tears could dry, supporters experienced the first of many fabled European nights at Anfield when Inter Milan were beaten 3–1 in the semi-final of the European Cup.

It was glorious. Swashbuckling style and challenging for top honours in a city becoming world famous for its music. Shankly was more easy listening than the new sound dominating the hit parade, but with the Beatles as the backdrop to his team's success he embraced it as enthusiastically as any Cavern Club regular. Not that Liverpool had a monopoly on moptops. At Manchester United, a new star shone bright. George Best had come from Northern Ireland, his young talent drawn to the attention of Joe Armstrong and watched by Jimmy Murphy, who deliriously told Busby they wouldn't need to coach this young man because 'He is a genius.'

Murphy as ever was right, and three years later, one night in the early spring of 1966, Best put on an individual display of such skill that talk of greatness moved giddily towards that of *the* greatest. Benfica were beaten 5–1 in their own Stadium of Light with Best dazzling. '*O Quinto Beatle*' – the Fifth Beatle – screamed the Portuguese public. The nineteen-year-old had scored twice to see off their team. Best arrived back in Manchester wearing a sombrero and sunglasses. Busby had a talent on his hand that would later ask more of a manager than any before it, but for now one that perfectly complemented the rest of his wonderful football team.

Chemistry. It was a word that perfectly described Busby's third great United side. Very different people away from the pitch markings but totally in tune within them, Best, Law and Charlton were the men who created the headlines, and the combinations they created stirred the public. Busby though demanded and worked on all his team. At centre half, Foulkes combined with

Nobby Stiles, a new type of midfielder, not quite half back but a more modern, holding player. Stiles in turn combined with his fullbacks and the more forward-thinking Crerand, a player able to look up and pass the ball with delightful precision. 'It was Matt's thing,' recalled Crerand.

He wanted us all to be in tune with each other. It was all about our chemistry. George, Denis and Bobby were one thing and rightly celebrated, but we had great relationships all over the pitch. Yeah, it was the same off the pitch. Before a game, Matt would talk to us. It would be calm, informative, tactical, and quietly reassuring. Then, he'd put his coat on and walk out the room to let Jimmy let rip at us. Matt didn't like bad language so he'd leave because Jimmy had a foul mouth. Matt was gone and Jimmy would go to town on us all, the message to me always being the same. Make sure you let them know you're there. Make sure your first tackle is a good one. Whether it's fair or unfair, it really didn't matter.

With Murphy's curses ringing in their ears and Busby's nurturing warming their hearts, United achieved greatness. They played with a free spirit that dazzled supporters all over the country. They were an extension of their manager and the expression of his dream. Liverpool were the same. They played with the intensity of Shankly and at a level of fitness that suggested they trained so hard just to keep up with him. Phil Chisnall, a striker signed by Liverpool from Manchester United in 1964, was able to compare both men and both set-ups, telling Stephen F. Kelly in his biography of Shankly that it was the ferociousness of the training at Liverpool that stood out. 'There was nothing like that at Old Trafford,' he said. 'The training there was much lighter, but at Anfield it was back-breaking.

'At United, Busby simply let us play our own game. He encouraged individualism; he let us do what we wanted. He had signed players because they could play football. But at Liverpool everything was done collectively. You were playing for each other.'

Two contrasting styles, two managers who had started from similar backgrounds but taken different routes to the top, but that's where they now found themselves. They were the talk of the game – Stein too, by the mid-1960s, as both Scotland's international manager, albeit for a short time, and the Celtic boss. Newspapers and television followed their every move, chronicled their every word. They were modern football managers. Tacticians, motivators, coaches with something to say, be it directly or through their brilliant teams, although modernity wasn't a tag they would embrace. Labels were for other people to tie on. These were men of the old school: Busby with his trilby and Woodbine cigarettes, Shankly wearing his tailored suits and polished brogues, Stein with Brylcreemed hair and white overcoat. They knew football though. Inside and out. They knew how to manoeuvre within it, keeping it simple, keeping its essence while making the changes necessary to compete and to win, not only at home but against Europe's finest minds too.

Modern managers though had the modern footballer to deal with, and at Old Trafford, Matt Busby had the most contemporary of them all. George Best had been a celebrity since that night in Lisbon. The great players of the past such as Stanley Matthews had been household names, but this was different, and with every swivel of his hips his fame rose quicker than a Mary Quant hemline.

'That was hard for Matt,' remembered Paddy Crerand. 'No manager had ever had to deal with someone like George before. This was a player on the front of newspapers as well as the back and Matt had to learn quickly. Matt though was brilliant. He was a father figure to us all who gained our instant respect and what helped the manager was his huge affection for George. We all loved him. He was this shy kid from Belfast but things got crazy, and Matt had to deal with it all.'

Although the modern player wasn't just boutique clothes shops and champagne fountains, Best epitomized just how famous a footballer could become. Away from the glitz, even your everyday player, now that the maximum wage had been abolished, wanted more. Meanwhile film stars such as Michael Caine and Sean Connery were spotted at Chelsea and celebrity football matches were played in front of thousands. Busby himself showed his keen eye for football's glamorous potential when, having watched sport in the United States, he sanctioned plans for a rebuild at Old Trafford that included executive boxes for the new type of corporate supporter.

All three managers had a complex relationship with the money that could be earned from football. They were staunch socialists with a passion for the welfare of the working man and wanted their players to get their fair share, but they refused to sanction sky-high wages. The bottom line – it was a privilege to play for the three clubs they managed.

'His marriage to the game has been the greatest love-match in its history,' Busby later wrote of Shankly. 'He loved football as a boy, and possibly no more than many another boy. I doubt that he lived it any more than I did. But the love became an even deeper affection, a passion, when he was told that, instead of working down a mine digging for coal and fitting in his football when he could, somebody was anxious to *pay* him for playing the game he would have walked miles to play for nothing.'

That was the thing. Men like Shankly, Busby and Stein loved the game and those who worked within it, and they could smell out those being tarnished by the riches now on offer. 'Us players at United and Liverpool had an inkling that Matt and Bill had got together and talked about wages,' recalled Crerand. 'The maximum wage had long been abolished, but even at our clubs, who were winning the championship regularly, we didn't get loads more.

'The two managers talked and agreed to cap the money they would pay. They came from working-class backgrounds and football in their minds shouldn't be about money. They were socialist men but to them football wasn't about huge wages. They weren't on that much either though. Even when we won the European Cup, I think Matt was on about £12,000 a year.'

Stein – who at Celtic paid his players forty pounds a week, but with a bonus of £1,500 for reaching the European Cup final – was also one to keep an eye on the pennies and was quick to pull up a player he thought was getting above himself. His footballers were put up in the best hotels but Stein would intervene if he heard an order at dinner suggesting delusions of grandeur. Jimmy Johnstone once ordered steak Diane. 'Come 'ere, son,' Stein called to the waiter. 'Give the wee man fish 'n' chips like the rest of them.' When his captain Billy McNeill had a prawn cocktail, Stein was on to him. 'You're from a mining family in Bellshill,' he shouted. 'They never had bloody prawn cocktails!'

Football was changing on the pitch as well as in the dining rooms. For all the romance of the sport Busby and Shankly had fallen in love with, a more pragmatic, conservative approach was creeping into the game. In 1966 and leading Liverpool to another championship, Shankly and Bob Paisley walked out of a coaching convention. Not ones for sitting at desks both men left dismayed at what they saw as purely a talking shop.

Later that year, England would win the World Cup, but away from the bunting Shankly was dismayed at the style of football on show that summer. 'I thought the World Cup was played in a negative sense and England won with negative football,' he declared, bemoaning the absence of his beloved wingers. Indeed, when Roger Hunt returned to training as a World Cup winner he was met by his manager at Melwood with, 'Come on, lad, you've got more important things to worry about.'

Scottish patriotism might have played its part in downplaying England's momentous achievement, but the idea of glory at the cost of beauty will have concerned these men. During a decade that had seen so many cultural and political upheavals, those who spent their Saturdays following the fortunes of Liverpool and Manchester United had been treated to their own form of psychedelia. Two teams competing for honours amid a blur of red and white but doing it in swashbuckling style.

Chapter 12:

Immortality

A large dark jacket and a white shirt hang on dressing-room pegs like two exhausted soldiers. They belong to Jock Stein. Creased and crinkled, they are casualties of not only the eighty-five-degree heat that has roasted Lisbon that May afternoon, but also their owner's full-throttle involvement in a football match in which he blocked every shot, bemoaned every bad decision and ran every mile. It's 1967 and Celtic have won the European Cup.

The dressing room is still packed. The sound of back-slapping accompanies the Celtic songs being chanted by jubilant players, staff and directors. The European Cup gleams, its sparkle added to by the champagne that fills it. 'Have you had a bevvy from this?' one player asks another.

Hugh McIlvanney of the *Observer* is in the room joining in the celebrations, congratulating the half-naked newly crowned kings of Europe. A fellow writer from Glasgow leans in to him so he can be heard above the din. 'They've all got Stein's heart,' he says. 'There's a bit of the big man in all of them.' McIlvanney nods in agreement.

Stein has worked with many of his players since they were reserves. He's trained them; he knows their lives; he's made them tick, but if there's a bit of Stein in all of them, the sweat that now soaks the manager's suit proves that each and every one of them is a part of him too.

Bill Shankly walks into the room, the only manager from England to have flown to Portugal. He seeks out his friend Stein. They embrace. 'John,' Shankly says, 'you're immortal.'

A story that started with a phone call from Glasgow to Llanelli has reached its peak under a sunny Lisbon sky. Prior to that call, a young jobbing footballer was preparing for a life back underground, but now with Internazionale, Milan's princes, made to look like paupers, the name Jock Stein will never be in the dark again.

It was in the light of Bermuda, 378 days prior to the sunshine of Lisbon, that Stein embarked on his quest for European Cup glory. At the end of the 1965/6 season – in which both the league and the cup were won – Stein had taken his team to the Atlantic island for what was planned as a break, a chance for his players to rest at the end of the long season before a tour of the US and Canada.

'Yeah, that was supposed to be a holiday,' laughed centre half John Clark. 'Not with our manager around. There we were, hoping for some relaxation and some time on the beach, but after a couple of days Jock has arranged a game against the Bermuda national team on the local cricket ground.'

If his players had swimming and pina coladas on their minds, Stein, his Burnbank work ethic never far away, was thinking about the next season and the tour of North America. Games in Ontario, New York, San Francisco and in the heat of Los Angeles against local teams, but also two against England's FA Cup winners Tottenham and one against Bayern Munich. In the event, Celtic returned unbeaten and primed for the season ahead.

'Training was intense,' said Clark. 'Even out in America, we worked so hard. Jock liked a bit of needle in there, he liked it competitive and it always was. We weren't a squad who liked to lose. There was some downtime and I remember being in Hollywood and Richard Attenborough, who was filming out there, would join us and mix well with the boys. Jock enjoyed his company but otherwise we trained hard. Jock started getting us to play fourteen-a-side games with two balls. Sometimes you wondered what he was doing, but it would always work. It got us all thinking quicker.'

Stein had been offered the Celtic job – the board finally realizing that in him, no matter his religion, they had a candidate who could turn the club from also-rans into something bigger and better – in the January of 1965. It had been announced that he would stay at Hibs until the end of the season, or at least until the Edinburgh club found a new man. They quickly did. Bob Shankly took over. It was March 1965, and the manager's office at Celtic Park had its new tenant.

As ever, Stein brought with him his knack for immediate brilliance with a 6–0 win at Airdrie, and while an embarrassing 4–2 home defeat to Hibs allowed the capital city a degree of Schadenfreude, Stein's desire for instant success was satiated with a 3–2 win over his other former employers Dunfermline in the Scottish Cup final. It was the club's first trophy since 1957, and like Matt Busby's 1963 FA Cup victory, was the perfect start to the manager's ambitious plan.

The following season's double of league and League Cup, plus a run to the final of the Scottish Cup and the semi-finals of the Cup Winners Cup, where they lost 2–1 on aggregate to Liverpool, spoke of a team destined for a shot at immortality. Indeed, in the two games against Shankly's men the energy and the ability his team showed against England's champions-elect raised the eyebrows of the hitherto-sneering pundits, who had to admit that Stein's side were unfortunate to go out.

Further signs of Celtic's potential came against Matt Busby's Manchester United when they came to Glasgow for a pre-season friendly. 'I don't think you could call it a friendly,' said John Clark. 'Far from it. United brought all the big boys up: Paddy [Crerand], Charlton, Law, Best, Stiles; they all played. My God, the tackles went in that day. It was in the right spirit, but the tackles went in and they went in hard. Both managers were very close, but like their teams, neither liked to lose. We won 4–1 and that proved just how good we might be that year.'

Busby left Scotland in no doubt of Celtic's chances in the competition he so wanted to win. 'Celtic will do well in the European Cup,' he declared. 'They have a good, all-round side and the way they go about their work is bound to bring success. I was impressed by their half-back line of Murdoch, McNeill and Clark. Gemmell was an outstanding fullback. And that support . . . I thought I had seen and heard everything from Everton and Liverpool supporters, but those Celtic fans beat the lot. Their enthusiasm seems to give the players additional energy and they never stop running.'

After Busby's trail-blazing in European competition, other English clubs had experienced success in Europe. Tottenham had won the Cup Winners Cup in 1963, West Ham following suit in 1965. With Liverpool and Manchester United swapping league titles between 1964 and 1967, Shankly and Busby had chased the big one, but with Liverpool losing to Amsterdam's Ajax and a teenage Johan Cruyff, after Christmas the 1966/7 season continued with Celtic the lone British club reaching for the stars. Stein had had a brush with the Dutch club when in early 1966 he was visited by the young Ajax manager, Rinus Michels. Stein's methods had reached the ears of Europe's coaching fraternity, and while Stein had gone to Helenio Herrera when he started out, now he was welcoming men eager to learn from him.

The 1966/7 League Cup had been won in October with a 1–0 win over Rangers, the first vindication of Stein's confidence about the season. 'I think we could win everything in front of us,' he had said before a competitive kick had been taken. 'I think this could be a season to remember.' Stein's capacity for understatement matched his ability to organize and manage a football team, for this was more than a season to remember. This was a season to shake a continent, a season to propel a nation's game to new heights, a season that even over half a century later lifts the spirits of those who were there and those who wish they had been.

The Glasgow Cup was won shortly after the League Cup, followed by the Scottish Cup in April and the league title in early May, before the glory of Lisbon later that same month. Geoffrey Green of *The Times* later remarked, 'Celtic had swept the board clean north of the River Tweed,' and, 'under the astute managership of Jock Stein they had won everything bar the Grand National and the Boat Race'. Green might have agreed that had Stein hoisted Jimmy Johnstone onto a decent steed or instructed his half-back line to crew a boat on the Thames, even those honours might have been achieved that year.

Celtic were so well drilled, so expansive and for those lucky enough to follow them week in week out, so thrilling. 'It was all about tempo,' said John Clark. 'In training if the tempo slipped, Jock was on to us. He'd stop things and tell us that's not what he wanted, and we'd start again. The team had pace, it had width from its fullbacks and wide men, it had plenty of guile with the likes of Bertie Auld in midfield, and it entertained.'

Entertainment was vital to Stein. He had grown up watching the game before the war. Names like Alan Morton, Rangers' blistering winger of the 1920s, would have been regularly lauded in Burnbank, as would local Hughie Gallagher, the Bellshill genius who shone in Scotland and England. Football was for the masses, a weekend art form accessible to those longing for brighter experiences. Things might have got more colourful in the 1960s but the game's task mustn't change, and Stein feared it had.

Like Shankly, Stein wasn't keen on what he had witnessed in England during the World Cup. 'The big difference between the 1966 World Cup and the first World Cup tournament I saw,' he said after returning home, 'was that in Switzerland twelve years ago there was entertaining, attacking ideas galore. Celtic took their team players to that 1954 World Cup in order that they should learn.'

Stein had certainly been educated. In 1954 he returned mesmerized by the Hungarians and the attacking patterns they wove. A philosophy had formed in his mind, and the ambition to win as much as he could was never going to dent it. A Stein team had scored a goal within ten seconds of starting his managerial career, and that day with Dunfermline set the tone for all his future teams. Now he was going for the European Cup, but nothing would change.

Stein had that summer shown his mettle. Winger John Hughes had gone public with his desire for an improved contract, flirting with English clubs and not committing to the club. Newcastle were offering a record £72,000 for his services, and Stein made it clear that no one was too good to be sold, using the opportunity to reiterate his desire to play expansive football. 'The fact that John Hughes is for sale does not mean that we are planning to follow the Alf Ramsey line of discarding orthodox wingers,' he told the press. 'We still have Johnstone, Auld, Chalmers, Lennox, Gallagher, who can play the old-fashioned wing game.' Hughes soon signed his contract.

'Old-fashioned' was the key here. The style of play he had grown up with was one thing, but Stein had also shown an old-fashioned strength. Player power was increasing, but here was a manager who wouldn't be dictated to. The plans for his 'special season' were in place, and no individual, however talented, could change them, although when it came to game preparation, some did see a change in Stein. League games – with the players at his disposal and their knowledge of their opponents – while not looking after themselves, could be simple. Instructions were always given, but there was, as Archie Macpherson put it, a 'uniformity of approach'. It was in Europe though that Stein's coaching muscles could be flexed, and an extra spring came to his step when he pulled out his magnetic tactical board and told his players how best to dismantle an overseas team.

He certainly not only had eager ears to preach to but also the most talented of footballers. All over the pitch and within the squad Stein could see footballers whose desire to play the game in the most brilliant way matched his own, and their talents had been spotted by football's aristocracy. 'This little man is a magnificent player,' Alfredo Di Stéfano said of Jimmy Johnstone in 1964, 'and one I would be proud to have in any side in which I was too.' It wasn't only Stein's attackers catching the eye. John Clark – the Brush, as he was known for his brilliance as a sweeper – was receiving plaudits. 'You maybe do not always notice him,' said Pelé after a friendly between Scotland and Brazil in 1966, 'but he is covering quietly for other players and always there to stop a man.'

These were players more than ready for Europe's best. Not that they were too good not to benefit from their manager's frequent pearls of wisdom. On the eve of their first away trip, a second leg in Zurich at which Celtic would defend a hard fought 2–0 win at Parkhead, Stein told his players their hosts would once again play a compact and physical game. His players didn't believe that a team would be so pragmatic at home, and some even told him so. Stein was right of course, and Celtic, armed with their manager's knowledge and tactics, ran out 3–0 winners.

The French champions Nantes were beaten comfortably in the next round, but it was the tie against Yugoslav opposition FK Vojvodina that convinced Celtic and Stein that they had arrived at the business end of the competition. 'They were a brilliant team,' recalled Clark. 'They beat us 1–0 and had some great players. Their goalkeeper Panteli was class, and Stani up front was a great player. That was the hardest game in the whole run.' Stein went into the second leg with a rare feeling of concern. The Yugoslavs had proved themselves a fine team, technically and tactically, and Stein, for all the confidence in his team, knew that a huge challenge lay ahead of them. Nearly 70,000 fans crammed into Celtic Park to see if their heroes would rise to it. Archie Macpherson, sitting up on the stadium's commentary gantry, noticed Stein fidgeting in the dugout. 'I recall him, above all, looking down at his wristwatch,' Macpherson noted, 'holding it up to the floodlights as if he wasn't getting a proper sight of it, and doing it with growing frequency.'

Stein would have noted the hour mark on his watch when Steve Chalmers nipped in to equalize. Then, with a play-off in Rotterdam looking more than likely, a roar of delight filled the Glasgow sky when Billy McNeill rose to head home a corner and send his team into the European Cup semi-final.

'Next up were the Czechoslovakian side, Dukla Prague,' said

Clark. 'We played well at home and won 3–1, but the trip out there was notable for the crowd being mainly military.' Stein was never going to let tens of thousands of soldiers sway his thinking, but on this occasion the manager seemed confused about whether to stick or twist. The Czechs had all the ball, while Celtic seemed happy to restrain their attacking instincts – so much so that after a tense 0–0 draw Stein came off the pitch and declared, 'I'll never resort to tactics like that again – never.' It was hard to know why Stein had said this. Some thought it wounded pride – dislike in admitting his team had simply been dominated.

'There was no game plan,' said Clark. 'We were perhaps a little bit over-cautious but not because the manager had asked us to be. They had a lot of the ball, but I never felt we were under a big threat. You take it as it comes. They had all the ball and we didn't have our attacking moments but it wasn't ever a big worry for me.'

The Scottish title was sewn up at Ibrox with a thrilling 2–2 draw, a game in which Bill Shankly's nephew Roger Hynd scored for Rangers and threatened to ruin the party, and for the final game, at home to Kilmarnock, Stein's demand for a high-tempo approach saw him declare, 'There will be no question of anyone taking it easy as that is how a player gets hurt.' After the 2–0 win, Stein was carried shoulder high on to the pitch. The domestic quadruple had been won, and so to Lisbon.

Preparing for Inter never seemed too arduous for the players, who had taken on their manager's self-belief. 'We knew about them,' said Clark. 'They didn't really worry us too much. They were the best in Europe so that sounds strange, but we were prepared, we were a confident team. Not arrogant, confident and even at half-time when we were losing, we felt that there was no way they could beat us.'

Stein had his players in the right frame of mind but his own ambition had been pricked by his managerial counterpart at Inter. Years after being nicknamed the 'big ant' by Helenio Herrera, their teams now faced each other. The Argentine had been seen at Ibrox observing Celtic clinch their league title, and had promised Stein use of Inter's private jet so he could see Inter do the same in Italy. This hadn't come to anything, and when Herrera's promise of a lift to the stadium and a match ticket also wasn't kept, Stein, who had to get a press pass for the game, was left in no doubt of his opponent's deviousness. 'My time will come,' Stein quietly told a Scottish journalist.

Celtic arrived in the Iberian heat as a relaxed group, unfazed by the task ahead. While not preoccupied by what others thought, they were eager to prove the doubters wrong. 'We felt good,' said Clark. 'We'd had two weeks off, and the days before the match we trained well. Jock sent us out onto the lawn outside the hotel, where we played five-a-side tournaments. Really competitive. We got right into each other but that would have pleased Jock.' The Inter officials watching Celtic train were disarmed by their opponents' antics.

Training was the only time Stein's players were allowed to be in the sun. Following advice from Matt Busby, whose Manchester United team had been beaten 5–0 by Benfica, a defeat he had attributed to the heat prior to kick-off, the players were only to go outside after five, and even standing near a window was discouraged. 'If there's as much as a freckle on any man's arm, he's for home,' Stein growled. But he was relaxed too. He joked about the huge church attendances for the celebration of Our Lady of Fatima: 'Those priests should give Celtic half the gate.'

Shankly joined the squad on the team bus to the stadium, sitting up front with Stein and Fallon, offering words of encouragement to the players soon to be the first Brits to contest a European Cup final. Stein had done the hard work and now it was time for him and his players to make history. 'I have no ambitions for myself,' he said. 'I am completely impersonal [*sic*] about the glories of winning the European Cup. The praise is for Celtic. I have worked around the clock for my club because I believe they are one of the greatest in the world and deserve nothing but the highest honours.'

Stein's confidence, his belief in what he was trying to do, rubbed off on his team. Changed and ready to walk out for the biggest game of their young lives, his players felt an air of normality amid the completely abnormal. 'Jock wasn't excited before the game,' remembered Clark. 'There was no big team talk. Jock knew how Inter would play and had calmly told us. We weren't going to change the way we did things.' In the tunnel, eleven men, all born within thirty miles of Celtic Park, stood and waited, their sun-starved limbs looking paler still next to the oiled tans of their Italian opponents. 'You could smell the Ambre Solaire off them,' noted Jimmy Johnstone. Bertie Auld looked a leggy Inter player up and down and shouted to Johnstone, 'Wee man, look at this big yin!' and then turned to the Italian and said, 'You tell your maw you're going to be late. Your eyes will be burling!' Then came Auld's rendition of 'Hail, hail!' gleefully joined by his teammates, and the tone was set for Inter's players. 'If you ask me, we won it in the tunnel,' Auld would later boast.

The task got that much harder for Celtic when after seven minutes Jim Craig brought down Renato Cappellini in the box. Penalty. Stein was up remonstrating. His players surrounded the German referee, the language barrier broken by facial expressions and hand gestures. Shankly in the crowd must have been taken back to the San Siro two years before, when a series of strange decisions saw Inter knock Liverpool out in the semi-final.

While Stein prowled the touchline making his feelings known, his skipper took his manager's anger to spur on his teammates. 'We felt it was an injustice,' recalled McNeill. 'We thought it was wrongly given, and from there on in we knew there was only one way to win the game, and that was to take it right to them, and that's what we did.' If that early goal didn't make the Italians sit even deeper than *catenaccio* demanded, the pulsating nature of Celtic's attacks certainly did. Stein's team, having gone behind to officially the best club team on the planet, brushed themselves down and attacked their opponents as if training back on the hotel lawn.

McNeill and Clark at the back, aided somewhat by the absence of Inter's great Spanish playmaker Luis Suárez, were charged with starting attacks rather than stopping them. Tommy Gemmell at left back was a constant forager in the Inter half, while Craig matched him on the right. Auld and Bobby Murdoch were having fun in the sun, ignoring Inter reputations and concentrating only on creating chances. The BBC commentator Kenneth Wolstenholme marvelled at Jimmy Johnstone's desire for the ball and ability to beat Giacinto Facchetti, calling him a 'little trickster'.

The heat was searing, but Celtic blood refused to boil. Chances came. Giuliano Sarti in the Inter goal was playing well but was in a minority of one within his team, and by the end of the half it was the Italians who were desperate to reorganize, regroup and ask why the hell they hadn't been better briefed about just how good their green-and-white opponents were. At half-time Stein approached the referee, furious with what he – wrongly – felt was an injustice. 'You're a Nazi bastard,' he growled. 'A penalty kick? You were conned! Where are you gonnae get your villa?'

His players would later agree that Craig had tackled Cappellini unfairly and it was indeed a penalty, but no matter. Stein's blood was up. More of the same was the half-time message.

Even for a seasoned and classy professional like Sandro Mazzola, more of the same was a big surprise. 'We had the strong impression,' the Italian playmaker recalled, 'especially during the second half, that the match was being played solely in one half – ours.' Celtic continued to swarm forward. Sarti continued to earn his lira. Johnstone on the wing was still full of running but started to think maybe this was going to be one of those days, but then, before 'glorious failure' could be scribbled onto notepads in the press box, Celtic struck. And what a strike. Jim Craig had a keen ear, and when the former university man carried the ball at the Inter defence he waited and waited, and then with Gemmell screaming for a pass, he pulled it to the edge of the box. His fellow fullback slammed the ball beyond Sarti.

At the restart, as Gemmell gleefully took his place at left back, Stein motioned to him with a message of calm. 'We can take them in extra time,' he said with a hint of uncharacteristic caution. Gemmell was having none of it. There were twenty minutes left, and Celtic were ready to conquer Europe. The attacks and the tempo wouldn't let up.

The winner on eighty-four minutes spoke again of Stein's nous. This time Gemmell attacked the fullback on the left, then pulled the ball back to Murdoch, who shot at goal, where Steve Chalmers diverted the ball into the net. It might have looked fortunate but it wasn't. Training drills under Stein worked time and time again on midfielders supporting their wide men and drilling the ball into the box, where anything could happen.

Inter had ran out of juice long before the winning goal and they wouldn't find any reserves. Celtic had won the European

Cup. Most important to Stein, they did so in a manner that made everyone sit up and take notice. They had entertained. Gloriously and beautifully.

Kilted Celts ran onto the pitch with beaming pink faces. The players rushed to Simpson's goal, where many of them had left the false teeth they now required for smiles of victory. Stein in vain asked the supporters to vacate the playing area, but the green-and-white sea was at high tide. The players fled to the dressing room for cover then realized that a trophy needed to be picked up.

Billy McNeill finally lifted the big old thing, its handles as wide as the Glaswegian smiles that greeted him doing so. Somewhat ungraciously, the winners' medals would be given out later from a shoebox at a banquet – 'That was the worst part of the whole thing,' John Clark recalled – but for now little else mattered other than a party.

'Hey, Ronnie Simpson, what are we?' shouted a half-naked Bertie Auld to his goalkeeper. 'What are we, son? We're the greatest. That's what we are. The greatest!'

A Portuguese official smiled with them. 'This attacking play, this is the real meaning of football. This is the true game.'

His words filled Stein with pride and joy. 'Go on,' he said to the man, slapping his shoulders. 'I could listen to you all night.' He then turned to everyone and said, 'Fancy anybody saying that about a Scottish team.'

Chapter 13:

Odyssey

Bobby Charlton called him the old man. Not so much because of the years that he carried with him, but for the almost ever-present paternal figure that he had become. Ever since walking through the bombed-out doors at Old Trafford, Matt Busby's fatherly grip on the club had been steady and sure. Now, sitting in the same stadium's dressing room, his players noticed something new in his eyes, and on his face. It was defeat.

'We're never going to win the European Cup now . . .'

Manchester United had been beaten by Partizan Belgrade in the semi-final of the 1966 tournament. A defeat is never greeted with anything but disappointment at Old Trafford, but as Busby stood and said those words to his players – his usual calming authority absent – they knew this was different.

Munich wasn't talked about at Old Trafford. It never had been. Soon after the tragedy, new players would arrive and notice that the survivors' moods were changeable, but they knew enough not to ask why. Jimmy Murphy might use the name Duncan Edwards to illustrate to a young footballer the real meaning of attitude and hard work, but Busby wouldn't talk about what had happened.

It was present though. As the decade wore on, a new team had enthralled, but the memories of that team and how they had died were always there. The 1965/6 campaign had been Busby's first foray back into the European Cup since the crash, and while losing at such a tantalizingly late stage must have hurt, it was Belgrade and all that place meant in relation to Munich that, as Bobby Charlton put it, 'hurt down to his bones'.

Three days later, United lost to Everton in the FA Cup semi-final; ten days later they lost the title to Bill Shankly's Liverpool. The season finished under a cloud, but it was Belgrade and the European Cup that most darkened Busby's skies. 'I think Matt was ready to quit,' said Paddy Crerand. 'He was low, and it wasn't like him. Us players had the strong impression that he was going to retire and us players got to him and we cajoled him back, saying very confidently, "Boss, we're going to win the league next year, and the European Cup the year after that."'

On that balmy evening in May 1967, as Billy McNeill hoisted the European Cup towards the blue Iberian sky, Matt Busby and Manchester United were up high themselves, cruising at 35,000 feet above the Pacific, on a flight from Hawaii to New Zealand. The manager and players only heard about Celtic's success in the competition when Paddy Crerand, still a Celt at heart, phoned the *Manchester Evening News* from his Auckland hotel room to find out the score. A less-than-well-informed switchboard operator said she didn't know but had heard that some team had become the first British team to win something.

So the competition that Busby had foreseen would change the game, the competition he had demanded his United team enter, had finally come to Britain. He would have loved to have been the first British manager to win the European Cup, but Celtic had been his team growing up and Jock Stein was his friend. He wasn't jealous, but his competitive edge was further sharpened, and as his team toured the USA and Australasia as champions of England, Busby could start to plan another go at it.

Manchester United had won the 1966/7 championship after a keenly fought battle with Liverpool. The crowds flocked to Old Trafford – the average attendance was 54,000 that season – to see their holy trinity. Although West Ham had a trio they could boast had won England the World Cup, the threesome of Charlton, Best and Law was seen in Manchester as something far more divine. The thrilling title race had added to the spring in the steps of the fans who flocked to the stadium every other Saturday.

On Boxing Day 1966 Liverpool had beaten a fine young Chelsea side at Anfield, while United had lost at Sheffield United, and Shankly's men would, as ever, battle hard, winning games and staying on course to retain their title. The thing is, United wouldn't go away. David Herd was adding goal after goal to the brilliance of Best, Law and Charlton, and in March, when Liverpool surprisingly lost at Burnley, United, 5–2 victors at home to Leicester, went top. There they would stay.

United had gone top of the league by beating Leicester, but they had lost David Herd with a broken leg. His goals had been invaluable, but even with the European Cup beckoning there would be no mad rush into the transfer market. A world-record fee for Geoff Hurst was mooted but it wasn't the right time. A year earlier goalkeeper Alex Stepney had been signed from Chelsea, and from the academy, eighteen-year-old striker Brian Kidd would make his debut in the 1967 Charity Shield against Tottenham. Otherwise the squad was settled and as eager as their manager to see their continental ambitions met.

In contrast to Busby's glum demeanour and talk of retirement just twelve months earlier, United's players were now working for a manager overjoyed with their work. If Paddy Crerand had helped lift Busby's spirits in the spring of 1966, his team's thrilling form – especially since Christmas – had him eulogizing his team. 'There are times when all the uncertainties of football disappear,' Busby said after a dazzling 6–1 win at West Ham that won him a fifth championship. 'You have the sense that your players can do anything. That is the most wonderful sensation for a manager.'

By reassuring their forlorn manager that they would win the league and then the European Cup, the players had certainly helped lift his morale, but now they had done more than merely talk, and Busby could plan for a crack at the big one. 'So once again the European Cup was there to be won,' he'd later write. 'There it was, high in the sky shining at us, twinkling like a star, almost beckoning us.'

United had long fluctuated between the exceptional and the less exceptional; Frank McGhee of the *Daily Mirror* had dubbed them 'the team you can't trust'. Such was the swashbuckling way Busby had them playing, many of his players wouldn't disagree but nor would they change it. 'McGhee was absolutely right,' said Bobby Charlton later, 'but what a marvellous experience.' Like the supporters, Busby's players were simply having fun. It was how Busby had always envisaged the game. It was why he had travelled miles from Orbiston to wherever a game was being played. After his decision to continue in football following the Munich crash, Busby had talked about his 'obsession' to get the club back to the top. The top meant being the best in Europe, but that ambition would never be achieved by sacrificing exciting, attacking football.

'I can remember waking up on the morning of every game at Old Trafford and thrilling to the prospect of playing there in front of a huge crowd,' recalled Charlton. 'Compared with what leading footballers earn now, we weren't paid that well, but there was nothing like the excitement of playing for United. If George Best was on song, if Denis Law was in a mood to rattle them in, if I was onto a game, then nobody could stop us. If it turned out to be one of the bad days, then Matt sucked on his pipe and waited for the next time.'

Busby understood that perfection wasn't something he could demand. He had the players; he had built the club; the fans flocked to see them, but patience was needed too. In George Best, that young man who had drawn the word genius from the mouth of Jimmy Murphy – not a man for hyperbole – Busby had a player who embodied all that flair, all that talent, but who also underlined the fact that perfection was not to be merely drawn from a tap. Best, more than any other player, would have Busby sucking on his pipe and waiting for the next time.

'Don't let Matt kid you,' wing half Maurice Setters told journalists earlier in the decade. 'You may imagine he's easy-going. Perhaps a soft touch. But don't ever take Busby on. He's cunning and tough. There isn't a trick he hasn't come across or an excuse he hasn't heard before. You don't take liberties with this fella.'

Paddy Crerand once kept the team bus waiting. Climbing aboard, clearly embarrassed, he met his manager's eye. 'You must be a very important person,' Busby said sarcastically. 'Only an important person could keep the directors, the manager and the players of Manchester United waiting so long.' That was the thing. Manchester United had become everything to Busby. Bill Shankly would one day say that a club was built on players, manager and fans; directors were there just 'to sign the cheques'. Busby would have smiled at his friend's scorn for the board but would not have agreed. To him, the whole club was there to be respected.

While that stance would be severely tested by Best in the years to follow, for now the young man's talents were pushing Busby's team towards glory. Best's two goals in a 2–0 win at Anfield put United top of the table in November 1967, a spot they occupied for months as Busby strived to keep his team focused on domestic matters, calling the title 'the bread and butter that leads to slices of cake'. It was hard though. Busby's own focus was on Europe, and as much as he tried to keep the club's day-to-day focus steady, his dream of being Europe's finest was on the line, and his players knew it.

'There was definitely a feeling that we had to do it for Matt and also for one or two of the senior players who were running out of time,' George Best would later say about that season's quest for the European Cup. 'A lot of us felt that this was the last chance for this particular team. If we hadn't done it that year, I don't think we would have ever won it.'

Despite his efforts, Busby's bread and butter was sacrificed in the European quest. After their European Cup quarter-final first leg, United lost at home to Chelsea. After the quarter-final second leg, they lost at Coventry. After the semi-final first leg, they lost at West Brom. Busby's old pal Joe Mercer (more than assisted by Malcolm Allison) was quick to take advantage, and when United lost their last game of the season at home to Sunderland, the championship made the short journey across Manchester to Maine Road.

But there could be no disappointment, no sense of loss. Just days later, Manchester United were taking a slender 1–0 lead to Real Madrid, and no one dared imagine yet another semi-final defeat.

To reach such tantalizing heights, United had started in less grandiose surroundings. A goalless draw in Malta against

Hibernians secured a 4–0 aggregate win in the first round. United then became Britain's only hope when Jock Stein's champions were knocked out by Dynamo Kiev in a second-leg game in the Soviet Union that would have had Shankly on the phone to Busby bemoaning the shortcomings of foreign referees. Some observers decided Celtic and Stein had lost their magic touch, but while Stein would have to plan for the following season, Busby moved his mind's eye onto FK Sarajevo. Once again United played out a goalless draw on foreign soil – after a flight to Dubrovnik, followed by a six-hour coach journey through the Bosnian mountains – before a violent fixture at Old Trafford that saw swinging fists and red cards ended in a tight 2–1 win.

Compared to all that, the trip to Poland for the quarter-final must have seemed like a breeze, but Polish champions Gornik Zabrze had impressed through the campaign, knocking out Celtic's conquerors Dynamo Kiev in the previous round. United took a 2–0 cushion into the snows of southern Poland, but with 105,000 people braving the weather (Busby considered asking for a postponement) this was never going to be an easy ride. Busby had his team digging in. Law was out injured, but with David Herd back at centre forward and Best working tirelessly, the whole team followed suit. The Polish champions managed one goal, but once again Busby could plan for a European Cup semi-final.

Heady heights, but with the league title slipping away, Busby had to convince some fans that he and his squad were up to the task. One local in the *Evening News* derided Busby's lack of action in the transfer market and his need to rely on youngsters such as Kidd and John Aston. 'It is maturity that wins the European Cup,' declared the knowing reader. 'It won't be won with key positions filled by young boys yet to learn their job.' Not quite

Alan Hansen's 1995 declaration that United would never win anything with kids, but Busby did use his right to reply with a sarcastic interview in the *Daily Express*: 'Why didn't I think of it before? It had dawned on me what Manchester United should have done to win every match by six clear goals. We should have bought Tom, Dick and Harry, not to mention Hamish and Andy, Dewi and Dai and Pat and Mick. Then we should have had the entire staff immunized against injury so that we should have won the league by September, be well on the way to winning the Cup and the European Cup and be favourites for the Derby.'

Busby had proved he could use humour to put down the know-it-alls, but he was keenly aware that his team that season were yet to win away on their European travels. He had created a football club based on entertaining football but during the campaign had shown a rare pragmatism. If the year before, Jock Stein had been visibly unhappy with the manner of his side's semi-final 0–0 draw in Prague, Busby tried to see the bigger picture.

'Away from home we have to contain the opposition,' he said, but after the 1–0 win over his old enemy Real Madrid at Old Trafford in the first leg, Busby must have wondered if containment alone would see them through. Nobby Stiles would try anything. Visiting a Madrid church with Paddy Crerand on the morning of the match, Stiles stuffed 400 pesetas into the collection box. 'Nobby, that's bribery,' shouted his Scottish teammate.

Half-time at the Bernabéu, and it seemed Stiles' financial investment was yet to be banked. Madrid, cheered on by 125,000 fans and spurred on by their brilliant winger Amancio and their ageing maestro Gento, had taken a 3–1 lead. A fourth semi-final, and once again it looked like Busby was going to fall short. Feeling sick as he walked into the away dressing room, Busby found his players with their heads 'between their legs'. He sat down. His trilby remained on; a small plume of smoke drifted from his pipe. The players started to wonder what he would say.

After what seemed an age Busby stood up and laughed. 'What's going on?' he said. 'It's your greatest chance of reaching the European Cup final. You should be enjoying yourselves.' And then, perhaps forgetting his own pragmatic approach to European away games, he continued, 'You've been attacking teams all season, why aren't you doing it tonight?'

Busby's smile, belying the anxiety he had felt just minutes before, remained as he told his men the facts as he saw them. 'You're letting me down,' he said. 'You're letting the club down, and the supporters down. Go out and enjoy yourselves.' And then, like a maths teacher explaining a simple formula to his pupils, he said, 'By the way, it's 3–2 on aggregate. If you get an early goal, you'll win.'

United went out with renewed zeal. They were by no means suddenly on top, but Madrid's threat was being better dealt with, especially by Stiles. The injured Denis Law, sitting along-side Busby, noticed something as the second half took shape and leaned into his manager's ear. 'I'll tell you what,' he said. 'We've got a chance here. They've jacked it in.' David Sadler had been encouraged by a gung-ho Busby to get further forward, and when he scored after a Crerand free kick, the famous old stadium fell into a worried silence, only broken by the 3,000 United fans starting to share Law's enthusiasm. It was 3–3 on aggregate, and a play-off in Lisbon looked likely.

If Sadler had been given licence to roam, his defensive partner Bill Foulkes was being screamed at to be less adventurous. The screams fell on deaf ears. Foulkes had never been a footballer of finesse, but with time running out and his own ambition driving him on, he ignored orders and set off one last time. Best, tormenting his markers, took the ball to the byline and lofted an inviting cross high into the box.

Knowledgeable onlookers must have thought the invitation was about to fall into the wrong hands. Foulkes had continued past defenders and his teammates alike and suddenly was under the ball. Would he panic? Would he simply head the ball anywhere? With Law-like authority, the big man who had survived Munich settled himself and side-footed the ball into the Madrid netting. 'The sight of Big Bill,' Busby would later write, 'tearing down the pitch and then connecting with George Best's cross will be a memory I shall cherish to the end of my days.'

Manchester United were going to a European Cup final, to be played at Wembley against the Portuguese champions Benfica. Two weeks would pass between Madrid and the final, a fortnight in which some players might stew on the enormity of pending events. 'Winning the trophy had become an obsession,' said Crerand. 'Of course it had. For Matt and the club. Not only because of Munich but also because Matt had desperately wanted to win it from the start. There wasn't pressure though. There was expectation and emotion, but we were playing in London. That made it feel like a home fixture and that was massive for us. We felt confident.'

Busby was exuding calm authority. Benfica had been taken apart in Lisbon in the same competition two season earlier, and while he knew enough about the game of football to take nothing for granted, Busby felt that his club was ready to meet its destiny. Not that the Portuguese opposition would just lie down. Eusébio (or Yew-see-beeeo as Busby would pronounce it) would have to be looked after, but in Nobby Stiles Busby had a willing counter-puncher and one with recent experience. In the 1966 World Cup semi-final Stiles had had similar orders from Alf Ramsey but also underlined by the young Alan Ball. 'That Eusébio is a PR player,' he'd said to Stiles. 'He's always shaking hands, always clapping the other team. It's a con. He wants to be everybody's friend. Sort him out, wee man.' Surely Stiles could again?

Matters on the pitch were matched by matters of the heart. Busby, on the eve of his biggest night in football, understood that this moment was about much more than the here and now. The relatives of those who died in Munich were invited to travel down to London with the squad, and those players who had survived but moved on – Harry Gregg, Jackie Blanchflower, Johnny Berry and Albert Scanlon – were all there too. Then there was Denis Law. The cartilage in the striker's right knee had been a long-term problem, and he would miss the final. He was in hospital, devastated that he could only watch from afar. Before the party left for London, Busby came to visit him at St Joseph's in Manchester. It wasn't easy. Law later said he was traumatized by his bad luck, but Busby sat with him, his affection some relief to his player's pain and disappointment.

Busby had become more than a manager. In parts of Manchester there was now reverence at the very mention of his name. In 1968 Arthur Hopcraft wrote *The Football Man* and made this observation about the man and his people:

To watch Sir Matt Busby move about Manchester is to observe a public veneration. He is not merely popular, not merely respected for his flair as a manager. People treat Busby in the way that middle-aged priests of compassionate and sporty nature are often treated: the affection becomes rapidly more deferential as they get nearer to the man. Small boys rush noisily towards him, holding their picture books out for his autograph, and fall silent and shy once they get up close and he calls for less jostling and settles the word 'son' upon them like a blessing. Adults shout his name and grab his hand. They wave at him in his car.

And it wasn't just in Manchester. On the way from their Surrey hotel to Wembley the players started to notice, as the twin towers got closer, that the pavements were getting busier. 'We drove through the streets of London to get to Wembley, and there were thousands of well-wishers cheering us on,' Paddy Crerand remembered. 'That wouldn't happen today, but the country was so behind Matt. People wanted him to win it and wanted Manchester United to win it.' In the ground a huge banner shouted, SIR MATT FOR PRIME MINISTER, and such was the national affection now felt for this manager of a northern football club, Harold Wilson must have been grateful that Busby's ambitions lay only in being in charge of Manchester United's trophy cabinet.

Busby and his chairman, Louis Edwards, had flown to watch Benfica beat Juventus in their semi-final, and while the manager felt he knew lots about his opponents, their right back particularly caught his eye. Adolfo Calisto, he noted, was fine at tackling wingers, but should the ball be knocked past him, was slow to react. Young Johnny Aston on the left wing was duly informed.

And then there was the calming team talk. In 1956, the year Busby first took his team on a European adventure, his Babes had faced Bilbao and needed two second-half goals to progress. 'Don't panic, make your passes and keep your patience' had been the message. Now, nearly twelve years later, in the Wembley dressing room, the occasion might have been grander but the footballing advice was similar. The players were told to keep their concentration, that possession must be retained and passing spot on. Busby reiterated that Wembley might give them home advantage, but the pitch could, if you let it, be your enemy. 'It saps energy and plays havoc with morale,' he said. 'Wembley is a place for real football, and that means accurate passing that keeps the ball and preserves confidence and energy.'

The match itself started nervously, the players on both teams tentative and fumbling like shy teenagers on a first date. An overly officious referee didn't help matters. Geoffrey Green of *The Times* called the first half 'busy dullness', going on to observe that 'both teams were clearly out of humour not only with each other but with officialdom'. Busby kept calm though, reiterating the message at half-time that patience was this team's best ally. And then, in the fifty-third minute, Charlton leaped to glance in a Sadler cross, and there it was: the game had its opening goal. But United didn't sit back. Best kept moving, getting in behind the Benfica defence and forcing a good save from José Henrique.

Time ticked on. Denis Law, sitting up in his hospital bed in front of a small TV, was surrounded by a few pals, a case of McEwan's and some Manchester-United-supporting nurses. Was it going to happen? Was the dream about to be realized?

With ten minutes left, Law might have been forgiven for throwing cans, pals *and* nurses across his room when José Torres nodded down a centre, and the lithe Jaime Graça smashed the ball in from an angle. Stiles dropped to his knees. 'Woe, woe, woe,' wrote Busby years later. 'I could have wept.'

It might have got worse. With just minutes left, Eusébio shrugged off his Stiles-shaped shadow, and was clear through. Trusting power over finesse, the great man put enough through it to send the ball through the net and out of the stadium, but Alex Stepney in goal stood firm, and while he later would say the Mitre emblem on the ball remained tattooed to his torso, extra time was forced.

Busby, his insides surely churning, kept calm. He told his team to take back the initiative. Win back the midfield. Feed the forwards. His words were heeded. Two minutes in, Kidd flicked the ball on and Best, clean through, strolled around Henrique as if walking into one of his boutiques to score his thirty-second goal of the season. United were in front again. Kidd, celebrating his nineteenth birthday, then effectively ended the contest, before a brilliant Charlton right-foot flick gave the scoreline a slightly flattering look.

The whistle that Busby called 'the blast in what seemed millions of decibels hit me' then went, and it was pure joy. Within Manchester United, Munich might not have been talked about, but the new players such as Stepney made a beeline for Charlton, for Foulkes and of course for the manager. Club captain Charlton only had thoughts for Busby. *The old man.* He wondered if his manager was seeing images of Duncan Edwards on that pitch, powering towards goal, or maybe Eddie Coleman dropping his shoulder and losing his marker. Captain and manager but so much more than that, met and embraced. Ten years had passed since they had lost friends and colleagues. Ten years had passed since Busby had had to look into the eyes of the parents of lost sons.

He had told them all that he would look after their boys, but instead had brought them home to be buried. Winning the famous trophy, being the best in Europe, wouldn't heal the pain – it could never replace those who had gone – but it was won, and everyone who had died on that Munich runway was an integral part of that glory. They always would be. And so there they stood, holding each other, Charlton and Busby celebrating the glorious present while remembering a tragic past.

'After Wembley they had a banquet, and the relatives of those who lost their lives in Munich were there,' Crerand said. 'That was really emotional. Jackie [Blanchflower] and Johnny Berry, players who had had to quit playing after the crash. You met these people who were so pleased we'd won, but I couldn't help but think about them and those who had died, that great team and the fact that if Munich hadn't have happened I might not have been there. It was a very emotional and poignant evening.'

As the night rolled on, friends celebrated. Busby's obsession had been satisfied; his football club were the best around. Not bad at all with a microphone, the manager took to the stage and with the audience eating out of his hands he began to sing.

'I see trees of green, red roses too'. He was right. It was a wonderful world.

Chapter 14:

Letting Go

His players were past their best. Change though was going to be painful.

Bill Shankly had watched his friends and rivals both lift the European Cup. He'd hardly sat on his hands, even spending the sort of money that would once have made his heart thump: £96,000 for Tony Hately from Chelsea, £100,000 for Alun Evans, a young striker from Wolves. Shankly was open to improvement – he always had been – but wholesale change? That was harder to envisage, harder to implement.

Liverpool finished First Division runners-up in 1967, third in 1968, runners-up again in 1969. In that last season of a memorable decade, St John, Hunt, Lawrence, Thompson, were still close to ever-present, but those looking on could see something had changed.

Standing on the Kop in the late 1960s was future captain, Phil Thompson. Given fifty pence by his big brother to get to the match, Thompson was infatuated by the team and especially Roger Hunt. In March 1969, during a 1–0 defeat to Leicester in an FA Cup replay at Anfield, things weren't going well. 'Shanks substituted Roger and he wasn't happy,' said Thompson. 'Roger threw his shirt at the dugout and stormed down the tunnel. We'd never seen anything like it. On the Kop though for a while you could hear the voices: "Hunt is finished, his legs have gone." It was hard but they were right. Then though when he was off, the ball would go in the box and we'd all shout, "Hunt would have scored that!" A lot of the team was in the same boat. Shanks had hard decisions to make.'

While the game's big moments take place in front of hundreds of thousands and in footballing meccas from Buenos Aires to Wembley, the lesser events that lead to them can occur in more modest surroundings. The Northern Midweek League fixture at an empty Maine Road in 1931 when Matt Busby – a man with an eye on home and the end of any meaningful footballing career – filled in at right half changed the course of many lives. The reserve game one night at Celtic Park when Jimmy Gribben noticed a competent centre half playing for Albion Rovers inadvertently glued the name Jock Stein to the club he'd make great. And then there was Liverpool's FA Cup quarter-final at Vicarage Road on a late February afternoon in 1970.

It was there, following the team's 1–0 loss to Watford, that Shankly knew what had to be done. 'Pathetic,' wrote one reporter. Malcolm Allison, the new and flamboyant manager of Manchester City, had called Liverpool 'trial horses', living off yesterday's achievements and no longer relevant. Shankly would call him a 'maniac', but travelling north from Hertfordshire he was finding it hard to argue. 'After Watford I knew I had to do my job and change the team,' Shankly said. 'I had a duty to perform for myself, my family, Liverpool Football Club and the supporters . . . It had to be done, and if I didn't do it, I was shirking my obligations.'

One man had already felt the cold wind of change, someone whose arrival from Scotland had done so much to facilitate the warmer variety. Ian St John was left out of a fixture at Newcastle but only found out after bumping into local legend

Jackie Milburn. 'Bonnie lad, you're not playing' were words that rocked the striker, especially as they hadn't come from the man he saw as something close to a father.

When St John stormed into the dressing room, Shankly wasn't around. Perhaps expecting a scene he didn't want to experience, the manager had named the team quickly while St John was out of the room and headed up to the stands. It wasn't until the Monday morning that the two men had it out with a row unbefitting the great times they'd shared. St John argued he deserved better treatment; Shankly argued no player did but found it impossible to meet the forward's eye.

The very notion that the football team that he'd built would one day crumble pained Shankly. This team had taken, as if by osmosis, all the enthusiasm he had for football and lit up the stadiums of England and beyond. He loved it. But it was ageing, and while he knew that, the reality was hard to accept. The one player that embodied the team's spirit, the player whose arrival had convinced Shankly that this was a great project, was St John. To drop him, to look him in the eye and to say, 'That's that,' well, even a forthright man such as Shankly found it impossible. Picking a team without Ian St John was to admit that an era had ended.

'I knew what I had meant to him,' St John said, 'and what he had meant to me. I suppose the last few months had been like a marriage breaking down, when you have to wonder where has all the love gone.' Shankly and St John would remain distant for some time. The love would return, but all three managers had the sometimes necessary knack for coldness. In 1960 Matt Busby unceremoniously sold left-winger and Munich survivor Albert Scanlon to Second Division Newcastle United. 'Matt basically cut us off, and I thought he was getting rid of what was left from Munich.' Harsh words, and perhaps missing the point that when it comes to management there can be no sentiment.

All three men were willing to discard the niceties if it meant gaining an advantage for their clubs. Shankly was known to ignore a footballer who was laid up through injury. However big the player, if he was unable to contribute, he was temporarily meaningless. 'You didn't exist,' said Denis Law of injured players working with Shankly. The club and those who could affect its fortunes – fit players, staff, fans – were everything, and while replacing such loved names such as St John, Hunt, Thompson and Yeats will have tugged at Shankly's heart strings, his desire to bring glory to Liverpool FC far outweighed that sentiment. And so steps were taken.

John Toshack, an imposing Welsh forward, came in from Cardiff City for £111,000; Ray Clemence, a promising goalkeeper, was bought from Scunthorpe; Steve Heighway and Brian Hall, two forwards of differing styles, joined from university; Larry Lloyd came in to replace Ron Yeats; Alec Lindsey, a fine left back, transferred from Bury. Already there, signed in 1967 from Blackpool, was Emlyn Hughes, a young midfielder bristling with the sort of enthusiasm that Shankly craved from every human being. Like much of the country, Shankly had become aware of the young man's form at Bloomfield Road. Hughes had broken Peter Osgood's leg, and his combative approach to the game had drawn Shankly to the coastal resort.

Blackpool's recent sale of Alan Ball to Everton – 'At least you'll play near a great team,' Shankly had remarked – meant the Seasiders were in a position of power, but such was Shankly's passion for the player, he already regarded the young man as a Liverpool footballer. Hughes would be sitting at home eating his Sunday-morning fried breakfast when the phone rang. 'Hey

Emlyn, son,' Shankly would say, 'don't eat that stuff you've got on your plate there. I'll be signing you soon. I want you lean and hungry, son. Lean and hungry!'

Shankly's wooing of Hughes was intensifed by him spotting Matt Busby at a Blackpool match, the Liverpool manager more than aware of his adversary's keen eye for young talent. On that occasion, right there in the stadium Shankly offered Blackpool £25,000 but would eventually have to pay £65,000 for the services of a player who would become a favourite of the Liverpool fans.

Those supporters, deprived of a trophy for too long, could see progress and embraced Shankly's changes. In the spring of 1971 the FA Cup final was lost to Arsenal, but such was the faith the fans had for the manager and his youngsters that on the team's return they showed up in their thousands. It was a moment that reminded Shankly that football was nothing if there was no link to those who watched it. 'I have drummed it into my players, time and again,' Shankly said over a microphone to the crowd, 'that they are privileged to play for you.' The crowd cheered. And then he continued: 'If they didn't believe me . . . they believe me now.' Standing behind him were his players, listening as intently as his adoring public.

One of them was Phil Thompson. 'It was presidential,' he recalled. 'He opened his arms up, like parting the seas. He was building something new, and that speech was, even after a defeat, a call to arms if you like. We all looked solemn because we'd lost, but then as we listened, and as he whipped the people up into a frenzy, telling them that we as players should be proud to play for you, the place went crazy and we fully believed every word and that we were on the verge of something special.'

Shankly would also look within the club, sometimes with hilarious results. He had watched one kid with interest – only seventeen years old but talented, perhaps a replacement one day for Ian Callaghan. There was one thing though: he was skinny, too slight, no match for hungry left backs willing and able to leave their mark. Wherever he went, Shankly had a knack for befriending butchers. During the war, while in the RAF and concerned with his own health, a nudge and a wink in the right direction could gain him a contraband sirloin. In peacetime – if there was ever such a thing with the well-being of Liverpool Football Club constantly on the line – such friendships were equally as helpful. Soon the young footballer had instructions to visit the local abattoir every week to pick up the meat that Shankly believed would turn potential into brilliance.

Time passed. The young winger ate his steak every day for six months. Shankly marvelled at the results. 'Jesus Christ,' he gasped. 'You're like physical poetry.'

The young footballer smiled but had some news. 'Boss, I need to have a week off. I'm getting married.'

'Getting married?' Shankly said, slightly surprised.

'Yes, I have to,' the boy said. 'I got my girlfriend pregnant.'

There was a pause.

'Bob, Rueben, Joe, get in here,' Shankly shouted. 'We've created a monster!'

While Bill Shankly was rallying the troops and about to unleash his second great team, Matt Busby's desire to build a fourth had gone. The euphoria of Wembley would always be with him, but as the following season took shape, he began to think of change. He called himself the 'managing manager of Manchester United', a role that asked for so much more than merely coaching and picking a team. In the May of 1969 he would turn sixty, and thoughts – as they had so often with Busby – turned to promoting youth.

It was after a 2–1 defeat at Leeds, a club which had come to embody the new challenges being set in the top flight, that Busby announced his plans. 'United is no longer a football club,' he said; 'it's an institution. I feel the demands are beyond one human being.' That was the crux. Busby planned to remain in the role of general manager, while someone else dealt with team affairs.

Under Busby the team had followed Celtic into the two-leg Intercontinental Cup match against South American opposition, and like their Scottish counterparts experienced the games as a battle rather than a sport. Celtic had faced South American champions Racing Club of Buenos Aires. They won 2–1 at home, but were defeated 2–1 in Argentina before a play-off in Uruguay that Celtic lost 1–0. All three games had been littered with fouls. Stein and his team knew about and embraced the physical side of the game – letting your opponent know you were interested was as much a part of football as cleaning your boots – but this was different.

'I loved the physical side of a football match,' said Celtic's Bertie Auld. 'I'd played in England and in Scotland, and my God, you had to be tough, but that game against the Argentines, that wasn't right. They would spit in the back of your head, they were punching us on the back of our heads. After the first game, Bob Kelly our chairman came to Jock and said, "John, if they are so desperate to win this, give it to them. Let's not travel." Jock said no, we'd beat them over there, so we went. But Jock hated all that. To him football was about entertaining the people, and those games left a bad taste in his mouth.'

On their return, Stein vowed never to take a team to South America again, and in 1968 advised Busby not to take his United team to face Estudiantes, again in Argentina. If Stein's competitive streak had been too wide to listen to his chairman a year earlier, Busby's would never allow him to miss out on a crack at a world title, however unofficial it might be. Busby believed his stature within the game might ease tensions, that diplomacy might encourage a better game of football, so in Argentina he and his players attended a reception at which the teams could mingle and get to know each other. Estudiantes didn't turn up. The tone was set.

The Argentines won the game on home soil 1–0, but it was the headbutts and the spitting and kicking that were talked about. Things didn't change back at Old Trafford. George Best saw red in a 1–1 draw, and once again Argentina had won football's world club championship amid disgusting scenes. Meanwhile, Busby, by now a knight of the realm, was looking up at most of the league. United's form was poor, their holy trinity only sporadically brilliant, the only consistency coming from Best's by-now-routine social antics in a city now used to seeing him welcoming the sunrise. However, Law chipped in a few goals, and John Ashton returned from injury to bolster results.

A run to the European Cup semi-final fired the imagination for a perfect send-off, but defeat at the hands of AC Milan scuppered those dreams. Instead a 3–2 win at Old Trafford over Leicester that lifted United to eleventh in the table was the modest prelude to Busby's (initial) farewell. The crowd clapped; Busby returned the applause and with very little fuss disappeared into the tunnel. He had work to do: he needed to pick a successor. Big names had been mooted, but Busby had looked within. Perhaps influenced by Manchester City's success with Joe Mercer and Malcolm Allison, he went for Wilf McGuinness, a promising coach who had impressed him with the club's and England's youngsters. Only thirty-one, some had concerns about how he'd manage his own contemporaries.

On the eve of the announcement, new head coach McGuinness had been told to wear a tie. It was advice that a boy might receive from a father, but it was the last help the new man would receive for a while, such was the awkwardness of the situation. McGuinness felt that Busby, fearing he'd be interfering, wasn't forthcoming with help, while the new man, for fear of looking weak, didn't seek it out.

'Matt had been a great, great manager and was still a great man,' McGuinness would say. 'He couldn't be anything but the Boss. I should have gone to him more.' Managing the club's greats wasn't going to be easy, and even when he did make big decisions, eyebrows were raised. Dropping the popular Alex Stepney for Jimmy Rimmer in goal was particularly badly received. The new man had ideas. He wanted to buy youngsters such as Colin Todd, Mick Mills and Malcolm Macdonald. Instead he got an unfit Ian Ure, a player he never wanted but an addition he couldn't complain about; Matt Busby, after all, had brokered the deal. Busby's role was hard to fathom. Press would phone McGuinness and ask about his team, and the coach would refer them to Busby, who would say, 'I don't know – you'll have to speak to Wilf about team affairs.' Amid the transition, results continued to suffer.

They reached the 1970 FA Cup semi-final and the League Cup semi-final the following season but league form remained poor, and on Boxing Day 1970 McGuinness picked his last team for the 4–4 draw against Derby and their new charismatic manager Brian Clough. Busby returned as team manager but it wasn't a mantle he wanted for long. This time he would look further from home for a replacement.

In the spring of 1971 Busby and Jock Stein went to Anfield to see their old pal Bill lose a Fairs Cup semi-final to Leeds, and after the game agreed to meet on the East Lancs Road, where the talk was of Stein taking the Manchester United job. Paddy Crerand had sown the seed in Busby's mind and the player then went to Stein to sound him out. The two men sat in Busby's Mercedes and spoke frankly. Busby, always loyal, was adamant that much of United's coaching staff must keep their jobs. Stein must have had doubts about this demand, but as the European Cup winners shook hands in the lay-by that night, Busby was sure he had secured a coup.

'Matt always said they had an agreement after that last meeting,' said Crerand.

But then the following day he came to me, and I could see he wasn't happy. 'Your mate, Jock,' he said. 'Some friend he is.'

'What's he done?' I asked.

'He's turned us down. Can you believe that? He's said no to the job.'

Matt was bitter about that. He thought Jock had used the situation to strengthen his position at Celtic and maybe even get more money out of them.

Stein would deny that. It was a chat with his wife, coupled with his deep-rooted affection for the club at which he worked, that decided him against going south. 'I like being manager of Celtic,' he had said when asked about moving elsewhere. 'I like the people, I like the players, the directors are very good, but most importantly I like the people who support us.' Moreover, he had too many ambitions still to fulfil with Celtic, even though they seemed to have peaked in 1967, not just in the sunshine of Lisbon but days later when they played Real Madrid at the Bernabéu for Alfredo Di Stéfano's testimonial.

After Lisbon the Italian paper *Corriere della Serra* declared that the European Cup had gone to 'a new team of the soccer aristocracy', and being invited to participate in such an occasion spoke volumes for Celtic and Stein's place in the game, but it was their performance that night that showed just how brilliant the team had become. It was a friendly but only in name. Bertie Auld had been told by Stein to watch out for the Madrid play-maker Amancio. 'The big man came to me and said, "You watch out for him, he likes to leave a foot in." As ever, he was right. Amancio did leave a foot in on me, but I left a right hook in on him. We were both sent off. Walking off the pitch, I shouted at him, "Hey pal, your team are going to miss you, more than mine will miss me."'

Auld, like the rest of the team, gasped at how brilliant Jimmy Johnstone was, with a performance Auld still relishes as the greatest individual display he's ever seen. 'I was glad to have been sent off,' Auld said. 'I sat back and watched Jinky destroy the Spanish team. Oh he was brilliant. You can talk about Messi and Ronaldo today, but I've never seen anything like the wee man that night. Jock enjoyed it too.'

The Lisbon Lions returned to dominate the Scottish game, winning a third title in succession in 1968, the treble in 1969 and a fifth title in 1970, a year in which they reached another European Cup final. The semi-final pitted them against Leeds United – hyped as the 'Battle of Britain' by an eager press and public. 'The hype was justified,' said Auld with relish.

Those games were great. Packed stands, two great teams, great players getting stuck into each other. Jock loved it. He loved these big occasions. It was what he had been brought up watching as a boy, and you could see how excited he was, and how used to the big occasion we'd all become.

We beat Leeds at Hampden, but big Jackie Charlton was in the press saying they'd batter us in England. They'd been dirty, which Leeds could be, but we matched them and outplayed them. I wore my fedora hat that night in Yorkshire – that raised a few eyebrows – but I liked to smoke my cigars under that hat.

That night Auld savoured his Havanas after a 1–0 win and the prospect of another European Cup winner's medal. Holland's Feyenoord would be the opponents in Milan, but if the team's relaxed attitude in Lisbon had helped them win it in 1967, this time observers thought it bordered on slacking. The game was lost 2–1. People wondered if Stein had underestimated his opponents. The players would have none of that, arguing that they simply hadn't performed, but what was obvious was this was a massive opportunity lost. No matter; the ambition that had burned in Stein even in the days he worked the pits was as intense as ever, and by now a new crop of players was emerging to keep the man's passion alight.

Stein had always been interested in the club's youth. The lions had been under his charge as mere cubs, and with players such as Danny McGrain, David Hay, Kenny Dalglish and Lou Macari playing with style and vigour in the reserves, it wasn't long before they got their chance in the first team. 'Nobody would say to you, you were doing well in the reserves,' said Macari, a striker of promise. 'I think they feared you might change your attitude if they praised you. You'd be asked to look after the first team's kit, look after the skips, carry the bags, lay out the kit. That was a wee indication from Jock that you were doing quite well.'

Macari would do more than quite well. He was an eager scorer, a direct runner who relished taking defenders on. Stein liked him. Stein would watch a young player, see they were good at something and then make them brilliant at it.

'The key was being told what you are good at and doing it,' Macari said. 'I remember players trying something different. If you did something you were crap at, you were told. If you were a bad passer and then you sprayed the ball from one side of the pitch to another . . . even if that pass found its target, Jock would rip your head off.'

Supported by players whose kits he used to care for, Macari settled straight in, and his goals started to get noticed. Stein, as ever, took precautions to stop a young head swelling. 'One day I scored a hat-trick, and after the game this press guy came over to me to chat and Jock was on him. The big man barked at this poor wee journalist, grabbing him by the lapels and said, "If you write anything positive about him, you'll never be allowed in Celtic Park again!" It was to keep my feet on the ground. There I am thinking I'm this and that, and Jock is telling this poor wee guy to not write about it.'

Praise was a rare commodity for footballers under Stein but so were pay rises. By 1973 Macari had got into the Scottish team and heard from those who had ventured south of the sort of money on offer down there. Macari was getting married; his father had died and he was looking after his mum. The fifty-five pounds a week he was getting wasn't enough, and he simply told his manager he was off.

Soon he was in a car with Sean Fallon and heading south. 'I had no idea where I was going,' Macari said.

Sean wouldn't tell me. We passed Carlisle. Good. We passed Blackpool. Good. My geography was crap so I had no idea where it might be, but eventually we were in Liverpool. At Anfield.

I met Shankly, who was brilliant. He said he had always wanted to sign me, that he and Jock were great pals and that I'd do great in his new team. Brilliant. Liverpool were playing that night so I took my seat in the directors' box and Paddy Crerand sat next to me.

'What are you doing here, wee man?' he said. Paddy was by now the assistant manager at United and so when I tell him I'm signing for Shanks, he says, 'No you're not. Tell Bill you'll think about it, but you're joining me at Old Trafford.'

That was the most uncomfortable ninety minutes I've spent because even though I'd agreed with Bill, I knew I was going to Manchester United. I'd grown up with the names Law, Best, Charlton, and Matt Busby of course. Paddy can talk you into most things but I knew straight away I was going there.

When asked by the press how he felt about missing out, Shankly simply said, 'I only wanted him for the reserves anyway.' His cockiness was not misplaced. By early 1973 the name Manchester United still had pull, but Shankly's new Liverpool were on their way to another championship. The team had an energy that on its day even the great sides in the country couldn't live with. Those players who had been brilliantly scouted and patiently settled in to the club were now thriving, and among them was Shankly's jewel, Kevin Keegan.

Shankly's old boss at Huddersfield Andy Beattie scouted

for Liverpool and had alerted them to an eighteen-year-old at Scunthorpe. Every one of the coaching staff at Anfield went to have a look at Keegan. Some thought maybe he lacked the courage for First Division football, but Bob Paisley told his manager to make it happen. Keegan, the son of a miner, and clearly in possession of a work ethic befitting his father's trade, was the very embodiment of the way Shankly saw football and with Paisley's endorsement, Liverpool's manager would act fast.

A £33,000 bid was accepted. 'Robbery with violence' Shankly called it. Keegan was invited to the 1971 FA Cup final and took defeat to Arsenal harder than some of the players involved. Shankly saw the dismay in this raw young man and thought, *He probably thinks if he had been playing we would have won – and we would have!* Keegan was straight into the first team, a rarity at Anfield for a lower-league prospect, but scored within twelve minutes and started a passionate six-year love affair with the club.

The team, Keegan's effervescence bubbling away at its core, was a mixture of sublime movement and pragmatic comradeship. Steve Heighway, a brilliant winger, gave it width, but early in his career, having lost possession that led to a goal, Shankly was on to him for not helping his fullback. 'If you're neighbour's house was on fire, wouldn't you grab a bucket and try to help put it out?' he asked.

'When you ask me a sensible question, I'll give you a sensible answer,' replied the graduate.

The dressing room winced. 'You might have letters after your name,' skipper Tommy Smith said, 'but you're a stupid bastard.'

Heighway learned quickly, and that team ethic coupled with brilliant individuals won Liverpool the 1972/3 championship. The same season at last brought a European trophy with the Uefa Cup won after a 3–2 aggregate win over Borussia Mönchengladbach. Shankly's new team were flying, and continental success brought a continental style. Going into the following season, Shankly's emphasis was very much on keeping the ball, with everyone including Ray Clemence expected to be at ease with the ball at his feet.

'It wasn't all about rhetoric with Shanks,' said Phil Thompson.

He drummed into us to play from the back. Larry Lloyd had got injured, and Shanks threw me, a defensive midfielder, into centre back alongside another midfielder, Emlyn Hughes. You normally had a commanding centre back with a ball player next to him, but now Shanks had two ball players.

That was the clue to the type of football that Shanks had us playing. It was so patient. We'd play a high line but Clem would sweep behind us, get the ball, give it to us, we'd feed the fullbacks and it would go from there. Later that summer, the world thought the Dutch had started Total Football, but they learned from Shankly!

If it is his way with words that has kept Shankly's legend alive, it is also important to note the tactical nous he could also call upon. The team that reached the 1974 FA Cup final underlined a footballing mind every bit as sharp as his tongue. In the run-up to Wembley, Newcastle played the role of confident would-be victors. Malcolm Macdonald told the press how he'd be too much in the air for Liverpool's two centre backs, but Shankly, at the top of his profession, kept his cool. In a TV interview – Shankly quickly mastered the medium – he said that his Newcastle counterpart Joe Harvey 'looked terrified'. 'Go and drop hand grenades all over the pitch,' he told Keegan.

Keegan obliged, and Newcastle's confidence ebbed away with each Liverpool pass. Death by possession, people called it. Liverpool's new style and patient control of the game followed by sudden and thrilling thrusts at goal was too much for their opponents, and the 3–0 scoreline hardly did justice to the cruelty inflicted by the victors upon the defeated. 'We were Barcelona with attitude,' Thompson remarked. The last goal in particular, a sweeping move that touched the boot of every player in the team, saw Keegan drop his final grenade from two yards out.

Shankly sat on the sidelines, his hands moving like those of a puppet master as he watched his team carry out his methods with clinical precision. Could it get better than this? Maybe not. The cup won, he ordered his players to pay tribute to the Newcastle fans as well as their own, and as he walked away from the celebrations in reflective mood, two Liverpool supporters ran on and dropped to their knees at his feet. 'Give the shoes a quick polish, lads,' Shankly joked almost apologetically.

Outside the dressing room he saw a fan in a wheelchair. He went over to him, shook his hand and helped him inside to meet the players. With hindsight there was something different about Shankly that afternoon: even more emphasis was put on football being for the people. 'I'm a people's man, a socialist,' he said in an interview. 'I'm sorry I couldn't get among them and speak to them. I'm glad that we worked religiously and that we didn't cheat them and that we have something to take back to them tomorrow.'

Liverpudlians had their cup, they had their manager, and they had a team bursting with brilliance destined only for even greater things, but a little over two months later television's Tony Wilson was on the streets of Liverpool gathering opinions about the shocking press conference he had just come from. 'Bill Shankly's retired,' he told the locals.

A teenage boy with a feathered haircut, fashionable at the time, looked aghast. His mouth hung open. 'You're having me on, aren't ya?'

Shankly was finished.

Chapter 15:

The Kings Are Dead

May 1967 and Celtic have a game to prepare for. Lisbon might be on every Celt's mind, but Jock Stein has his eye on other club matters. Sean Fallon, despite it being the night of his wedding anniversary, is in a house in Milton, Glasgow, next to Rangers' training ground. At Stein's behest, he sits talking to a father, while a boy sits quietly in the corner.

That boy is Kenny Dalglish. Stein had seen this slight, blond midfielder playing for Glasgow United against Celtic's youngsters at his training ground, and a simple 'I like the number 4' was enough for Fallon to visit the Dalglish home to meet the family – Protestants and Rangers fans – in order to persuade them Celtic Park was the place for their son.

Fallon and Dalglish Senior simply talked football while young Kenny sat enthralled before it was agreed that, yes, he would sign provisional forms at Celtic. The boy's mother walked into the room. 'Can I show you around the house?' she said proudly to her guest.

The boy suddenly panicked. His room was covered in Rangers posters. He ran upstairs and started to pull pictures of Jim Baxter and Ian McMillan down from the walls. What if Fallon saw them? What if it got back to Stein? Dalglish needn't have worried. Unlike Rangers, Celtic had no policy preventing them signing a player for reasons other than talent, and Stein's own disdain for bigotry and sectarianism had been in his bones from his days on the often angry streets of Burnbank.

As with Busby and Shankly, the childhood had shaped the man. Busby, the Great War asking so much of him as a fatherless boy, always showed faith in the capabilities of youth, while Shankly's view of football as belonging to the masses stemmed from watching the men of Glenbuck returning from their dark work, bathing in the light and arguing over Saturday's match. Stein may have locked away the memory of a supposed friend walking out of his mother's house when he signed for Celtic, but his sole aim in his working life was to make Celtic the best team, not only in Glasgow, not only in Scotland but in Europe too, and any player who could make that happen would be signed, no matter what school or church he went to.

Dalglish actually wanted to attend the local Catholic school because they had laid a new gravel football pitch. Such enthusiasm for the game, mirroring his own, would do Stein just fine. So Dalglish joined the group of young players – known as the Quality Street Gang – that would eventually rattle the lions' first-team cage.

While Busby had been accused of misplaced loyalty to the players and staff who had helped him win the European Cup, and Shankly had faced the same accusations when it came to his team of the 1960s, Stein, it was said, broke up his great team too soon – a point of view understandably taken by the players who were dropped. Like Shankly with Ian St John, when charged with closing the door on a player, Stein preferred an awkward slam rather than a sentimental goodbye. In the early years of the 1970s Bertie Auld left for Hibernian, John Clark and Stevie Chalmers for Morton, John Hughes and Willie Wallace for Crystal Palace, and Tommy Gemmell for Nottingham Forest.

Auld would go on to manage and would know the complexities of the manager–player relationship, but he admits that the abruptness with which Stein finished his Celtic career came as a shock. 'I have nothing but love for the Boss,' he says, 'but yes, most of us were on the end of sudden departures with very little said.'

Busby would scoff at talk of him being too loyal. 'Loyalty is, I think, being human,' he'd write. 'I should have been less than human had I not been concerned about Manchester United's loyal servants.' But whether it was allowing players to stay too long or cutting them adrift with hardly a word, it seemed that all three managers struggled to deal with any sort of ending.

For now, Stein only had thoughts for his club's future, and the group of young players he had assembled was more than good enough. Dalglish joined the likes of Danny McGrain, David Hay and Lou Macari in making the step up. The always forward-thinking Stein had wanted his reserves to play in Scotland's second tier and such was his belief in them was adamant they'd have won it. Even though the youngsters were taking the dressing-room pegs from so many club legends, the old guard who remained were nothing but helpful.

'Jock and his players had built a dressing room with such warmth and camaraderie that it was easy for us youngsters to step into it,' said Macari. 'I remember walking in, sitting in the corner, saying nothing, getting into my kit, playing, coming back and getting dressed and still saying nothing, but the senior players were so supportive and you soon came out of your shell. We didn't have big ambitions to match the lions; we were just kids and we just wanted to get out there and play.'

That suited Stein. The new players offered a blank canvas for his skills, and in the case of Kenny Dalglish he could concentrate on getting the best from an already wonderful prospect. 'Big Jock was the most important figure in my football education,' Dalglish wrote in his autobiography. 'He was a visionary. He had the idea of putting number 9 on my back and then withdrawing me into the middle of the pitch. My role was to take the ball from the back four and link with the front two.'

For years to come Dalglish's brilliance would indeed be in his ability to not only score goals, but to create space by dropping into midfield pockets. Stein's ever-keen eye for where his players' strengths lay saw his new Celtic team of the 1970s continue to win honour after honour.

At Old Trafford such glorious continuity was a faraway memory. United's woeful form in the 1970/1 season picked up under Busby's renewed stewardship, but they were nowhere near challenging. The final game of the season, Busby's last ever in charge of the team, was a 4–3 win at Manchester City, with George Best at his finest. This was now a rarity. The City defenders chased him around Maine Road like the red-top reporters who chased him around Manchester's bars.

Depending on how you looked at it, the troubled Irishman's glittering performance that day could be seen as either an apology to a manager to whom he'd recently given so much cause for worry, or thanks to the patient man who had nurtured his incredible talents. Best scored twice, and the fact that the other names on the scoresheet that day were Charlton and Law gave the match added poignancy. Bobby Charlton left Maine Road with nothing but admiration for Busby. 'I had the satisfaction of feeling that, on his last day as the manager of Manchester United, Matt Busby had almost certainly been reminded of what his work would always represent most strikingly: a willingness to nourish talented players, to give them freedom to express all their ability.'

The question now was, could the new manager – Frank O'Farrell, a likeable Irishman who had done well at Leicester – foster a similarly nourishing environment. On his first day what he found was Busby in the manager's office. Busby was now on the board, but O'Farrell, unlike McGuinness, who had taken Jimmy Murphy's office, insisted the office was his, and as Busby had assured the new man that he was in complete control of team affairs, it was vacated. It was an end of a glorious era.

O'Farrell wouldn't be able to get too comfortable at his new desk. This was a troubled club, and managing brilliant but ageing legends loyal to their old manager – who happened still to be a huge presence – was always going to be a challenge, although Busby showed nothing but contempt when it was suggested that his remaining at the club somehow hindered progress. Form though was poor. Best, still able to show flashes of genius, was very much a problem, and his presence at training often regarded as a bonus. Law and Charlton were prone to injury and fading, but when the latter was dropped eyebrows were still raised. None any higher than Busby's, who, despite promising O'Farrell total control, told the new man he had been wrong to do so.

O'Farrell also discovered that Best had had a meeting at Busby's home that he was unaware of, and the feeling of those outside looking in was that this was a football club being steered in two different directions and so going nowhere.

Derby won the title in 1971/2, and their brash young manager Brian Clough, who had wanted the United job after McGuinness, taunted Busby. The calm old man wouldn't be drawn. Clough's cockiness didn't sit easily with Busby, and there were no regrets about not welcoming him to Old Trafford.

Halfway through the following season though, the word relegation was floating around the stadium like some mischievous will-o'-the-wisp, and O'Farrell's job was on the line. David Meek of the *Evening News* wrote a piece asking United to show patience, saying that the manager deserved more than the eighteen months he'd had. 'The club didn't like it,' Meek told Patrick Barclay in his biography of Busby. 'Matt might have moved aside as manager but he was the power behind the throne. In fact, he was the throne itself. And I think the decision to sack Frank had already been made when my piece came out.'

O'Farrell was replaced by Tommy Docherty, who had done fine managerial jobs at Chelsea and Scotland. Relegation was staved off – for now – and new signings made. Lou Macari's capture from under the nose of Liverpool suggested the new man had some pull, but while Docherty and his assistant Paddy Crerand had worked hard to persuade the young striker to join United, the aura of the club and of that of Busby still had much to do with it.

'Of course Matt's presence at the club added to the allure,' said Macari. 'It was like going to Hollywood and seeing Cary Grant strolling around. I couldn't tell you if the Doc struggled with it, but I doubt it. The thing was, Matt was far too clever to interfere, too streetwise to do anything that would hinder progress. He never got in the way of training, and from what I could see, was there to offer advice if needed.'

Paddy Crerand agreed. 'We were delighted to have Matt there. Who wouldn't be? He was club president really and he had to be, he *was* Manchester United. It was no problem for us at all, and anyone who says it was is a liar.'

Those close to the situation might have known the truth about Busby's role at Manchester United, but at Anfield things turned out differently. By the autumn of 1974, with United by now relegated, Liverpool were facing their own dilemma. After the shock waves of Shankly's unexplained (many reasons were given but none ever confirmed) retirement had subsided, the board had looked to the old manager's quiet lieutenant Bob Paisley. By promoting from within, the club was hoping to avoid any seismic change, but very soon it became obvious to all that maybe things hadn't changed enough. Phil Thompson recalled:

> We'd turn up for training and there was Shanks' car, and there was Shanks, in his shorts. "Mornin', lads,' he'd say to us. 'Let's get going.' I was young and at first it wasn't a problem. It felt familiar. 'Mornin', Boss,' we'd say. Yeah, it became awkward but what else could we call him?
>
> In time I started to feel very uncomfortable. You'd spend time wondering how the situation was going to develop. We hadn't started well under Bob, and things got a bit fraught. We were still a very good team but there was this real sense of uncertainty. I was too young to ask, so I don't know who said what, but one day Shanks wasn't there.

However inaccurate their understanding of what had happened down the East Lancs Road, Liverpool were worried that their fortunes could nosedive like United's. The board backed Paisley, who reluctantly took Shankly to one side and said his presence at Melwood was 'embarrassing' the new man and confusing the players. He was of course welcome to the place he had built, but it needed to be done differently – Paisley suggested Shankly do some scouting for him – but the talk convinced the former manager that he simply was no longer wanted.

He was wrong, but the fact that the club didn't even give him his own seat at the ground (Busby had one with his name engraved upon it) was a shocking misjudgement. Shankly felt cut adrift and wondering where he might get his football fix from. He would still put on his red tracksuit of a morning; and the image of him in red playing games against Everton's youngsters decked in blue is both amusing and melancholy.

In November 1974 Shankly began consulting for Tranmere Rovers' new manager Ron Yeats. Results were mixed, and after about six weeks Yeats' assistant John King asked Shankly for his thoughts. 'You're making a fundamental error,' he said.

'What's that?' asked King.

'You're changing at Bromborough; you should be changing at Prenton Park.'

It was a strange observation, but, a stickler for detail, Shankly had always had his Liverpool teams change at Anfield before travelling to Melwood. He suggested Tranmere do the same and travel together to their Bromborough training ground. For a while results picked up.

On one occasion, sitting on the bench next to Yeats, he asked the manager, 'Ron, who's your slow right-winger?'

'That's Alan Duffey. He's our PFA union rep.'

'Christ!' yelled Shankly. 'Why are you paying him if he's on strike?'

Still sharp of tongue, Shankly did some media work, co-commentating on Liverpool's further triumphs in Europe, but the lack of day-to-day work within the game left a void he was struggling to fill. To Shankly football was about people, and by being in it he had been able to surround himself with what he saw as the best of them. 'When I did my cartilage after he retired he would be on the phone to me,' said Thompson. '"Jesus Christ, you'll be back better than ever, son. You're a star, you're going to be a great player." Even though he'd been my manager, I was still thinking, *Bill Shankly is on the phone in my house!*'

Having won the 1972/3 Championship, Liverpool's players did a lap of honour, but that day it was Shankly, in the hearts and minds of the supporters more than a manager, who was the object of most of the love. At the Kop end scarves fell from the terraces like ticker-tape, but when Shankly spotted a policeman kicking one away, he was on to him. 'What do you think you're doing?' he rasped. 'That's someone's life.'

All three managers understood the connection between those who came to watch football and those they paid to see. Matt Busby's thoughts were always on entertaining the people. He feared for the game in the 1970s, an era that he thought had lost its ability to smile. Stein too was driven to succeed by the hordes in green and white, who were as much a part of Celtic Park as the players and staff.

'He had them training with us,' Bertie Auld said. 'The fans, he'd invite them in, and at times the big man would say, "Come on lads, join in." And they would. There was this one guy who would come along in his overcoat and suede shoes and get stuck in. It was great. We were a huge part of what happened on those terraces, of course we were, but they, them fans with their songs were a big part of us. Jock never let us forget that.'

After occasions such as that in 1956 when Busby famously said that Old Trafford was his heaven, supporters can't be blamed for regarding successful managers as superhuman. In his heyday Shankly certainly had Liverpoool supporters almost believing he could turn water into wine. Brian Clough, having left Leeds United in 1974, when asked by David Frost who in football management he most respected, turned to Shankly. 'He's a one off,' Clough said. 'They'll never be another like Shanks. He was a one off, and [Clough pointed up] the last guy that was one off was the one that rules us all.'

Not that Shankly was comfortable with such comparisons. He was a man *of* the people, not *above* them. He would often visit Alder Hey children's hospital, visits he would cherish but that left him feeling drained and often upset. On one occasion he was asked by a local journalist to visit a particularly sick child. He would of course, but because all he could do was be there, he remarked, 'I'm no god. I'm no miracle worker.'

In the summer of 1975 Jock Stein needed a miracle. Lying in a hospital bed, he was fighting for his life. Like most battles he took on, Stein won, but such was the severity of the injuries he had sustained in a car crash driving home from the airport after a holiday in Spain, he effectively missed the whole of the coming season. Discharged in August 1975, Stein's need for continued treatment saw Sean Fallon step in, but the team lacked its rudder. Rangers had stopped Celtic reaching their goal of ten consecutive titles the season before, and in Stein's absence held on to the championship.

The following season Stein had to convince a changing Celtic board that he was fit enough and strong enough to step back in. His ankle, that age-old problem from his playing days, would cause him further pain, but with Billy McNeill leaving to start his own managerial career, the sight of Kenny Dalglish wearing the captain's armband, scoring and eventually lifting the title, Stein's tenth, must have worked wonders.

The smiles though were about to run out. Dalglish wanted away. Stein was devastated. Not just because he was losing a footballer he had educated and guided to the very top of the game, but because Dalglish was desperate to test himself at the business end of the European Cup – an indication to Stein that while he had been the first to make British European

Cup dreams a reality, realistically he could no longer hope to repeat the feat.

The 1977/8 season brought more frowns. Post-Dalglish performances on the pitch were dreary and relations with the chairman, now Desmond White, cool. Stein no longer had the allies of his past at the club and changes were being demanded. It says a lot for the insecurity felt by even the best managers that because of a barren year Stein, still a relatively young man, was being forced out. Would the move be a sideways one or complete separation?

Stein made suggestions for a successor and a role for himself that involved developing young players, but the club had other ideas. 'You'll never guess what they want me to do,' Stein said to his family. 'They want me to sell pools tickets.' Stein had been offered a place on the board, but his role would be that of a fundraiser. Stein knew the importance of raising money for the team but he couldn't and wouldn't accept the role, so instead, perhaps on the rebound, he took the manager's job at the now ailing Leeds United.

Stein had long been admired in England – Busby hadn't been the only man wanting him for a manager – but he had been always too settled to move on. John Clark would travel to England with Stein on scouting trips and was always struck by how officials at English clubs were almost in awe of him, and it wasn't just football that paid its respects. Clark remembered:

> We were driving to see Liverpool, and this road in the city was closed off with cones. Jock wasn't having it. He gets out the car and moved the cones and started to drive. Suddenly there's blue lights behind us and a big plain-clothed inspector is holding out his hand in front to stop us. Jock wound down the window, and the big inspector

has his head in the car, takes a look and says, 'Jock Stein, how are you getting on?'

'I'm good, thanks, just trying to get to Anfield.'

The inspector turns to his officer and says, 'Please escort Mr Stein to Anfield.'

Anyone else would have been escorted to jail.

English respect might have pleased Stein, but the job at Leeds, a club a world away from its recent glorious past, was immediately not right. In 1978, just two months after taking the job at Elland Road, Stein was heading home. The national team job was once again his. It seemed the perfect fit.

Stein had been too busy deriding the offer made to him by the Celtic board during the summer to pay too much attention to his predecessor's efforts at the World Cup in Argentina, but those who felt humiliated by the efforts of Ally McLeod's team were more than pleased to have Stein's reassuring presence in charge.

Bill Shankly, unlike Busby and Stein, never managed Scotland, but he was always quick to fight his country's corner. 'If Scotland went to war, I'd be the first to sign up,' he once said, and when asked about the Scottish squad going to Argentina in 1978, he declared that if they were to compete in the English First Division, 'It would be over by Christmas.'

In the summer of 1981 Shankly took a phone call from Paddy Crerand. 'We were organizing a dinner for Matt, and I called Bill to invite him,' Crerand recalled.

Matt wanted special people at this dinner, and the first he mentioned was Bill Shankly. Bill was well up for it and asked what date.

'Monday the thirtieth November, Bill' I said.

We talked a bit more and Bill asks for the date again.

'Thirtieth November, Bill,' I said.

We chat a bit more and again he brings the date up. 'That date,' he says.

'The thirtieth November, Bill?' I say. 'What about it?'

There's a pause. He then starts to tell me off. 'Pat, have you forgot about the thirtieth November?'

'What?' I say.

'That's the day of the patron saint of Scotland. That's St Andrew's Day!' Oh he gave me such a bollocking.

Shankly accepted the invitation, but that night his chair remained empty. A month before Busby's dinner, a month before St Andrew's Day 1981, Bill Shankly had suffered a second heart attack and died. Nessie was at his side.

Obsessed with his health, Shankly had long joked he'd be the fittest man in the cemetery, and his sudden death shocked the footballing community. 'I think Bill died of a broken heart,' his former coach Joe Fagan said years later, and many would agree. 'I think there is something in that,' Phil Thompson said. 'Liverpool was his life, and I think he lost some of his strength when he left.'

Anfield had a minute's silence in honour of Bill Shankly. The opposition were Swansea, and their manager John Toshack removed his tracksuit top to reveal a Liverpool shirt. The city's flags flew at half-mast, and the Kop and fans all over the stadium, whether they'd borne witness to the man's genius or not, bowed their heads.

Jock Stein continued as Scotland manager. In 1982 the team once again failed to progress beyond the World Cup's group stage but unlike in 1978 flew home with a modicum of self-respect. Stein would stay in charge and have a crack at taking the country to Mexico in 1986.

'I don't think Jock was all that happy as Scotland boss,' said Paddy Crerand. 'I played for him in the 1960s with Scotland and he was great, but I really think he missed the day-to-day stuff he got with Celtic and at other clubs.'

Managing the very modern Graeme Souness highlighted Stein's still keen eye, both for a footballer and good character. Asked by Alex Mooney, a Scottish journalist, to name the best player he had worked with, Stein waxed lyrical about Bobby Murdoch but, when it came to best team player, that was Souness.

Souness, with his blow dried hair and fondness for life's bubbles, was on the face of it the antithesis of Stein's hard working and stringent approach to things. Stein though saw deeper than most and in Souness he noticed worthier traits than mere razzmatazz.

'There is seldom a moment when you play in central midfield that you are not involved but he still finds time to do things way above and beyond what's required,' Stein told Mooney. 'He helps players in his own side without them even knowing. If somebody has had a bad touch or makes a mistake, Graeme will be just a few yards away from him every time he gets the ball so he can take an easy pass.

'And he'll keep doing that till the player's got his confidence back. I've never known anybody do that. He's the best team player you could wish for. Oh aye, he's some guy. There's no doubt about that.'

Stein saw in his captain, a willingness to help colleagues, a willingness that he had grown up with while working in Lanarkshire's mines. Such teamwork and selflessness was the embodiment of what all three managers had set to achieve and none would ever lose sight of such attributes.

In 1984, travelling with the Scotland squad during the miners' strike, Stein saw a coal lorry about to cross a picket line. Stein flagged down the driver and sharply suggested he turn round. Bemused by the telling-off, the driver did just that. Stein would never compare the pressures on those charged with choosing football teams with the lives of miners and their families. He knew their plight better than anyone, but at the last of Scotland's qualifying matches for the 1986 World Cup, the pressure on him was immense. Scotland had travelled to Cardiff knowing that defeat by Wales would see them out. At half-time they trailed 1–0. The players noticed that their manager wasn't his usual bullish self. Graeme Souness, his suspended skipper, would later remark that Stein had even asked his advice.

The tension and the noise from Ninian Park rose as the locals dreamed of a first World Cup since 1958. Stein was a forlorn figure, far from the days when he sat with calm authority in his white overcoat. But then a penalty. A penalty for Scotland. Davie Cooper stepped up and Scotland were level. To Stein's annoyance, photographers surrounded his dugout. This wasn't glorious mayhem; there was something too intense about it all. Moments later, Stein collapsed. A cardiologist treated him in a nearby media room. Concerned players, press and staff gathered outside. 'It's all right, Doc,' Stein said. 'I'm feeling a bit better now.' They were to be his last words. Four days later, Celtic Park fell silent.

Matt Busby had attended both his friends' funerals. Jean, his wife, died in 1988, and when asked about his own health on trips to Old Trafford, Busby would simply say, 'Still battling along.' While not influencing the club's 1986 decision to recruit Alex

Ferguson as their manager, he will have approved of a man who had trained as a Govan toolmaker. Ferguson himself, during his early strained years at the club, would admit to feeling comforted by the familiar smell of the old man's pipe when walking into his Old Trafford office, knowing he was there to offer an ear.

Busby saw Ferguson turn Manchester United back into what he had always seen them as: the best. The league championship (now morphed into its Premier League manifestation) was won in 1993, United's first since 1967. In January 1994, a week after visiting Old Trafford for the last time, Busby went into Alexandra Hospital in Cheadle and on 20 January 1994, with his family surrounding him, he was gone. Old Trafford and the wider game paid their tributes. 'The spirit of Matt Busby will fill Old Trafford as long as it stands,' wrote Bryan Butler in the *Daily Telegraph*.

All three men will for ever haunt the clubs and the game they loved, but were you able to ask any of them to take you on a stroll through the reasons for their success each would proudly walk you among the shadows of their formative years.

Football men of the future may be shaped by academies and coaching courses, but here were three individuals who, when they walked out of Orbiston, Glenbuck and Burnbank, took the best of what those places had to offer. The mining communities in which all three grew up gave them a deeper understanding of life, people and of course football.

Hard work, discipline, honesty, total trust for the man working beside you, an appreciation for life's darker arts, humour and teamwork: all were discovered and cultivated in their younger years. From the pits to the pitches, these qualities brought them and their teams glory.

All three had football too ingrained in them to suppose they would not still be in love with it, even in its money-bloated modern guise. Any tribute which included 'Football was better in their day' would do them and their passion a disservice, and thanks to their lives, football fans of all ages are aware of the names Busby, Shankly and Stein. All they need do is close their eyes to conjure up images given to the game by these three incredible men.

Maybe it will be Duncan Edwards, smiling with his teammates, his pals. Maybe it will be Tommy Gemmell, marauding down Celtic's left flank, as hard as a green and white stick of rock, and just as much fun. It could be Bobby Charlton falling into Matt Busby's arms, the Wembley floodlights catching the tears on their happy cheeks. Perhaps it's Ian Callaghan taking himself to the byline and whipping in the cross that wins Liverpool the FA Cup.

They could just close their eyes and be in Lisbon on that famous May evening. The sun still warm in the sky. Celtic songs warming the air further still. Bill Shankly walks over to his friend. 'John, you're immortal,' he says. The big man would be the first to say, they all are.

Epilogue:

Long Live the Kings

But what are kings, when regiment is gone,
But perfect shadows in a sunshine day?

Christopher Marlowe

A Premier League ground. A goal. Manchester United have scored. Four thousand away fans erupt and fill the stadium with song. 'Twenty times,' they sing, reminding their hosts of the number of times they have called themselves champions. 'Playing football the Busby Way!'

Anfield. A European evening. The bus carrying the team inches its way through the heaving crowd. A fan in his early twenties stands on a makeshift scaffold. Red smoke billows from the flare he holds to the sky, and he begins to sing of the noise you'll hear from the Bill Shankly boys.

Celtic Park. A night match. The floodlights beam their moonlike rays onto the famous stadium. Green scarves glow like phosphorus algae. A huge banner is unfurled, and on it is Jock Stein, an image of the European Cup is cast from his ankles. IS IT COLD IN HIS SHADOW? it asks.

Three very modern images and three very modern football clubs, but each owing everything to three men from their pasts. Over the years the successes of Jock Stein, Bill Shankly and Matt Busby may have been matched or bettered, but the club that each created still marches to the beat of their drums.

Today the sound of those drums reaches far and wide. The modern game is a global phenomenon, and forward-looking men such as Matt Busby would have smiled at the knowledge that his team are idolized everywhere. It's said that a quarter of the world's population support either, Manchester United, Liverpool, or Celtic. You are as likely to hear a conversation about Manchester United's progress in Singapore as you are in Salford, and Busby would have been proud of that. Shankly too. It was he after all who spoke of building a team that would 'conquer the bloody world'. But that is not to forget the very local concerns all three managers had for what they were doing. Busby's remit as soon as he arrived at Old Trafford in 1945 was to build a team consisting of local talent. Stein followed suit with a European Cup-winning team with a label reading, MADE IN GLASGOW.

Shankly was drawn to Liverpool by the people there, and always held them dear, even if it was the bloody world he hoped to conquer. Cup final tickets would often quietly find their way to fans unable otherwise to get them, courtesy of a manager who knew that without the supporters such occasions meant nothing. Today, a Liverpool supporters' group set up to promote their rights is called Spirit of Shankly, and you sense he would have enjoyed their rage against the machine.

By being totally at ease with people, inside forward or tea lady, and therefore knowing how to get the best from them, all three managers prospered. 'They all came from working-class environments, and from there they all knew how to treat people,' said Paddy Crerand.

That sounds like the easiest thing in the world but it isn't. They treated human beings as human beings.

On a Saturday we'd have a lunch at the golf club and then drive to Old Trafford. At Trafford Park, thousands of people would be getting off work. Matt would always say to us, 'Look at these people. Look at them. We need to give them some enjoyment. They have been working for five and a half days and we need to entertain them, make their day better.' Matt was always thinking of the people and I know Bill and Jock were the same. They had nothing but respect for people.

After winning the European Cup in 1968, Busby had been introduced by Alex Stepney to his brother. Nine years later, after United won the FA Cup, he met the goalkeeper's brother again and greeted him with warmth. This was typical of a man who surely remembered those wartime meetings with General Montgomery well.

Not that they were soft; all three had a hard side and did not suffer fools. 'There was no bullshit,' said Lou Macari. 'They had to be tough and hard and nasty at times, but they liked and understood men. They were very clever. It was only years later that it dawned on me that I had been lucky enough to, in a very short space of time, cross paths with three of the greatest football managers the game has ever known.'

That greatness endured. In 1991, with Manchester United playing for the Cup Winners Cup in Rotterdam, the team bus arrived to a raucous reception. Songs were being bellowed, flags waved, hands thumped the side of the coach. The doors to the bus opened and there was immediate silence. Sir Matt Busby was leading the team out, so only polite applause would do – for now. 'I just followed behind,' wrote Alex Ferguson. '"I'm with him," my body language was saying.'

The 'Busby Way' is a tangible thing too. Managers are very much judged at Old Trafford by the way their teams play. They must entertain. Flair, width and dynamism are as desirable as success. Busby was the keenest advocate of the manager having full control of team matters, but through his own brilliance he will for ever peer over the shoulders of those charged with following him.

Shankly's presence at Anfield and beyond is similarly lasting. A stand is named after him at Preston's Deepdale stadium while Liverpool fans demand the manager understand their ways, they demand a connection. If the man in charge can empathize with their fanaticism, then their love is won.

In 2018 Phil Thompson went to Melwood to interview Liverpool manager Jurgen Klopp for Sky TV. In the manager's room, as the cameramen set up, the two men stood and talked. Pictures of Shankly, Bob Paisley and Joe Fagan hung on the wall. 'The one of Shanks dominates the room,' said Thompson. 'We were chatting about things and then Jurgen stops me, takes my arm and says, "Phil, why did Bill Shankly resign in 1974? His team were so brilliant and he was so young." I thought, *Christ, even now, my old boss fascinates people.*'

Just months before Shankly died, Liverpool won the European Cup in Paris. Thompson was their captain.

As I lifted the European Cup into the Paris sky, I was thinking of Bill. He was there working, and to know he was watching me, this man who always said I'd be a star, that was special.

I was lucky enough to support Shankly's great team and

then be part of another. I tell my sons today and people who come to Anfield for tours, just how special he was. These people come from everywhere. Asia, Australia, America. I tell them all, we wouldn't be standing here now, surrounded by so much greatness and history, if it wasn't for this amazing man, who from humble beginnings built a giant of a football club.

I'd give anything to see Shanks again because I'd like to say thank you. Not thank you for my own career but simply for what he did for my football club. I love the place and it is because of him I am so proud of it.

And what does Thompson think Shankly would have said about the fact that people are still talking about him nearly forty years after his death? 'What would he say? "Too fucking, right!"'

The success that Jock Stein brought to Celtic has ensured similar levels of devotion. Even when he was treated by the club's board with less than the respect he was due, he never showed any anger or hostility towards them. 'In all my experience of him,' wrote Alex Ferguson, 'I never once heard Jock criticize Celtic. It made me realize how much he loved that club.' Even when asked to explain how his side won the European Cup in 1967, Stein ignored his own brilliance but instead praised the players and fans. 'Everybody knows that his contribution – in finding and developing the players and then supplying them with tactics brilliantly devised to suit their strengths – was utterly crucial, but he shrugged off any attempt to give him a substantial share of the glory,' Ferguson said. 'His modesty was extraordinary and sincere.'

Stein would probably blush if he were to hear any suggestion that his brilliance had in any way contributed to Ferguson's glut of honours at Manchester United. But just as the lives of Shankly, Busby and Stein – from their shared background, through their playing days, to competing against each other as managers – were so intertwined, so was the unwitting influence they would have on the futures of the clubs they managed.

'I was working at United soon after Alex arrived,' said Lou Macari. 'I watched him on the training ground and I remember standing there and thinking, *Jock Stein*. It was scary. He was just like him. He talked like him, joked like him. Coached like him. When to laugh, when to use anger. It was all Jock.'

Matt Busby, Bill Shankly and Jock Stein created three great footballing traditions but all strived for so much more than self-acclaim. 'I'm happy for the multitudes,' Bill Shankly would say after another trophy was won. Politics and religion might have been different, but the shared desire to work both with people and for people linked them. And so three statues stand outside three football stadiums. Sir Matt Busby's shows him holding a football, a hand on his hip, that friendly, approachable smile on his face. Bill Shankly's has his arms held aloft, fists clenched, a fan's scarf around his neck. Jock Stein is simply holding Britain's first European Cup.

For centuries kings lay on their deathbeds, worrying about the legacies they would leave behind. Our three kings might have quietly enjoyed the idea of their sculptured selves standing outside the stadiums they so loved. The idea of permanent residence would surely have appealed. Who knows? What isn't in doubt is that their legacies are set in so much more than mere bronze.

Acknowledgements

Bill Shankly called natural enthusiasm 'the greatest thing in the world'. He'd have liked Jonny Owen. In the summer of 2017 I was introduced to Jonny and we spent an afternoon talking about Sir Matt Busby, Bill Shankly and Jock Stein. He was making a film about the three of them and their mining background, and would I write a book to accompany it? His eyes fizzed with excitement and I was in.

I'd like to thank Jonny for never letting that enthusiasm wane and inviting me to share in this wonderful project. Also a huge thanks to Jim Gill at United Agents, equally as passionate and a real driving force behind this book. Thank you to Richard Milner at Quercus for all his support and immediate enthusiasm for our three subjects.

Writing this book, it dawned on me just how many brilliant words have been written about these three men, and I'd like to thank the late Hugh McIlvanney for his consistent brilliance and for Stephen F. Kelly for a wonderful biography of Bill Shankly. A huge thank you to Jock Stein's biographer Archie Macpherson for not only his book but his support with mine. Thank you also to John Keith for his always unerring help. Patrick Barclay wrote a brilliant biography of Sir Matt Busby, which was invaluable, but I'd like to also thank him for his constant support and friendship.

I'd like to thank the following people for their help with the book: Mick Aitchison, Bertie Auld, Alex Bower, Simon Bristow, John Clark, Paddy Crerand, Peter Doherty, Pamela Dwyer, Peter Etherington, Nick Kerwick, Lou Macari, Gerry McElhone, Matt McGlone, Paul Minney, Clare Moynihan, Kevin O'Rourke, Sam Pilger, Struen Rodger, Craig Rooney, Jay Rossi, Iain 'Iggy' Shaw, Ian St John, Phil Thompson and Craig Williamson,

Finally, thank you to my daughter Daisy. As knowing as Busby, as brilliant as Stein and as mischievous as Shankly. I love you.

Leo Moynihan, October 2019

I'd like to thank Jim and Leo, who believed from the very start. As did James, Paul, Milly, John and everyone at Box to Box films. I couldn't have asked for more support and better people to work with. To Paddy, Archie, John, Gerry and Richard, who (along with Leo) all spoke so brilliantly about the three men. To Vicky and my family, the Owens, who ended up in Merthyr Tydfil, an iron and coal town in the industrial valleys of South Wales, and were miners there a hundred years ago, the same time as our heroes were underground in Scotland. To my film editor and right-hand man Owen Davies, who gave everything to this film. Finally to my father Brian and two grandfathers, Gwyn and Les, who, from when I was a young boy, always told me (when they appeared on our giant Rediffusion TV) that Matt, Bill and Jock all started out working underground and never ever forgot that. They were immensely proud of them and the profession that once ruled Britain in the same way as Manchester United, Liverpool and Celtic did when these three giants of men were their managers.

Jonny Owen, October 2019

Bibliography

John Arlott, *Concerning Soccer*, Longmans, Green and Co., 1952

Patrick Barclay, *Sir Matt Busby, The Definitive Biography*, Ebury Press, 2017

Matt Busby, *Soccer at the Top, My Life in Football*, Sphere, 1973

Bobby Charlton, *Bobby Charlton's Most Memorable Matches*, Stanley Paul, 1984

Sir Bobby Charlton, *Sir Bobby Charlton, My Manchester United Years*, Headline, 2007

Jeff Connor, *The Lost Babes*, Harper Sport, 2006

Kenny Dalglish, *Dalglish*, Hodder & Stoughton, 1996

T. M. Devine, *The Scottish Nation*, Penguin, 2012

Robert Duncan, *The Mine Workers*, Birlinn, 2005

Alex Ferguson, *Managing My Life*, Coronet, 2000

Ken Gallacher, *Jock Stein, The Authorised Biography*, Stanley Paul, 1988

Geoffrey Green, *Great Moments in Sport: Soccer*, Pelham Books, 1972

John Keith, *Billy Liddell, The Legend Who Carried the Kop*, Robson Books, 2003

Stephen F. Kelly, *Bill Shankly, It's Much More Important Than That*, Virgin, 1996

Denis Law, *The King*, Bantam Books, 2003

Archie Macpherson, *Jock Stein, The Definitive Biography*, Highdown, 2004

Graham McColl, *A Year and a Day*, Simon & Schuster, 2017

David Miller, *Father of Football, The Story of Sir Matt Busby*, Pavilion, 1994

Adam Powley and Robert Gillan, *Shankly's Village*, Pitch Publishing, 2015

Bill Shankly, *Shankly, My Story*, Trinity Mirror, 2009

Alex Shorrocks, *Winners and Champions*, Arthur Baker, 1985

Ian St John, *The Saint*, Hodder, 2005

Frank Taylor, *The Day a Team Died*, Souvenir Press, 1983

Jim White, *Manchester United, The Biography*, Sphere, 2008

John Williams, *Red Men*, Mainstream, 2011

Index

A

Aberdeen FC 72, 141, 153

AC Milan FC 133, 166, 216

A'Court, Alan 143–4

Airdrie FC 33, 182

Ais Gill rail accident (1913) 17

Ajax FC 183–4

Albion Rovers FC 60, 64, 65, 66–8, 69, 70–1, 210

Alder Hey children's hospital 236

'all-star' teams 79–80

Allison, Malcolm 199, 210, 216

Alloa Athletic FC 36, 153

Alpine Villa FC 33

Amancio 201, 219

Ancell, Bobby 148

Anderlecht FC 131

Anderson, John 82

Argentinian football teams 215–16

Arlott, John 120–2, 123

Armstrong, Joe 127, 174

Arsenal FC 13, 33, 49, 54, 77, 95–6, 101, 111, 123, 130, 133, 213, 223

Aston Jr, John 8, 200, 205, 216

Aston Sr, John 78, 82, 83, 84, 122, 123

Aston Villa FC 50, 128

Attenborough, Richard 182

Auld, Bertie 5, 163, 184, 186, 190, 191, 193, 215, 219–20, 228, 229, 235

Ayrshire, Scotland 12–14, 16

B

Ball, Alan 204, 212

Barclay, Patrick 31–2, 61, 77, 79–80, 86, 122, 232

Barnsley FC 80–1, 126

Barrass, Matt 48

Bayern Munich FC 181

the Beatles 149, 174

Beattie, Andy 100–2, 222–3

Bell, Alex 44, 51

Bellshill, Scotland 40

Benfica FC 7–8, 174, 189, 203–4, 205–7

Bennett, Reuben 105, 141, 147, 148

Bent, Geoff 134

Bermuda national team 181

Bernábéu, Santiago 129

Berry, Johnny 125, 129, 131, 134, 204, 208

Berwick Rangers FC 153

Best, George 171, 174, 176–7, 183, 196, 198, 199, 200, 202–3, 206, 207, 216, 230, 231

Bilbao FC 131, 205

Billingham, Jack 96

Bingham, Billy 156

Birmingham City FC 163

Blackpool FC 80, 87, 121, 212, 213

Blanchflower, Jackie 49, 123, 128, 134, 167, 204, 208

Blantyre Victoria 'the Vics' FC 39, 41, 66, 67

the Blitz 74–5

Bolton Evening News 62

Bolton Wanderers FC 46, 61–2, 75, 127

Boot, Eddie 101
Borussia Dortmund FC 131
Borussia Monchengladbach FC 224
Bothwell Castle pit 64
bowling championships 66
boxing 92, 139, 142
Brazil national team 186
Brennan, Eddie 118, 133, 143, 171
Britton, Cliff 79, 80
Brown, Alex 13
Buckley, Frank 54
Burnbank Athletic FC 41
Burnbank, Scotland 24–5, 40, 41–2, 107
Burnley FC 133, 196
Burns, Robert 37–8, 93
Burton, Richard 28, 35
Busby, Alex 16–17, 20–1, 40
Busby, George 16
Busby, Helen 'Nellie' 17, 20–1, 25, 34, 35, 40
Busby, Jean 29, 33–4, 44, 48–9, 52, 119–20,
    135, 241
Busby, Matt 4, 13–14, 49, 54, 59–60, 91,
    102, 244–7, 249
    'all-star' teams 79–80
    Alpine Villa FC (player) 33
    'Busby's Babes' 124–35, 205
    childhood and family background 12,
      16–17, 20–2
    coal mining 1, 6, 25, 27–8, 34
    death of 242
    early football influences 32–3
    European Cup campaign and final
      (1968) 5–8, 199–08
    European Cup competitions 5–8, 130–
      1, 133, 189, 194, 199–208
    football career (player) 29, 30, 33–4,
      43–5, 47, 48–9, 50–1, 52–3, 67
    friendship with Bill Shankly 133, 139,
      145, 146, 149, 169, 171–2, 177,
      238–9
    Hibernian FC (player) 35
    Liverpool FC (player) 47, 48, 52–4,
      59–60, 76–7, 78–9, 136, 159
    Manchester City FC (player) 29, 30, 35,
      43–5, 48–9, 50–1, 52, 210
    Manchester United FC (board
      member) 231, 232, 241–2

Manchester Utd (pre-Munich air
    disaster) 75–9, 80–9, 105, 120–
    35, 137, 142
Manchester Utd manager (post-Munich
    air disaster) 145, 166, 167–9,
    171–2, 174–6, 183, 189, 194–208,
    211–12, 213, 214–18, 229, 230
Manchester Utd vs Benfica (European
    Cup final 1968) 5–8, 199–208
Munich air disaster 118–20, 133–5,
    194–5, 207–8
religion/sectarianism 35, 40, 80, 120
Scotland national team (manager)
    166–7
Scotland national team (player) 60, 61
Second World War 47, 48, 59–60, 62, 79
Busby, Sandy 52
Busby, Sheena 52
'Busby's Babes' 124–35, 205
Butler, Bryan 242
Byrne, Roger 123, 128, 134

C
Calisto, Adolfo 205
Callaghan, Ian 144, 149, 173
Callaghan, Willie 152
Cann, Sid 49, 50
Cappellini, Renato 190–1, 192
Cardiff City FC 126, 212
Carey, John 78, 82, 83–4, 103, 123, 125
Carlisle FC 29–30, 36, 38, 56–7, 91, 93–6
Carruthers, Peter 38
Carter, Raich 58, 60
Catholicism 20, 35, 40, 69–70
Catterick, Harry 156
Cavett, Dick 28, 35
Celtic FC 13, 33, 35, 66–7, 84, 152, 154–5,
    162–3, 244–5, 248
    Jock Stein (coach) 113–17
    Jock Stein (manager) 164, 176, 178,
      180–96, 200, 215, 218–22, 227–
      30, 235, 236–7
    Jock Stein (player) 106–13
    vs Internazionale (European Cup
      final 1967) 1–5, 180–1, 188–93,
      195–6, 219

Celtic/Rangers sectarian rivalry 35, 107–8, 227–8

Central League 78

Chalmers, Stevie 4, 185, 187, 192, 228

Chamberlain, Neville 47

Chapman, Herbert 49, 54, 77, 130

Charity Shield 196

Charlton, Bobby 6, 8, 87, 127, 128, 132, 145, 171, 172, 173, 174, 183, 194, 196, 197–8, 206, 207, 230, 231

Charlton, Jack 145, 167, 173, 220

Chelsea FC 13, 33, 47, 60, 103, 128, 130, 196, 199, 209, 232

Chilton, Allenby 80, 83, 123, 125

Chisnall, Paul 175–6

Churchill, Winston 26

cinema 19, 32, 38, 86, 103

Clark, John 113–15, 116, 117, 181, 183, 184, 186, 187, 188, 190, 193, 228, 237–8

Clay, Cassius 158

Cleaton Moor Celtic FC 90–1

Clemence, Ray 212, 224

Clough, Brian 138, 217, 231, 235

Clyde FC 112

coal mining 1, 5, 6, 13–19, 25–8, 34, 40, 41–2, 48, 64–6, 241

Cockburn, Henry 123

Coleman, Eddie 128, 134, 207

Collins, Bobby 112

Connachan, Eddie 154–5

Connor, Jack 103

Cooper, Davie 13, 241

Cormack, Peter 161–2

Coronation Cup (1953) 111

Corrie, Joe 42

Corriere della Serra newspaper 219

Coventry City FC 199

Craig, Jim 190–1, 192

Crerand, Paddy 113, 114, 169, 171, 172–3, 175, 177, 183, 195, 197, 198, 201, 202, 205, 208, 218, 222, 232, 238–9, 240, 245–6

Crickmer, Walter 74–5, 78, 79, 81

Cronberry FC 38

Cruyff, Johan 183

Crystal Palace FC 228

Cullis, Stan 59, 91, 103, 130, 162

Cunningham, Willie 153, 156–7, 160

Cup Winners Cup 182–3, 246–7

Curry, Tommy 56, 75, 105, 129, 134–5

D

Daily Express 170, 201

Daily Mirror 134, 197

Daily Post 137, 138, 165

Daily Telegraph 51, 242

Dalglish, Kenny 220, 227–8, 229–30, 236–7

Davies, Donny 123–4, 132

Delaney, Jim 84, 86, 121

Derby County FC 231

Di Stefano, Alfredo 162, 186, 218

Dick Cavett Show 28, 35

Dickson, Andy 152

Dickson, Charlie 155

Docherty, Tommy 232

Doherty, Peter 52

Drake, Ted 103

Duffey, Alan 234

Dukla Prague FC 187–8

Dundee United FC 36, 71, 72, 145, 147, 159

Dunfermline FC 117, 151–60, 182, 185

Dunne, Pat 171

Dunne, Tony 171

Dynamo Kiev FC 200

Dynamo Moscow FC 83

E

Eastern European migrants 40

Edwards, Alex 158, 161

Edwards, Duncan 119, 126, 132, 134, 165–6, 194, 207

Edwards, Leslie 137, 138

Edwards, Louis 205

El Alamein, Battle of 62, 66

Elizabeth II, Queen 111

England national team 60, 61, 99, 111–12, 144, 179

Estudiantes FC 215

European Cup 130–2, 133–4, 159, 162,

166, 183, 194–5, 216, 220, 236–7
Celtic vs Internazionale (1967 cup
  final) 1–5, 180–1, 188–93, 195–6,
  219
Jock Stein's Dunfermline FC 155–6
Liverpool vs Inter Milan (semi-final
  1965) 174
Liverpool vs Real Madrid (1981) 247
Manchester United (1968 campaign)
  5–8, 199–203
Manchester United vs Benfica (1968
  cup final) 5–8, 203–8
Real Madrid vs Eintracht Frankfurt
  (1960) 36
European Cup Winners Cup 164
Eusébio 8, 203–4, 206
Evans, Alun 209
Evans, Dennis 133
Everton FC 47, 54, 103, 122, 133, 137,
  156–7, 195, 212, 234

F
FA Cup 53, 72, 77, 137, 223
Carlisle vs Arsenal (1951) 95–6
Liverpool vs Leeds United (1965) 9,
  172–4
Liverpool vs Newcastle United (1974)
  8–9, 10–11, 224–5
Manchester City vs Everton (1933) 50
Manchester City vs Portsmouth (1934)
  51
Manchester United vs Blackpool
  (1948) 86–7, 121, 137
Manchester United vs Bolton (1958)
  166
Preston North End vs Huddersfield
  Town (1938) 59
Preston North End vs Sunderland
  (1937) 58
FA Youth Cup 102
Facchetti, Giacinto 191
Fagan, Joe 105, 141, 239
Fairs Cup 217–18
Falkirk FC 36
Fallon, Sean 105, 109–10, 111, 142, 163,

189–90, 221, 227, 236
Ferguson, Alex 168, 169, 241–2, 247,
  248–9
Fernie, Willie 105, 154
Ferniegair pit 64–5
Feyenoord FC 220
Finney, Tom 79, 92–3, 132
First World War 20–1
Fleck, Neilly 72
Football Association, English 79, 130
football heritage, Scottish 30–2
Football League, English 72, 84, 85, 88, 130
The Football Man (A. Hopcraft) 204–5
Foulkes, Bill 6, 126, 128, 166, 167, 171,
  174–5, 202–3, 207
Frost, David 235
Fulham FC 122

G
Gallacher, Hughie 13, 32, 34, 87, 185, 186
Gallacher, Ken 24
Gazette 67
Gemmell, Tommy 4, 113, 183, 191, 192,
  228
General Strike (1926) 26
Gento, Francisco 162, 201
Gibson, Alan 125
Gibson, James 75–6, 77, 124–5
Gibson, John 39
Glasgow Cup 3, 184
Glasgow, Scotland 12, 15, 31–2, 37
Glasgow United 227
Glenbuck, Ayrshire 18–19, 22–3, 36, 38
Glenbuck Cherrypickers FC 38
Glenbuck Iron Company 18
Goldsborough, Jack 72–3
The Good Companions (J.B. Priestley)
  88
Gornik Zabrze FC 200
Goslin, Harry 46–7, 61–2
government, British 16
Graça, Jaime 206
Grandstand BBC television programme
  153
Great Depression 44, 51, 58

Greaves, Jimmy 103
Green, Geoffrey 87, 184, 206
Greer, Jimmy 17, 20, 21
Greer, Private Willie 21
Greer, Thomas 21
Gregg, Harry 132, 204
Gribben, Jimmy 106, 108, 210
Grimsby Town FC 96–7

H
Hall, Brian 212
Hamilton Academical FC 55
Hampson, Billy 56
Hanot, Gabriel 130
Hansen, Alan 201
Hardaker, Alan 130
Hardie, Keir 66
Hardman, Harold 81, 125, 168–9
Harvey, Joe 10, 225
Hately, Tony 209
Hay, David 220, 229
Heighway, Steve 212, 223
Henrique, José 207
Hepburn, Dougie 163
Herd, Alec 50, 55
Herd, David 167, 196, 200
Herrera, Helenio 3, 159, 184, 189
Herron, Allan 164
Hibernian FC 6, 35, 60, 111, 130, 151–2,
    160–3, 182, 200, 228
Hidegkuti, Nándor 99, 112
Hillan, Frank 26–7
Hodge, Peter 44–5
Hopcraft, Arthur 136, 204–5
Huddersfield Town FC 59, 80, 100–4, 129,
    130, 132, 139–40, 143, 145
Hughes, Emlyn 9, 212–13, 224
Hughes, John 185–6, 228
Hull City FC 58
Hungarian national team 99, 111–12, 156,
    185
Hunt, Roger 144, 149, 179, 209–10, 212
Hunter, Norman 173
Hurst, Geoff 196
Hynd, Roger 188

I
Ibrox Stadium, Glasgow 37, 158, 188, 189
Industrial Revolution 15
Inter-Cities Fairs Cup 156–8
Intercontinental Cup 215
Internazionale of Milan 2, 3–4, 5, 159,
    180–1, 188–93
Ireland 15, 16
iron works, Glenbuck 18

J
James, Alex 13, 32–3, 59, 87
Jeffreys, Bobby 72
Johnson, Tommy 43
Johnstone, Jimmy 4, 178, 184, 186, 190,
    191, 192, 219
Jones, Mark 128, 134
José-enrique 206
Juventus FC 205

K
Kane, Peter 139
Kay, George 52–3, 54–5, 61, 77, 96, 137,
    159
Keating, Frank 88
Keegan, Kevin 10, 11, 222–3, 224
Keith, John 144
Kelly, Bob 106, 109, 113, 117, 162–3, 215
Kennedy, John F. 167
Kidd, Brian 8, 196, 200, 207
Kilmarnock FC 153, 159, 188
King, John 234
Klopp, Jurgen 247
the Kop, Anfield 136, 170

L
Labour party 26, 66
Lanarkshire 12–15, 16, 64
Lanarkshire bowling championship 66
Law, Denis 8, 102–4, 129, 167–8, 170, 171,
    174, 183, 196, 198, 200, 202, 206,
    212, 216, 230, 231
Lawrence, D.H. 34
Lawrence, Tommy 209

Lawton, Tommy 47–8, 79, 144
Leeds United FC 145, 167, 172–4, 215,
    219–20, 237, 238
Lees, Webber 66
Leicester City FC 169, 196, 209–10, 216,
    231
Lennox, Bobby 164, 185
L'Equipe sports paper 130
Lewis, Eddie 125–6
Leyton Orient FC 99
Liddell, Billy 55, 85, 138–9, 144
Liddell, Phyllis 144
Lincoln City FC 139
Lindsey, Alec 212
Liverpool Echo 53–4, 140–1
Liverpool FC 84, 85, 96, 104, 122, 136–9
    1950s slump 137–40
    Bill Shankly (manager) 90–1, 104, 105,
        139–50, 164–5, 167–8, 169–74,
        175–6, 183, 191, 195, 196, 217,
        222–6, 244, 245
    Bill Shankly (post-resignation) 233–4
    Matt Busby (player) 47, 48, 52–6, 59,
        60, 76–7, 78–9, 136, 159
    relationship with Busby's Manchester
        Utd FC 170–2
    vs Leeds United (FA Cup final 1965)
        9, 172
    vs Newcastle Utd (FA Cup final 1974)
        8–9, 10–11
Llanelli FC 63, 71–2
Lloyd, Larry 212, 224
Lord, Bob 133
Low, Gordon 103
Lowry, L.S. 88
Luftwaffe 60, 74
Luton Town FC 36, 53, 61

M
Macari, Lou 220–2, 229, 232, 246, 249
Macdonald, Malcolm 10, 224–5
Macpherson, Archie 25, 39, 67, 71, 108,
    153, 155, 163, 186, 187
Manchester City FC 29, 30, 35, 43–5, 48–9,
    50–1, 54, 80, 141, 210, 216, 230

Manchester Evening News 128, 195, 200–1,
    232
Manchester Guardian 78, 123–4, 128
Manchester League 78
Manchester United FC 4, 44, 74–9, 111,
    244–7
    Alex Ferguson (manager) 241–2, 247
    European Cup campaign and final
        (1968) 5–8, 199–208
    first European Cup tournament 130–2
    Frank O'Farrell (manager) 231–2
    Matt Busby (board member) 231, 232
    Matt Busby (manager post-Munich
        air disaster-1971) 5–8, 145, 166,
        167–8, 169, 170–2, 174–6, 183,
        194–208, 211–12, 213, 214–18,
        229, 230
    Matt Busby (manager pre-Munich air
        disaster) 80–9, 111, 120–35, 137,
        142
    Munich air disaster 118–20, 133–5,
        165–6, 194–5, 204, 207–8
    relationship with Shankly's Liverpool
        FC 170–2
    Tommy Docherty (manager) 232
    vs Benfica (European cup final 1968)
        5–8, 203–8
Manchester United Junior Athletic Club
    (MUJAC) 78, 102
Mathie, David 72
Mathie, Harry 21
Mathie, Jimmy 22, 35, 54
Matthews, Stanley 87, 176
Mazzola, Sandro 2, 192
McBride, Joe 4
McClean, Adam 71
McCullan, Jimmy 35
McDade, Margaret (JS's sister) 24, 41, 42–3
McDonald, Tommy 152–3
McGahey, Mick 65–6
McGhee, Frank 197
McGrain, Danny 220, 229
McGrory, Jim 109, 112
McGuinness, Wilf 127, 216–17, 231
McGuire, Jimmy 119
McHale, Kevin 103

McIlvanney, William and Hugh 31, 180
McInnes, Jimmy 140
McInnes, Lachie 72
McLeod, Ally 238
McLoy, Phil 29, 43
McNeill, Alex 35
McNeill, Billy 4, 13, 113, 115, 178, 187, 191, 193, 236
McNeill, Jessie (JS's sister) 41, 42
McPhail, John 67, 109, 110
Meek, David 232
Melia, Jimmy 144, 148, 149
Melrose, Harry 158
Melwood training ground 142, 148, 233
Mercer, Joe 50–1, 59, 79–80, 199, 216
Meredith, Billy 77–8
Merthyr Tydfil FC 72
Michels, Rinus 183–4
Milburn, Jackie 211
Miller, George 152, 159–60
Milne, Gordon 145, 149
Mitten, Charlie 78, 82, 83, 86, 121, 122, 147
Mochan, Neilly 105, 112
Montgomery, General Sir Bernard 61–2
Mooney, Alex 240
Moores, John 156
Moran, Ronnie 149
Morris, John 86, 121
Mortensen, Stan 80, 99
Morton, Alan 185
Morton FC 228
Motherwell FC 72, 145, 147
Moynihan, John 131–2
Munich air disaster 118–20, 133–5, 165, 194–5, 204, 207–8
Murdoch, Bobby 113, 183, 191, 240
Murphy, Jimmy 80, 84–5, 86, 105, 128, 129, 133, 134, 139, 142, 165–6, 167, 174, 175, 194, 198, 231
Mutch, George 59

N
Nantes FC 187
Newcastle United FC 8, 10, 13, 33, 80, 111, 155–6, 185, 211, 224–5

Norris, Sir Henry 77
North Eastern League Cup 56
Northern Midweek League 44, 210
Norwich FC 61
Nottingham Forest FC 132, 228

O
Observer 180
O'Farrell, Frank 231–2
Old Trafford bombing (1941) 74–5
Olive, Les 81
Orbiston Celtic FC 32–3
Osgood, Peter 212

P
Paisley, Bob 55–6, 85, 105, 141, 142, 178, 223, 233
Partizan Belgrade FC 194
Peacock, Bertie 111
Pearson, Stan 78, 82, 86, 123, 125
Pegg, David 128, 134
Pelé 114, 186
Pius XII, Pope 80
politics 26, 65–6
Porter, Jack 92
Portsmouth FC 36, 51, 128
potato blight, Irish 16
Preston, Lancashire 57–8
Preston North End FC 48, 53, 57–9, 92–3, 128, 145, 247
Priest, Reg 127
Priestley, J.B. 88
Priory pit, Blantyre 64–5
Protestantism 37, 39, 109, 117, 163
Puskás, Ferenc 99, 112, 148, 162

Q
'Quality Street Gang', Celtic FC's 228
Queen, Tony 111

R
Racing Club FC 215
Raisbeck, Alex 136

Ramsey, Alf 185, 204
Rangers FC 13, 35, 37, 39, 67–8, 107–8,
    111, 112, 114, 158, 184, 185, 188,
    227, 236
rationing 92, 95
Rayment, Captain Ken 134
Reading FC 60
Real Madrid FC 6, 129, 130, 131, 133, 148,
    162, 199, 201–3, 218, 219
Red Star Belgrade FC 133
reserved occupations, WWII 48, 60
Revie, Don 167, 172
Rimmer, Jimmy 217
Rocca, Louis 76, 78, 125
Rodgers, Frank 33, 82
Rous, Stanley 59, 79, 130–1
Rowley, Jack 86, 121, 123, 125, 129
Royal Air Force (RAF) 60–1
Royal Irish Regiment 21
Rumney, John 18

S
Sadler, David 202, 206
Sarajevo, FK 200
Sarti, Giuliano 191, 192
Sawyer, Eric 146, 147
Scanlon, Albert 129, 204, 211–12
Scotland national team 59, 60, 61, 67, 112,
    147, 166–7, 232, 238, 239–41
Scott, Elisha 136
Scottish Cup 33, 154–5, 182, 184
Scottish Cup, under-18s 33
Scottish Football Association 130
Scunthorpe FC 212, 223
Second World War 46–8, 59–62, 64, 74, 79
sectarianism, Catholic/Protestant 35, 40–1,
    69–70, 82, 107–8, 163, 227–8
Setters Maurice 198
Shankly, Agnes 'Ness' (BS's wife) 92, 93,
    97, 98
Shankly, Alec 36, 37, 57
Shankly, Barbara 17–18, 20
Shankly, Bill 13–14, 26, 40, 75, 118, 133,
    247–8, 249
    birth and childhood 17–18, 20, 22–3
Carlisle FC (manager) 91, 93–6
Carlisle FC (player) 38, 56–7
coal mining 25–6, 28, 34
Cronberry FC (player) 38
death of 239, 241
early football influences 36–9
football career (player) 29–30, 38–9,
    48, 50, 53, 56–8
friendship with Jock Stein 159, 181,
    188–9, 200
friendship with Matt Busby 133, 139,
    145, 146, 149, 169, 171–2, 177,
    238–9
Grimsby Town FC (manager) 96–7
Huddersfield Town FC (manager)
    100–4, 129, 132, 136, 139–40,
    143, 145
Liverpool FC (manager) 90–1, 104,
    105, 139–50, 164–5, 167–8, 169–
    74, 175–6, 178, 183, 191, 195,
    196, 209–14, 217, 222–6, 235–6
Liverpool FC (post-resignation
    presence) 233–4, 235
Liverpool vs Leeds United (1965 FA
    Cup final) 9, 172–4
Liverpool vs Newcastle United (1974
    FA Cup final) 8–9, 10–11, 224–5
personal fitness/training 91–2
Preston North End FC (player) 48, 53,
    57–8, 92–3
Scotland national team 59, 60–1, 238
Second World War 48, 60–1, 62
team diet 94–5, 103, 214
Tranmere Rovers FC (consultant) 234
Workington FC (manager) 90, 97–100,
    105
Shankly, Bob 36, 141, 158–9, 182
Shankly, Jimmy 36
Shankly, John 36
Shankly, John (BS's father) 19–20
Sheffield United FC 36, 80, 196
Simpson, Ronnie 193
Sinclair, Jackie 152, 158
Smith, Bob 49, 64–5
Smith, Jimmy 67–8
Smith, John 68

Smith, Tommy 9, 10, 223
Souness, Graeme 240–1
Southampton FC 53, 149
Spanish Football Association 130
Sporting Chronicle 93
St John, Ian 104, 145, 146, 147–8, 149, 167,
    172, 173, 209, 210–11, 212
St Mirren FC 109, 153–4
Stanton, Pat 160, 161, 162
Steele, Harry 40–1, 43, 69, 70, 107
Stein, George (JS's father) 39, 41, 42, 107–8
Stein, George (JS's son) 116
Stein, Jane (JS's mother) 24, 34, 41–2, 69,
    107
Stein, Jean (JS's wife) 69–70, 71, 72–3,
    107–8, 117, 155, 160
Stein, John 'Jock' 13–14, 26, 105, 248–9
    Albion Rovers FC (player) 60, 64, 65,
        66–8, 69, 70–1, 210
    birth and childhood 24–5, 30
    Blantyre Victoria FC (player) 41, 66, 67
    Burnbank Athletic FC (player) 41
    Celtic FC (coach) 113–17, 129
    Celtic FC (manager) 164, 176, 178,
        180–96, 200, 215, 218–22, 227–
        30, 235, 236–7
    Celtic FC (player) 106–12
    Celtic vs Internazionale (European
        Cup final 1967) 1–5, 180–1,
        188–93, 195–6, 219
    coal mining 1, 5, 14–15, 27, 28, 41–2,
        64, 69, 115–16
    death of 241
    Dunfermline FC (manager) 117,
        151–60, 185
    early football influences 39
    European competitions 155–8, 180–1,
        186–93, 195–6, 219
    football career (player) 39, 41, 42, 60,
        63–4, 65, 66–8, 69, 70–3, 106–12
    friendship with Bill Shankly 159, 181,
        189–90
    friendship with Matt Busby 159, 200
    Hibernian FC (manager) 151–2,
        160–3, 182
    Inter-Cities Fairs Cup 156–8

Leeds United FC (manager) 237, 238
Llanelli FC (player) 63, 71–3
offered Manchester United managers
    job 218
Scotland national team 176, 238,
    239–41
Second World War 64, 66
sectarianism 40–1, 69–70, 107–8, 109,
    117, 227–8
Stein, Ray 71, 72, 155
Stepney, Alex 196, 206–7, 217, 246
Stevenson, Willie 167
Stiles, Nobby 8, 170, 175, 183, 201, 203–4,
    206
Stock, Alex 89
Stoke City FC 149
Stranraer FC 153
strikes, industrial 15, 16, 26, 65–6
Stubbins, Albert 136
Suárez, Luis 191
Summer Cup 161
Sunday Mail 164
Sunday Post 66, 109
Sunderland FC 58, 60, 199
Swansea City FC 239
Sweeney, John 154
Swift, Frank 50, 51, 119, 134
Swift, Joe 79, 80

T
Tait, Alex 13
Taylor, Frank 134
Taylor, Phil 138, 139
Taylor, Tommy 126, 127, 129, 131, 134
The Times 87, 184, 206
Thompson, Jimmy 103
Thompson, Peter 170, 209, 212
Thompson, Phil 209–10, 213, 224, 225,
    233, 234, 247–8
Thomson, Davie 154
Tilson, Fred 50, 51
Torres, José 206
Toshack, John 212, 239
Tottenham Hot Spur FC 13, 167, 181, 183,
    196

Trades Union Congress 26
Tranmere Rovers FC 234
Trevelyan, Charles 16
Tulley, Charlie 109
Twentyman, Geoff 94

U
UEFA Cup 224
Ujpesti Dozsa FC 156
United States Football Association 119
United States of America, Celtic tour
    181–2
Ure, Ian 217
Uruguay national team 112

V
Valencia FC 157–8
Victoria, Queen 15
Viollet, Dennis 126, 128, 131
Vojvodina, FK 187

W
Waddell, Willie 159
wages, players' 177–8, 221–2
Wales national team 85, 167, 241
Wallace, Dougie 71
Wallace, Willie 228
Warnock, Jimmy 139
Watford FC 210
Watson, Bill 98–9, 105, 141
Welsh, Don 137
West Bromwich Albion FC 85, 128, 166,
    199
West Ham United FC 53, 183, 196, 197
Whalley, Bert 105, 126, 127, 129,
    134–5

Whelan, Liam 128, 134
Whig government 16
White, Desmond 237
Whittaker, Tom 101
Whittle, Ernie 98
Williams, Captain Bill 75
Williams, Lizzie 63
Williams, Tom 138, 139, 140
Wilson, Ramon 'Ray' 102–3, 129
Wilson, Tony 225
Wolstenholme, Kenneth 191
Wolverhampton Wanderers FC 72, 103,
    127, 128, 130, 162–3, 209
Wood, Ray 132
Woodrooffe, Thomas 59
Worcester City FC 137
Workington FC 90, 97–100, 105
World Cup (1954) 111, 112, 185
World Cup (1966) 102, 111–12, 179, 185,
    203–4
World Cup (1978) 239
World Cup (1982) 239–40
World Cup (1986) 241
World Series, baseball 23–4
Wrigglesworth, Billy 82

Y
Yeats, Ron 104, 145, 146–7, 149, 167, 172,
    212, 234
Yeovil Town FC 88–9
Young, Alex 156
Youth Cup games 128, 102
youth players, support for 54, 77, 78, 85,
    95, 114–15, 138, 145, 152, 163, 214,
    220, 228
    see also 'Busby's Babes'
youth teams 33, 78